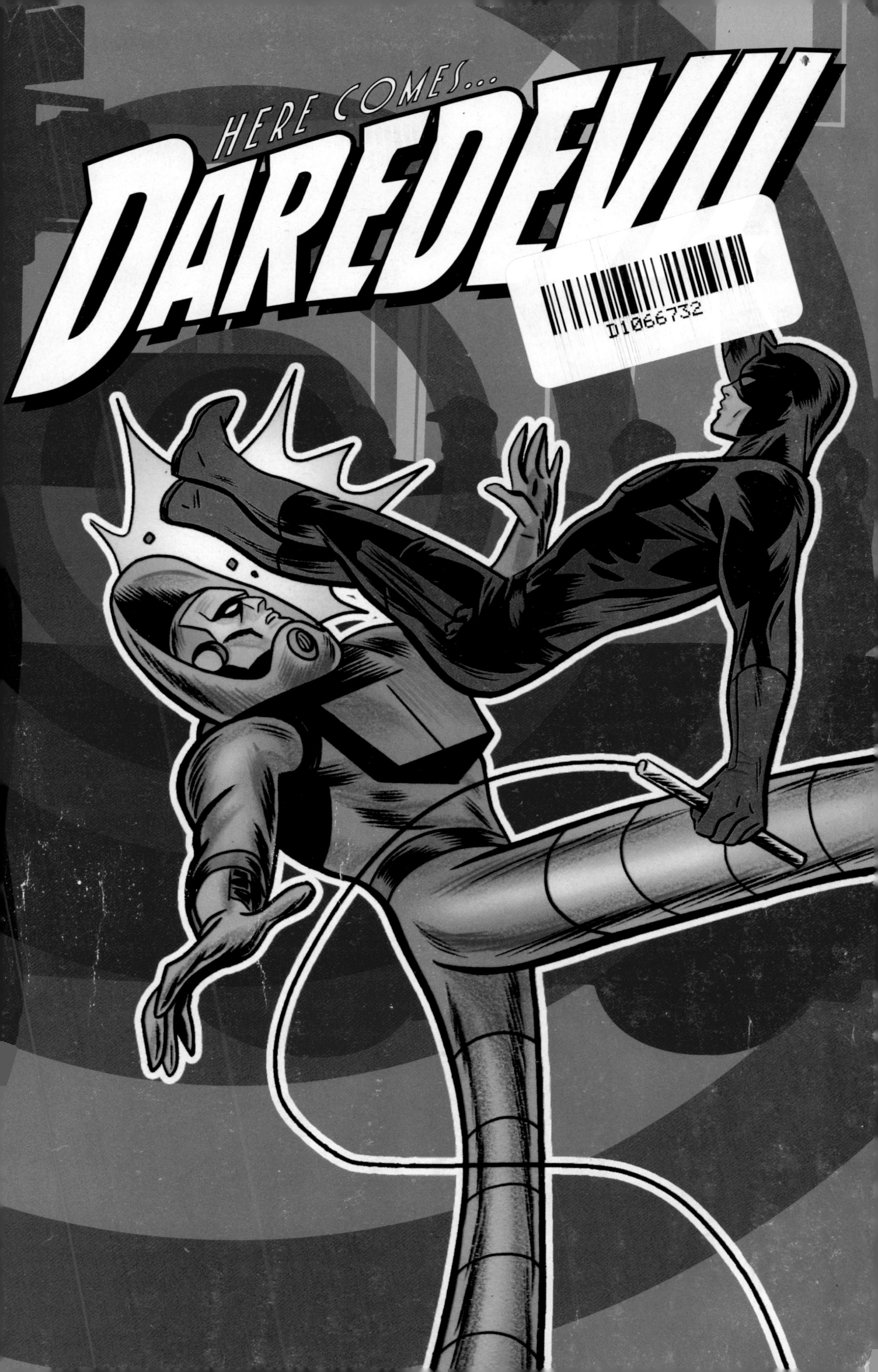
HERE COMES...
DAREDEVIL

COLLECTION EDITOR & DESIGN *CORY LEVINE*
ASSISTANT EDITORS *ALEX STARBUCK* & *NELSON RIBEIRO*
EDITORS, SPECIAL PROJECTS *JENNIFER GRÜNWALD* & *MARK D. BEAZLEY*
SENIOR EDITOR, SPECIAL PROJECTS *JEFF YOUNGQUIST*
SVP OF DIGITAL & PRINT PUBLISHING SALES *DAVID GABRIEL*

EDITOR IN CHIEF *AXEL ALONSO*
CHIEF CREATIVE OFFICER *JOE QUESADA*
PUBLISHER *DAN BUCKLEY*
EXECUTIVE PRODUCER *ALAN FINE*

DAREDEVIL BY MARK WAID VOL. 4. Contains material originally published in magazine form as DAREDEVIL #16-21. First printing 2013. Hardcover ISBN# 978-0-7851-6102-8. Softcover ISBN# 978-0-7851-6103-5. Published by MARVEL WORLDWIDE, INC., a subsidiary of MARVEL ENTERTAINMENT, LLC. OFFICE OF PUBLICATION: 135 West 50th Street, New York, NY 10020. Copyright © 2012 and 2013 Marvel Characters, Inc. All rights reserved. All characters featured in this issue and the distinctive names and likenesses thereof, and all related indicia are trademarks of Marvel Characters, Inc. No similarity between any of the names, characters, persons, and/or institutions in this magazine with those of any living or dead person or institution is intended, and any such similarity which may exist is purely coincidental. **Printed in the U.S.A.** ALAN FINE, EVP - Office of the President, Marvel Worldwide, Inc. and EVP & CMO Marvel Characters B.V.; DAN BUCKLEY, Publisher & President - Print, Animation & Digital Divisions; JOE QUESADA, Chief Creative Officer; TOM BREVOORT, SVP of Publishing; DAVID BOGART, SVP of Operations & Procurement, Publishing; RUWAN JAYATILLEKE, SVP & Associate Publisher, Publishing; C.B. CEBULSKI, SVP of Creator & Content Development; DAVID GABRIEL, SVP of Print & Digital Publishing Sales; JIM O'KEEFE, VP of Operations & Logistics; DAN CARR, Executive Director of Publishing Technology; SUSAN CRESPI, Editorial Operations Manager; ALEX MORALES, Publishing Operations Manager; STAN LEE, Chairman Emeritus. For information regarding advertising in Marvel Comics or on Marvel.com, please contact Niza Disla, Director of Marvel Partnerships, at ndisla@marvel.com. For Marvel subscription inquiries, please call 800-217-9158. **Manufactured between 12/31/2012 and 2/11/2013 (hardcover), and 12/31/2012 and 8/12/2013 (softcover), by R.R. DONNELLEY, INC., SALEM, VA, USA.**

10 9 8 7 6 5 4 3 2 1

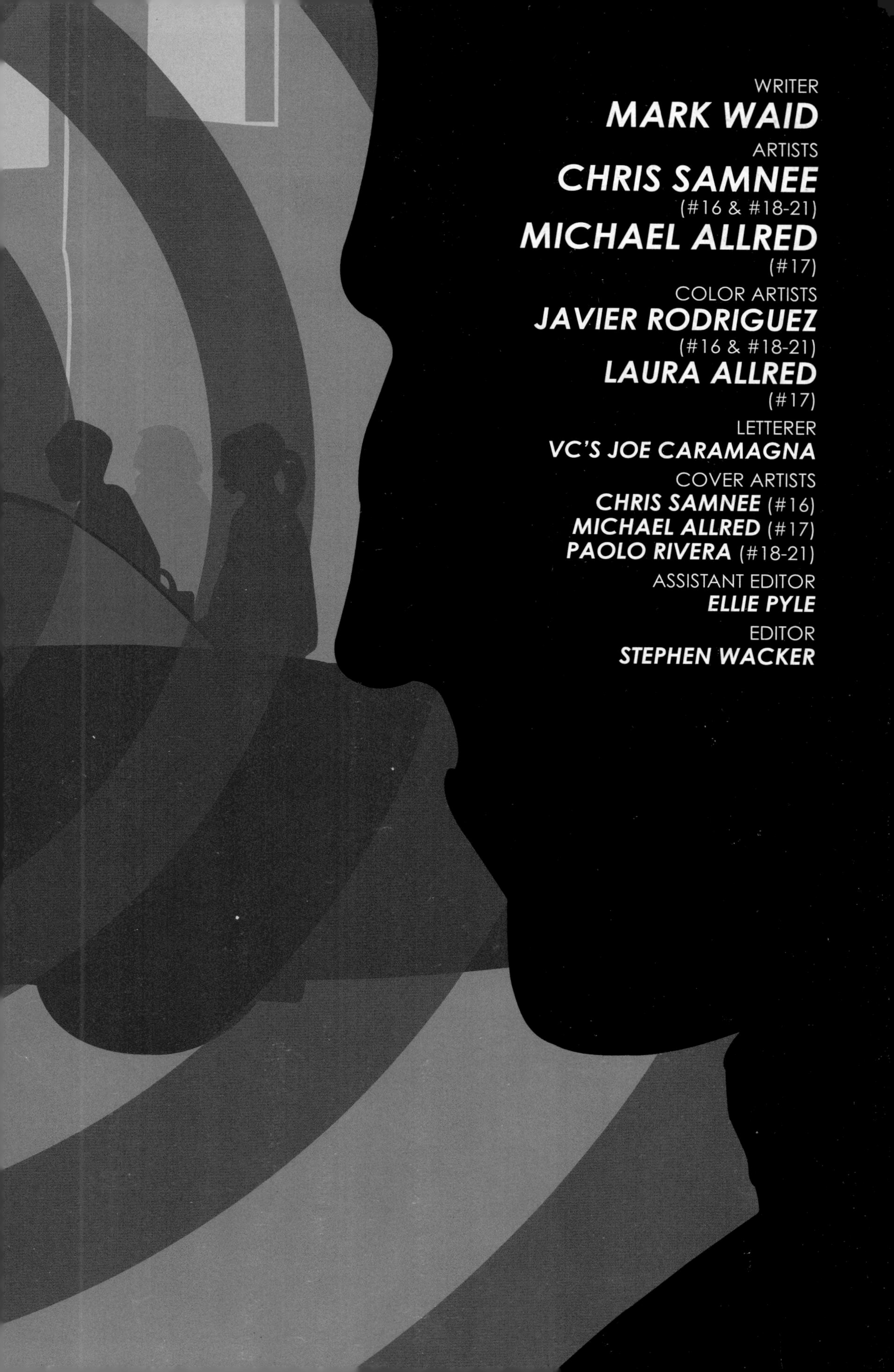

WRITER
MARK WAID
ARTISTS
CHRIS SAMNEE
(#16 & #18-21)
MICHAEL ALLRED
(#17)
COLOR ARTISTS
JAVIER RODRIGUEZ
(#16 & #18-21)
LAURA ALLRED
(#17)
LETTERER
VC'S JOE CARAMAGNA
COVER ARTISTS
CHRIS SAMNEE (#16)
MICHAEL ALLRED (#17)
PAOLO RIVERA (#18-21)
ASSISTANT EDITOR
ELLIE PYLE
EDITOR
STEPHEN WACKER

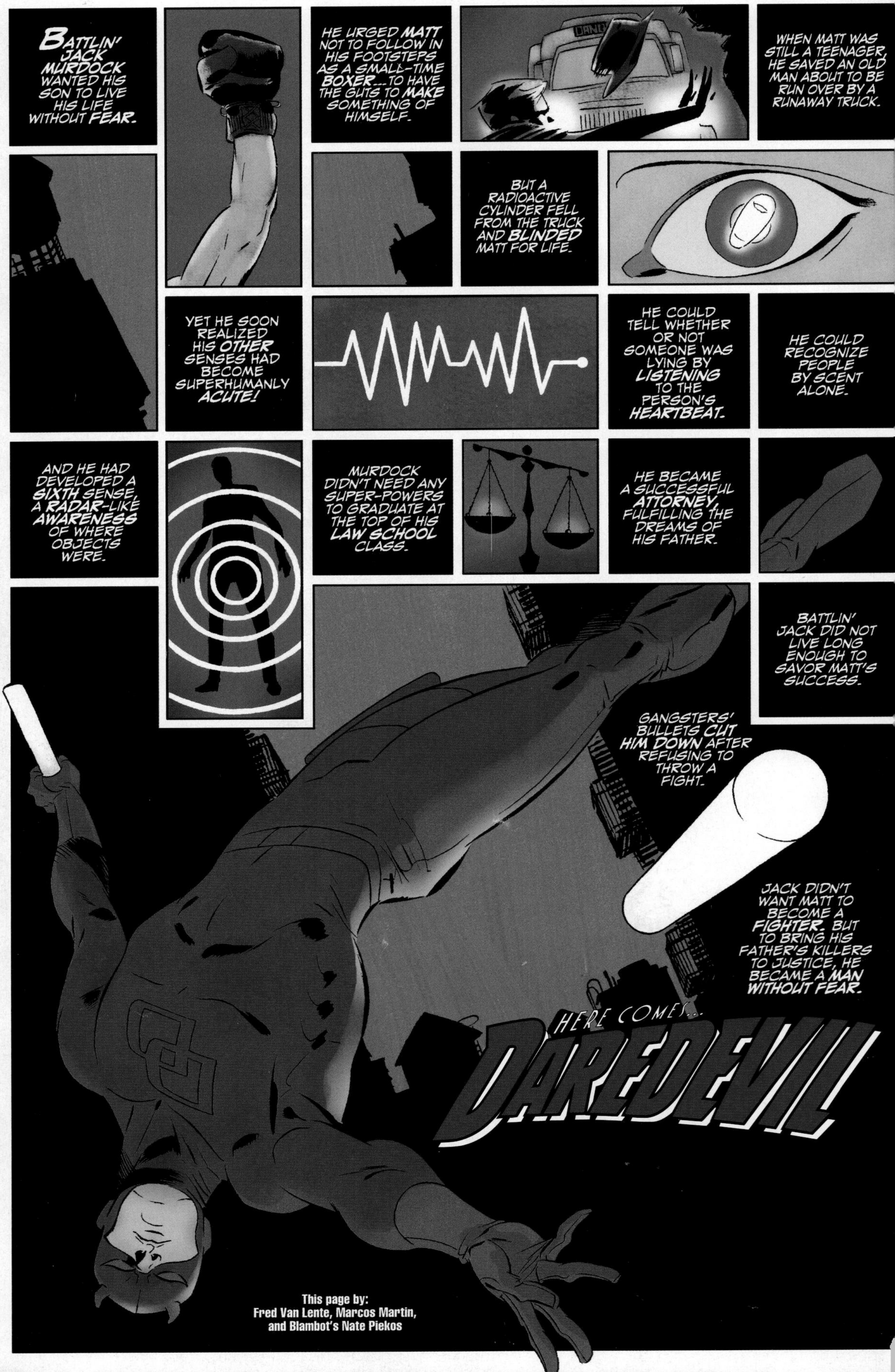
BATTLIN' JACK MURDOCK WANTED HIS SON TO LIVE HIS LIFE WITHOUT FEAR.
HE URGED MATT NOT TO FOLLOW IN HIS FOOTSTEPS AS A SMALL-TIME BOXER... TO HAVE THE GUTS TO MAKE SOMETHING OF HIMSELF.
WHEN MATT WAS STILL A TEENAGER, HE SAVED AN OLD MAN ABOUT TO BE RUN OVER BY A RUNAWAY TRUCK.
BUT A RADIOACTIVE CYLINDER FELL FROM THE TRUCK AND BLINDED MATT FOR LIFE.
YET HE SOON REALIZED HIS OTHER SENSES HAD BECOME SUPERHUMANLY ACUTE!
HE COULD TELL WHETHER OR NOT SOMEONE WAS LYING BY LISTENING TO THE PERSON'S HEARTBEAT.
HE COULD RECOGNIZE PEOPLE BY SCENT ALONE.
AND HE HAD DEVELOPED A SIXTH SENSE, A RADAR-LIKE AWARENESS OF WHERE OBJECTS WERE.
MURDOCK DIDN'T NEED ANY SUPER-POWERS TO GRADUATE AT THE TOP OF HIS LAW SCHOOL CLASS.
HE BECAME A SUCCESSFUL ATTORNEY, FULFILLING THE DREAMS OF HIS FATHER.
BATTLIN' JACK DID NOT LIVE LONG ENOUGH TO SAVOR MATT'S SUCCESS.
GANGSTERS' BULLETS CUT HIM DOWN AFTER REFUSING TO THROW A FIGHT.
JACK DIDN'T WANT MATT TO BECOME A FIGHTER. BUT TO BRING HIS FATHER'S KILLERS TO JUSTICE, HE BECAME A MAN WITHOUT FEAR.
HERE COMES...
DAREDEVIL!

This page by:
Fred Van Lente, Marcos Martin,
and Blambot's Nate Piekos

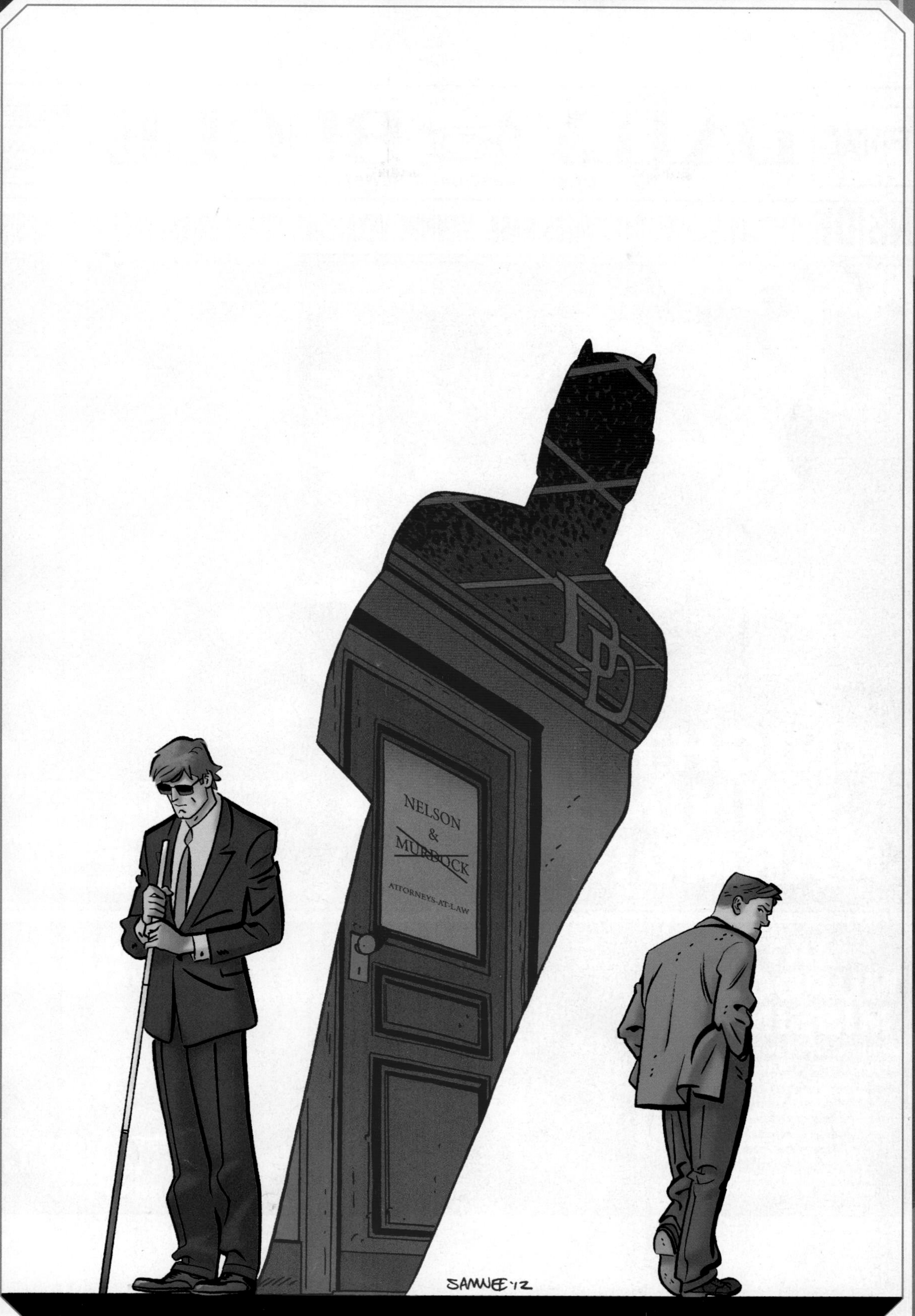
NELSON
&
MURDOCK
ATTORNEYS-AT-LAW
SAMNEE '12

SIXTEEN

FINAL ☆☆☆☆

DAILY BUGLE®

NEW YORK'S FINEST DAILY NEWSPAPER

SINCE 1897 ☆☆☆☆
$1.00 (in NYC)
$1.50 (outside city)

INSIDE: CAPTAIN MARVEL CAPTIVATES MASS., VAMPIRE VEXATIONS, PUNISHER(S?!) PRESENCE PERSIST

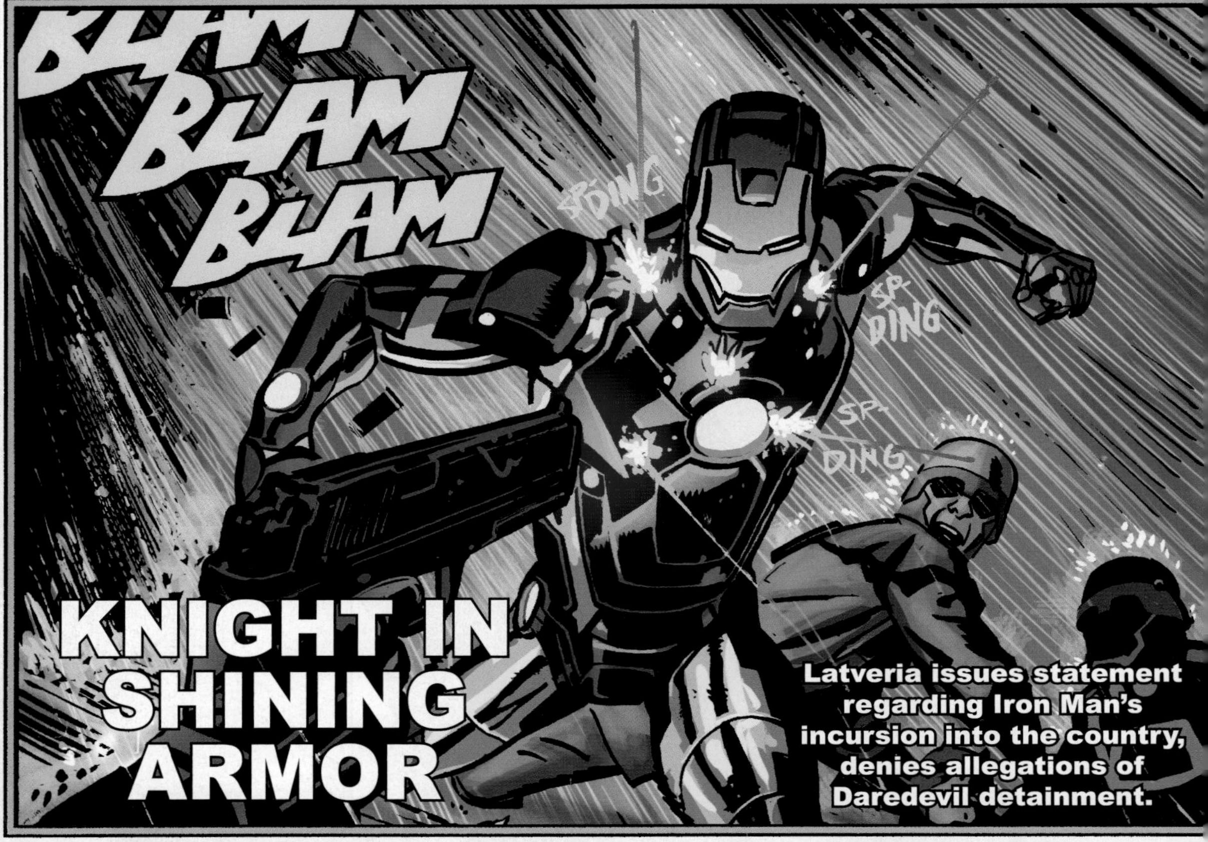

BLAM
BLAM
SPDING
SP-DING
SP-DING

KNIGHT IN SHINING ARMOR

Latveria issues statement regarding Iron Man's incursion into the country, denies allegations of Daredevil detainment.

MATT MURDOCK MISSING?

Manhattan's favorite blind lawyer, Matt Murdock, has been suspiciously absent from the legal (and singles!) scene. Could this have anything to do with the rumors that he's Daredevil?

(pictured here with law partner Foggy Nelson]

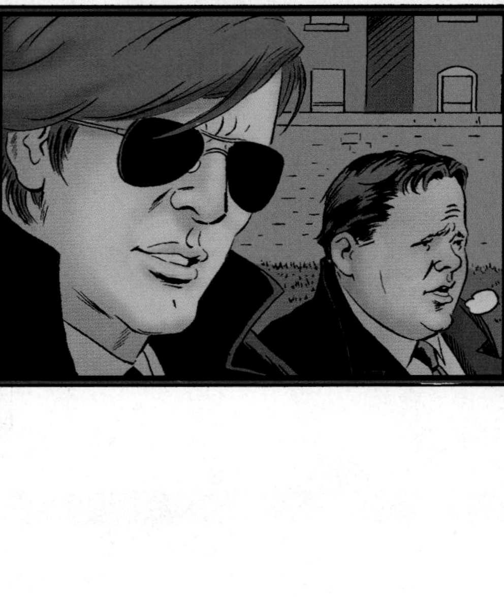

Remembering JANET VAN DYNE:

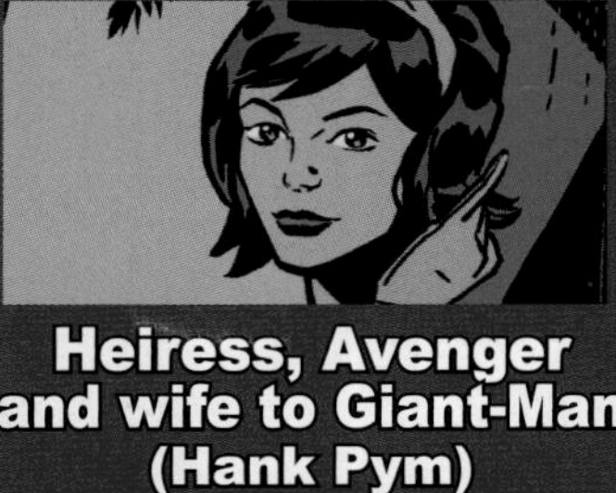

Heiress, Avenger and wife to Giant-Man (Hank Pym)

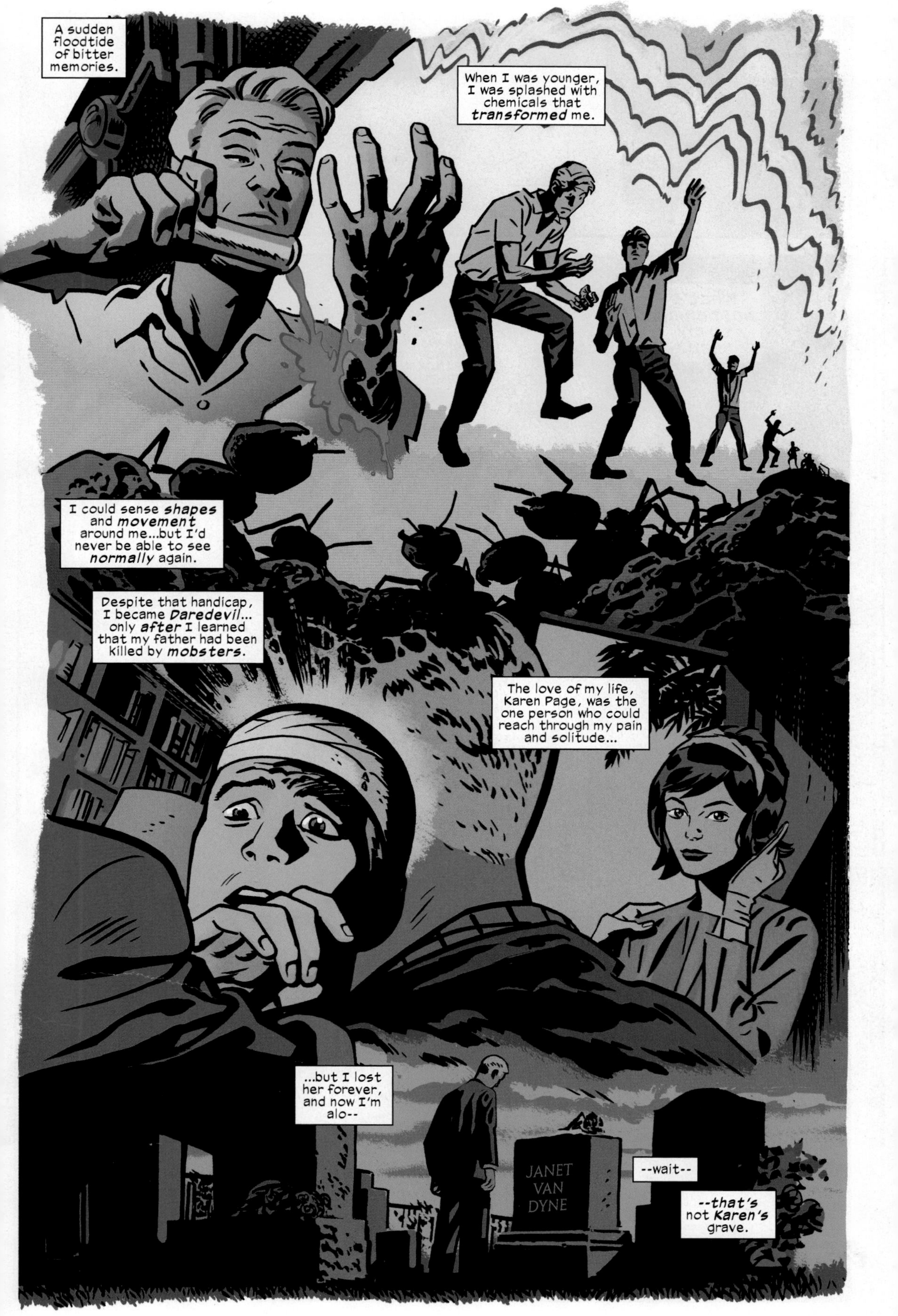
A sudden floodtide of bitter memories.
When I was younger, I was splashed with chemicals that *transformed* me.
I could sense *shapes* and *movement* around me...but I'd never be able to see *normally* again.
Despite that handicap, I became *Daredevil*... only *after* I learned that my father had been killed by *mobsters*.
The love of my life, Karen Page, was the one person who could reach through my pain and solitude...
...but I lost her forever, and now I'm alo--
JANET VAN DYNE
--wait--
--*that's* not *Karen's* grave.

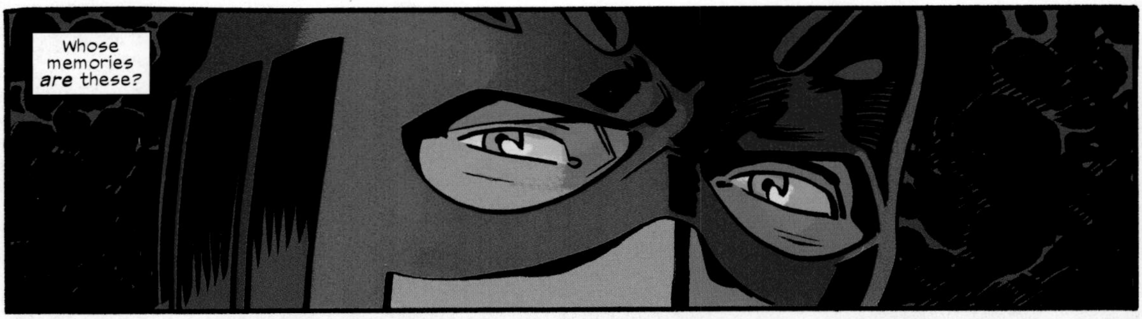
Whose memories are these?

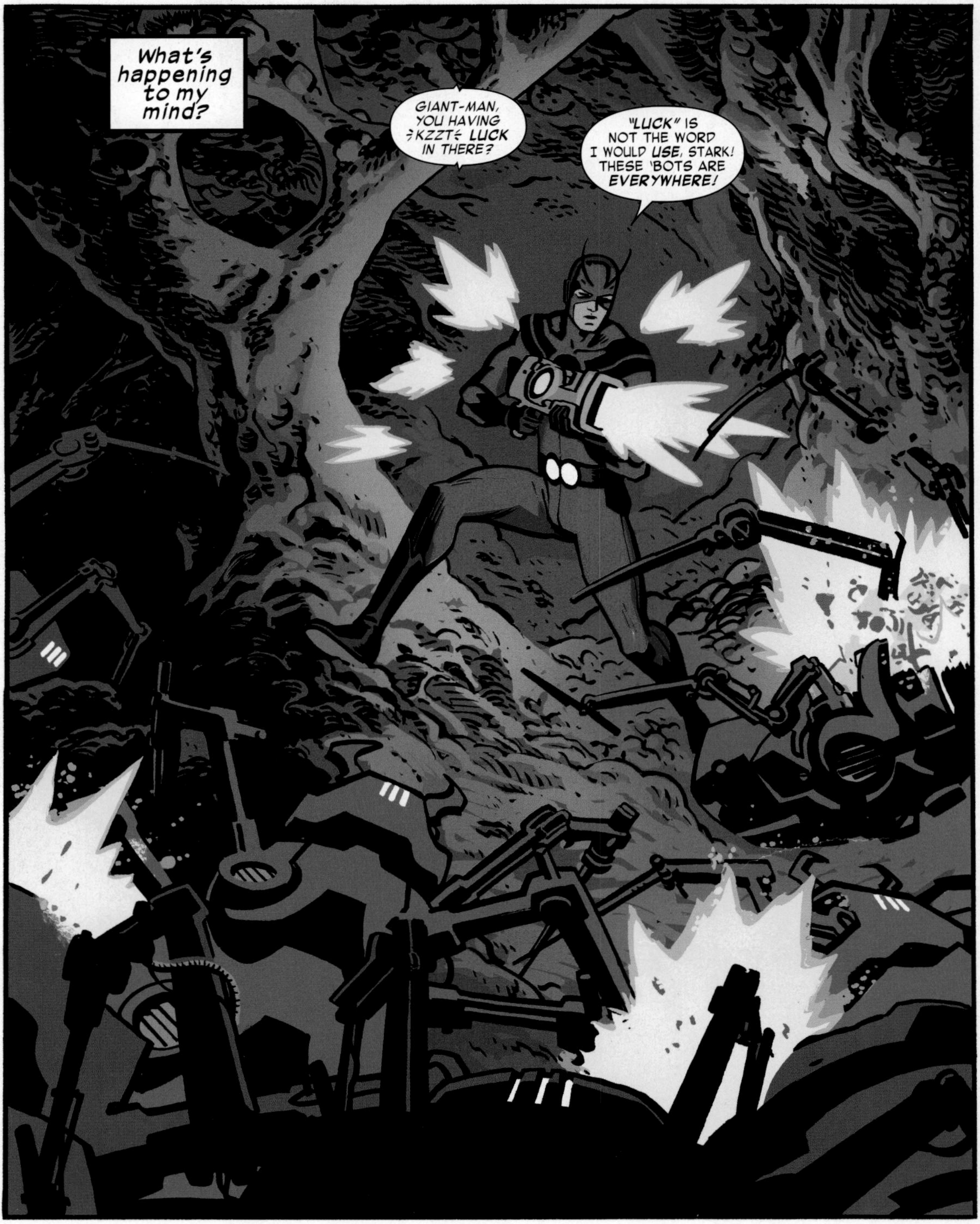
What's happening to my mind?
GIANT-MAN, YOU HAVING ≠KZZT≠ LUCK IN THERE?
"LUCK" IS NOT THE WORD I WOULD USE, STARK! THESE 'BOTS ARE EVERYWHERE!

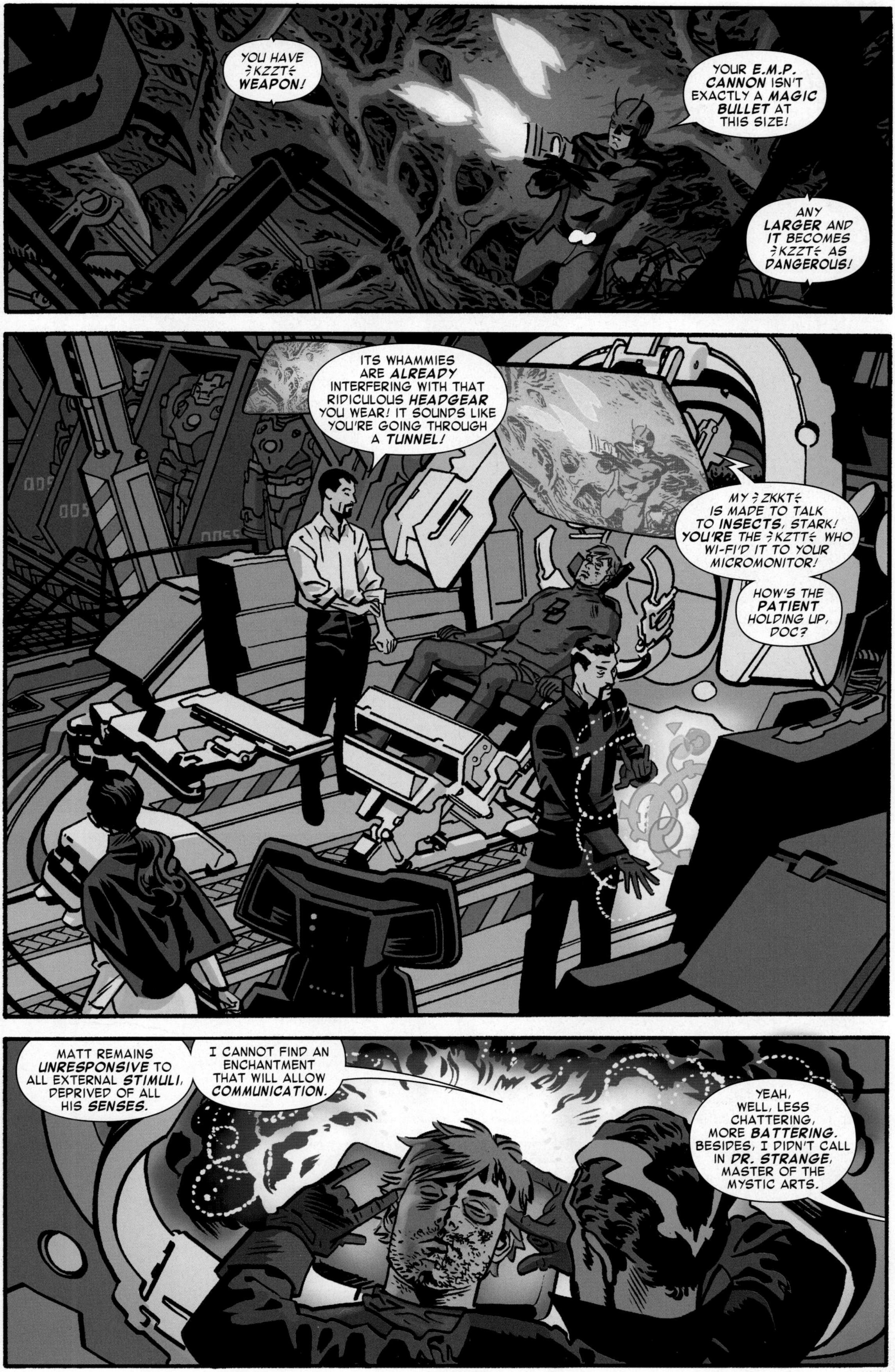
YOU HAVE =KZZT= WEAPON!
YOUR E.M.P. CANNON ISN'T EXACTLY A MAGIC BULLET AT THIS SIZE!
ANY LARGER AND IT BECOMES =KZZT= AS DANGEROUS!
ITS WHAMMIES ARE ALREADY INTERFERING WITH THAT RIDICULOUS HEADGEAR YOU WEAR! IT SOUNDS LIKE YOU'RE GOING THROUGH A TUNNEL!
MY =ZKKT= IS MADE TO TALK TO INSECTS, STARK! YOU'RE THE =KZTT= WHO WI-FI'D IT TO YOUR MICROMONITOR!
HOW'S THE PATIENT HOLDING UP, DOC?
MATT REMAINS UNRESPONSIVE TO ALL EXTERNAL STIMULI, DEPRIVED OF ALL HIS SENSES.
I CANNOT FIND AN ENCHANTMENT THAT WILL ALLOW COMMUNICATION.
YEAH, WELL, LESS CHATTERING, MORE BATTERING. BESIDES, I DIDN'T CALL IN DR. STRANGE, MASTER OF THE MYSTIC ARTS.

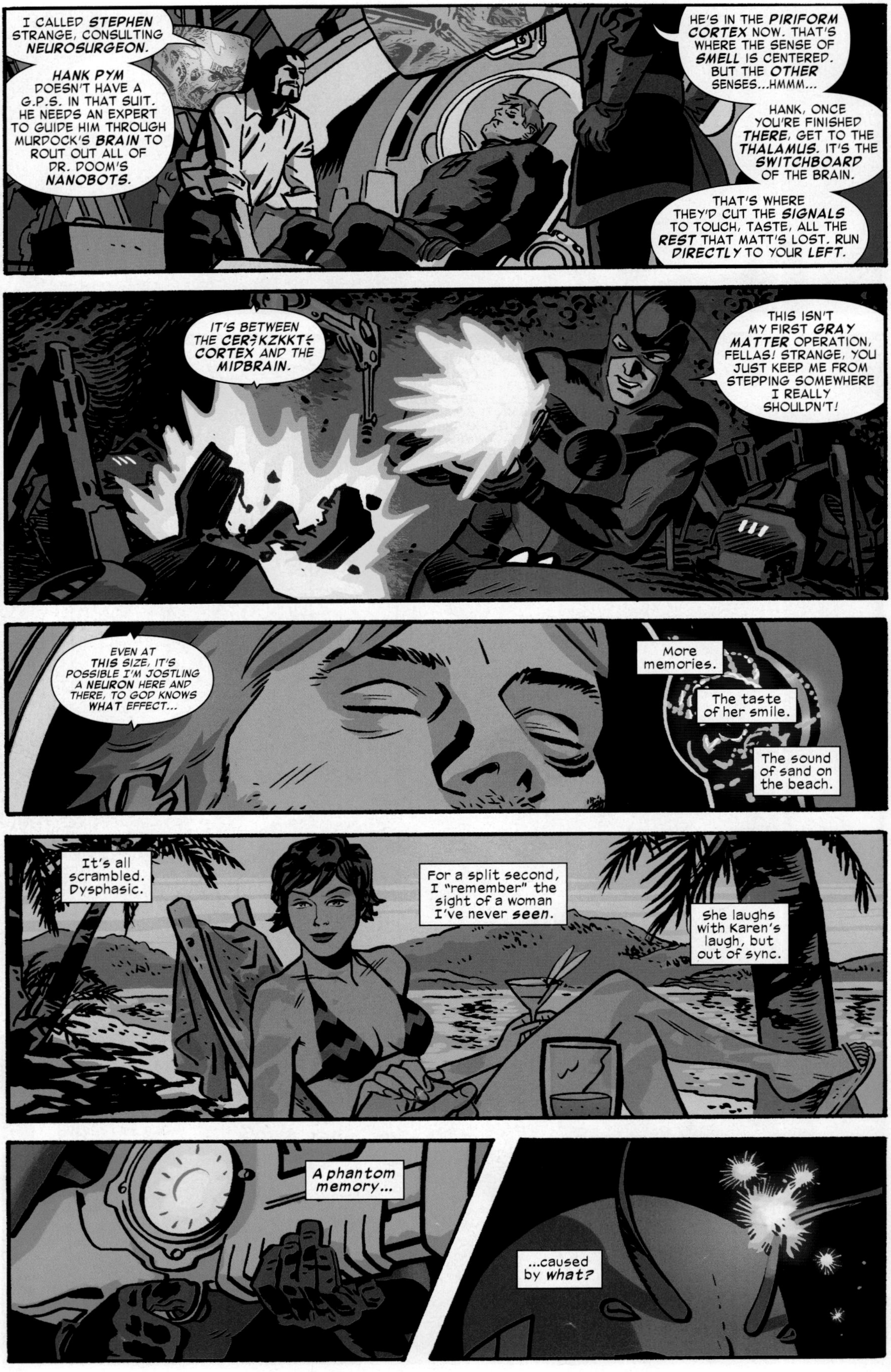
I CALLED STEPHEN STRANGE, CONSULTING NEUROSURGEON.
HANK PYM DOESN'T HAVE A G.P.S. IN THAT SUIT. HE NEEDS AN EXPERT TO GUIDE HIM THROUGH MURDOCK'S BRAIN TO ROUT OUT ALL OF DR. DOOM'S NANOBOTS.
HE'S IN THE PIRIFORM CORTEX NOW. THAT'S WHERE THE SENSE OF SMELL IS CENTERED. BUT THE OTHER SENSES...HMMM...
HANK, ONCE YOU'RE FINISHED THERE, GET TO THE THALAMUS. IT'S THE SWITCHBOARD OF THE BRAIN.
THAT'S WHERE THEY'D CUT THE SIGNALS TO TOUCH, TASTE, ALL THE REST THAT MATT'S LOST. RUN DIRECTLY TO YOUR LEFT.
IT'S BETWEEN THE CER-KZKKT- CORTEX AND THE MIDBRAIN.
THIS ISN'T MY FIRST GRAY MATTER OPERATION, FELLAS! STRANGE, YOU JUST KEEP ME FROM STEPPING SOMEWHERE I REALLY SHOULDN'T!
EVEN AT THIS SIZE, IT'S POSSIBLE I'M JOSTLING A NEURON HERE AND THERE, TO GOD KNOWS WHAT EFFECT...
More memories.
The taste of her smile.
The sound of sand on the beach.
It's all scrambled. Dysphasic.
For a split second, I "remember" the sight of a woman I've never seen.
She laughs with Karen's laugh, but out of sync.
A phantom memory...
...caused by what?

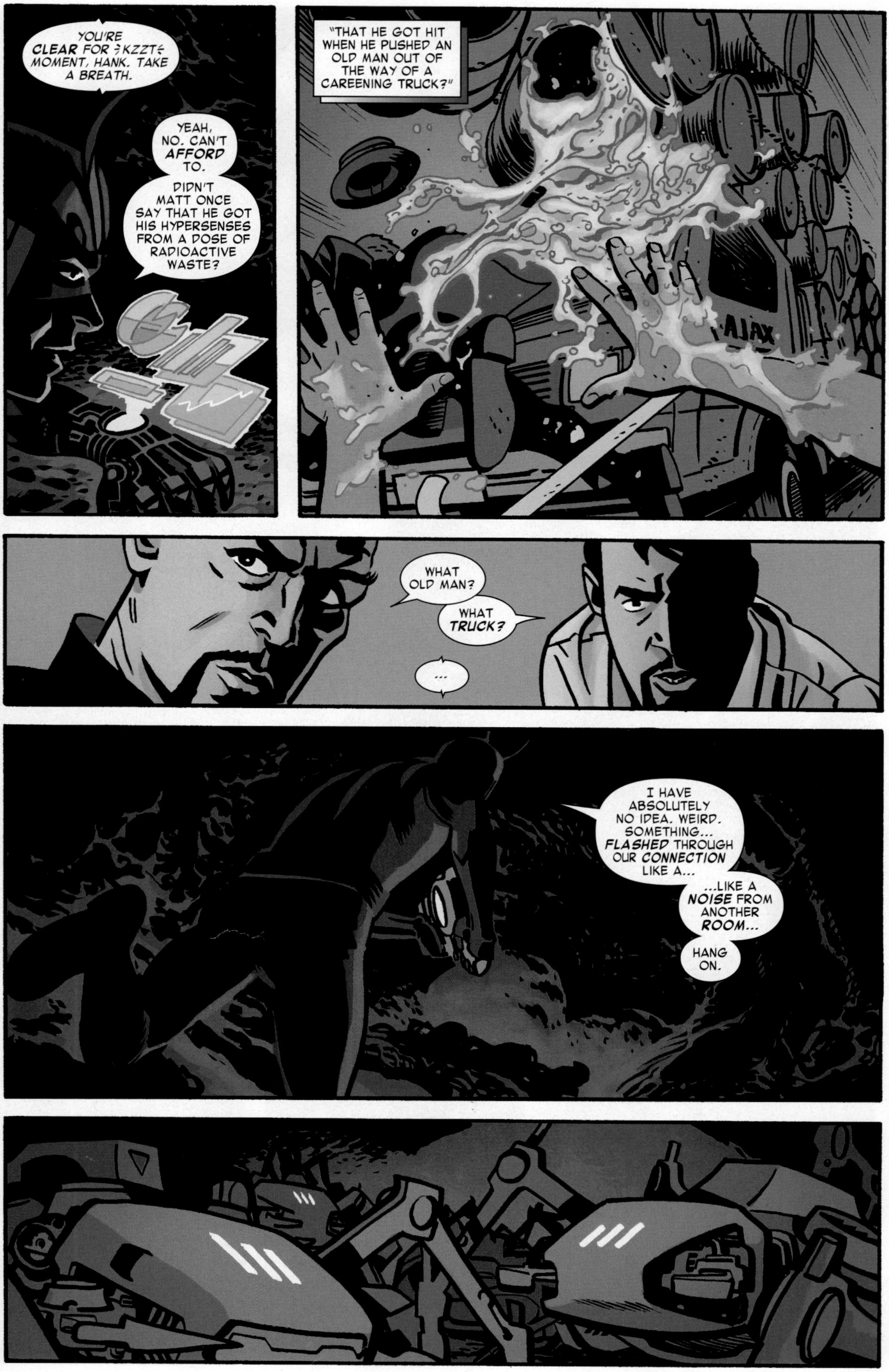

YOU'RE CLEAR FOR ⸗KZZT⸗ MOMENT, HANK. TAKE A BREATH.
YEAH, NO. CAN'T AFFORD TO.
DIDN'T MATT ONCE SAY THAT HE GOT HIS HYPERSENSES FROM A DOSE OF RADIOACTIVE WASTE?
"THAT HE GOT HIT WHEN HE PUSHED AN OLD MAN OUT OF THE WAY OF A CAREENING TRUCK?"
AJAX
WHAT OLD MAN?
WHAT TRUCK?
...
I HAVE ABSOLUTELY NO IDEA. WEIRD. SOMETHING... FLASHED THROUGH OUR CONNECTION LIKE A...
...LIKE A NOISE FROM ANOTHER ROOM...
HANG ON.

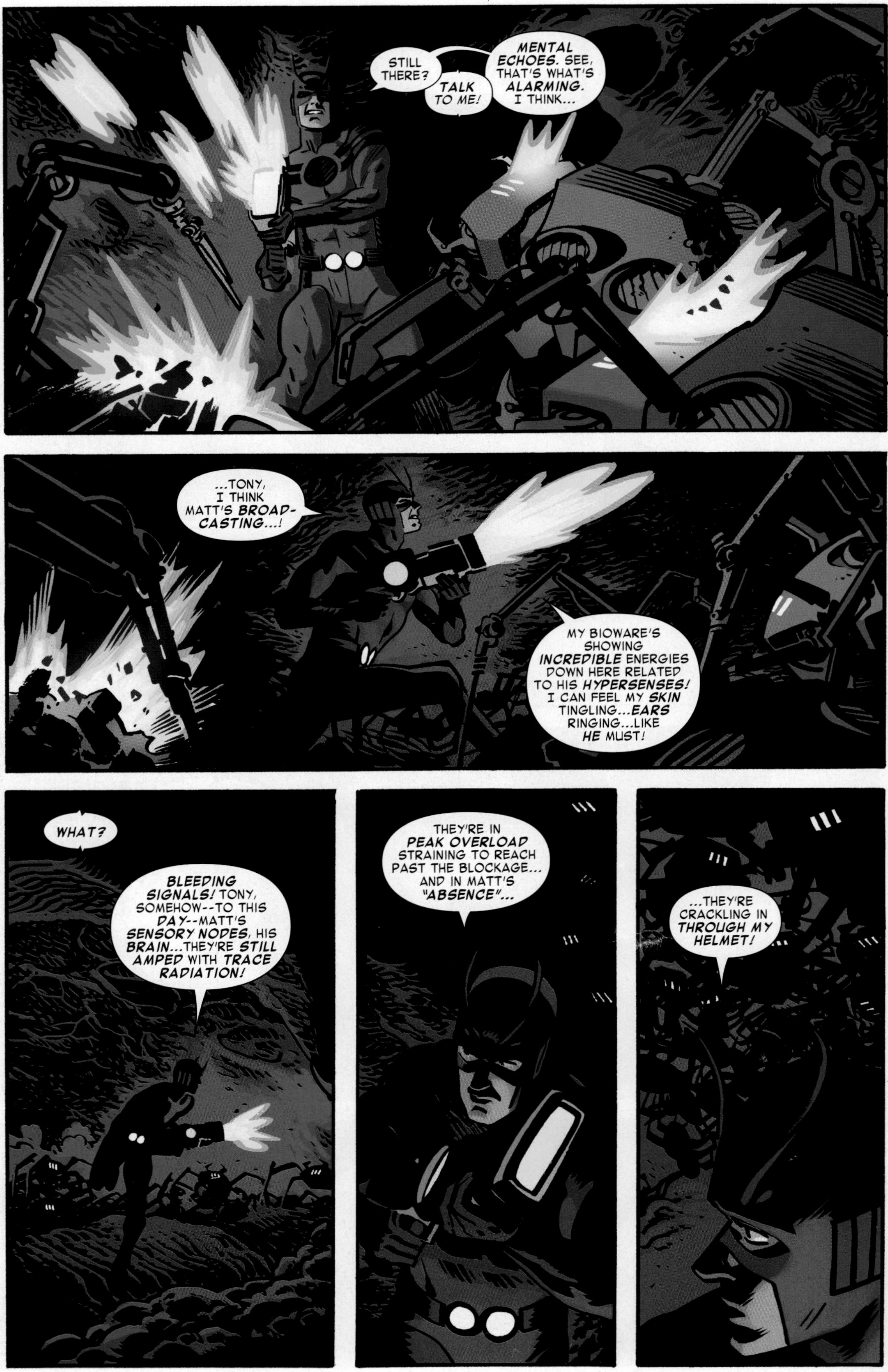
STILL THERE?
TALK TO ME!
MENTAL ECHOES. SEE, THAT'S WHAT'S ALARMING. I THINK...
...TONY, I THINK MATT'S BROAD-CASTING...!
MY BIOWARE'S SHOWING INCREDIBLE ENERGIES DOWN HERE RELATED TO HIS HYPERSENSES! I CAN FEEL MY SKIN TINGLING...EARS RINGING...LIKE HE MUST!
WHAT?
BLEEDING SIGNALS! TONY, SOMEHOW--TO THIS DAY--MATT'S SENSORY NODES, HIS BRAIN...THEY'RE STILL AMPED WITH TRACE RADIATION!
THEY'RE IN PEAK OVERLOAD STRAINING TO REACH PAST THE BLOCKAGE... AND IN MATT'S "ABSENCE"...
...THEY'RE CRACKLING IN THROUGH MY HELMET!

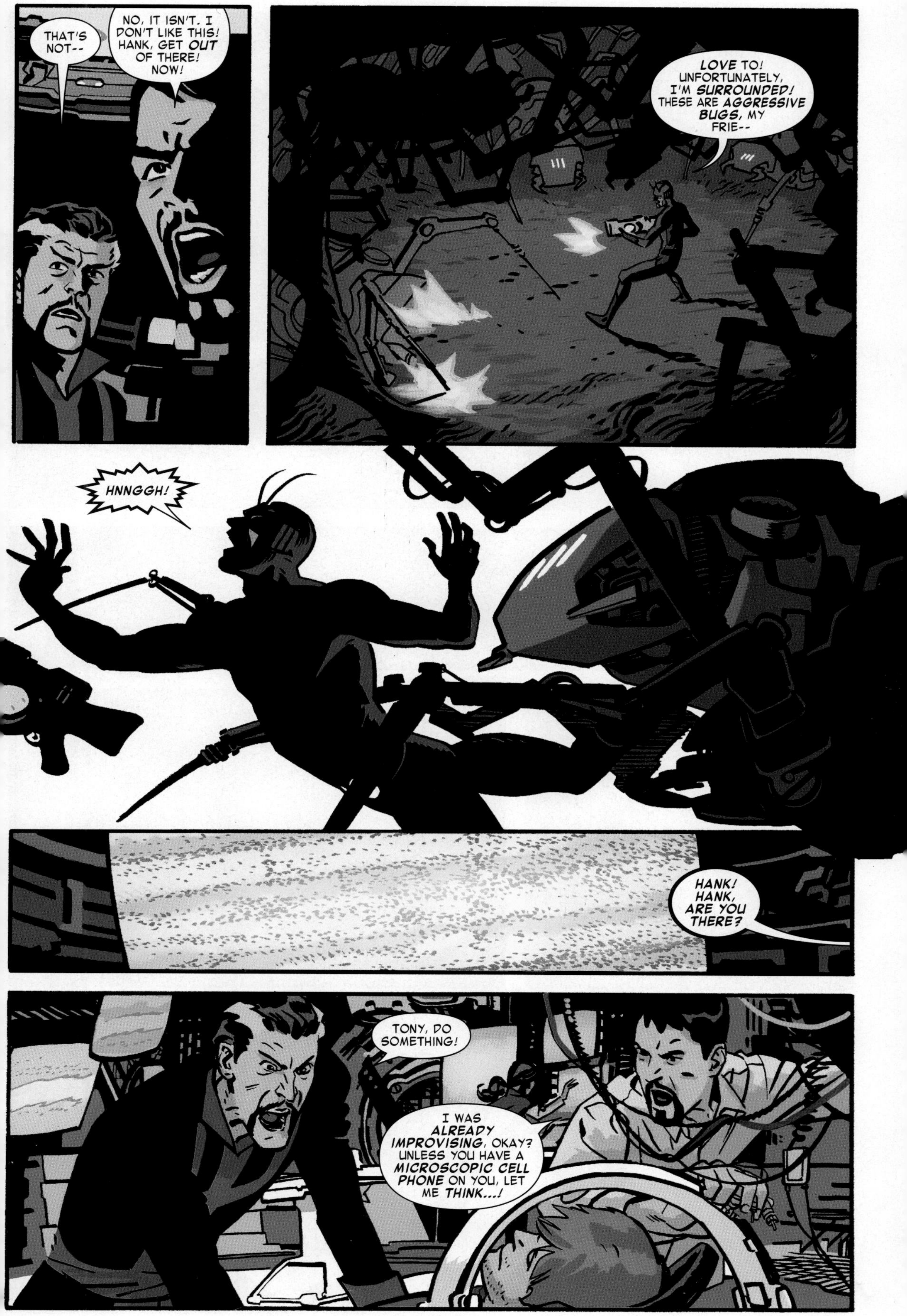
THAT'S NOT--
NO, IT ISN'T. I DON'T LIKE THIS! HANK, GET OUT OF THERE! NOW!
LOVE TO! UNFORTUNATELY, I'M SURROUNDED! THESE ARE AGGRESSIVE BUGS, MY FRIE--
HNNGGH!
HANK! HANK, ARE YOU THERE?
TONY, DO SOMETHING!
I WAS ALREADY IMPROVISING, OKAY? UNLESS YOU HAVE A MICROSCOPIC CELL PHONE ON YOU, LET ME THINK...!

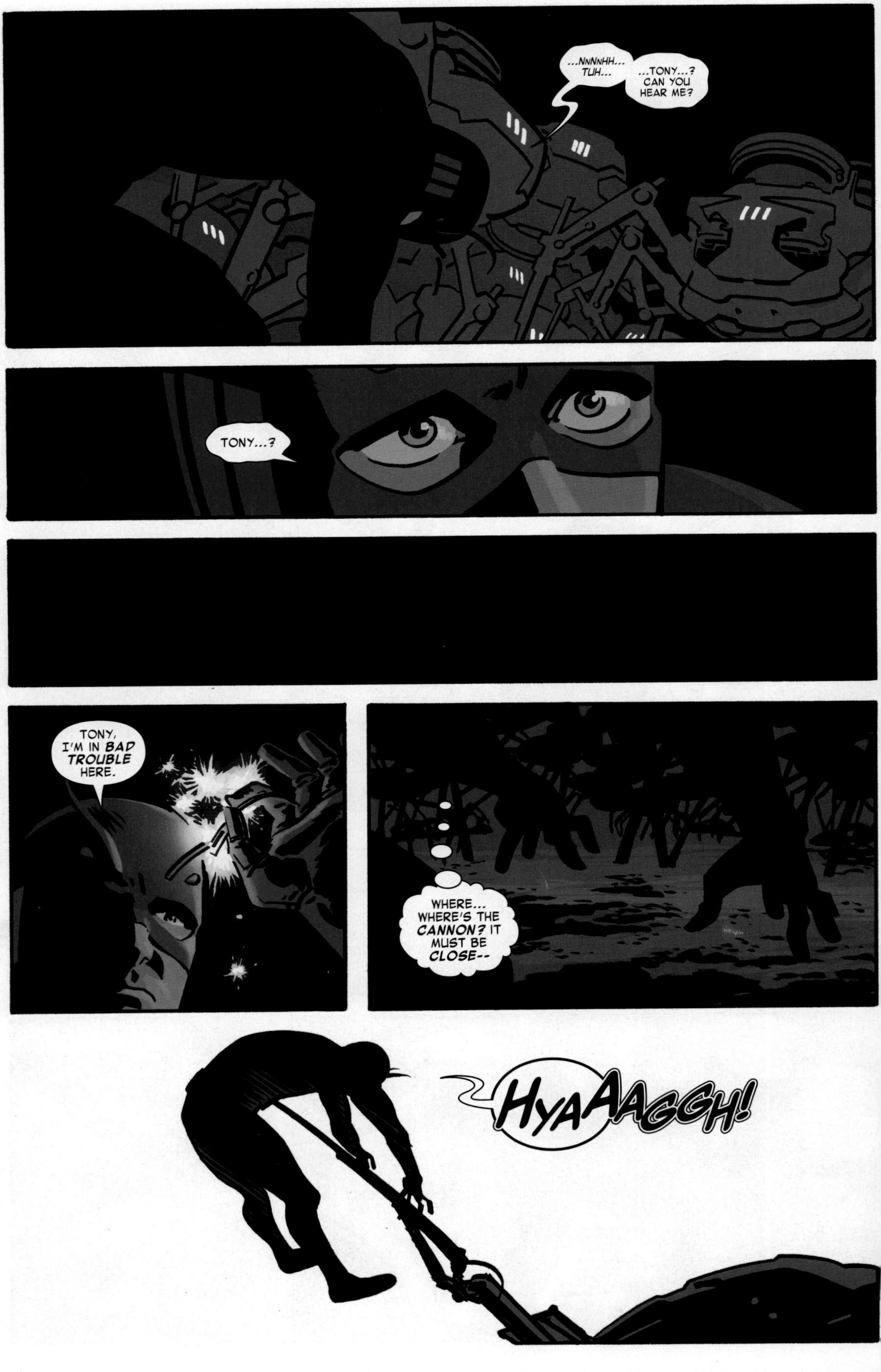
...NNNNHH... TUH...
...TONY...? CAN YOU HEAR ME?
TONY...?
TONY, I'M IN BAD TROUBLE HERE.
WHERE... WHERE'S THE CANNON? IT MUST BE CLOSE--
HYAAAGGH!

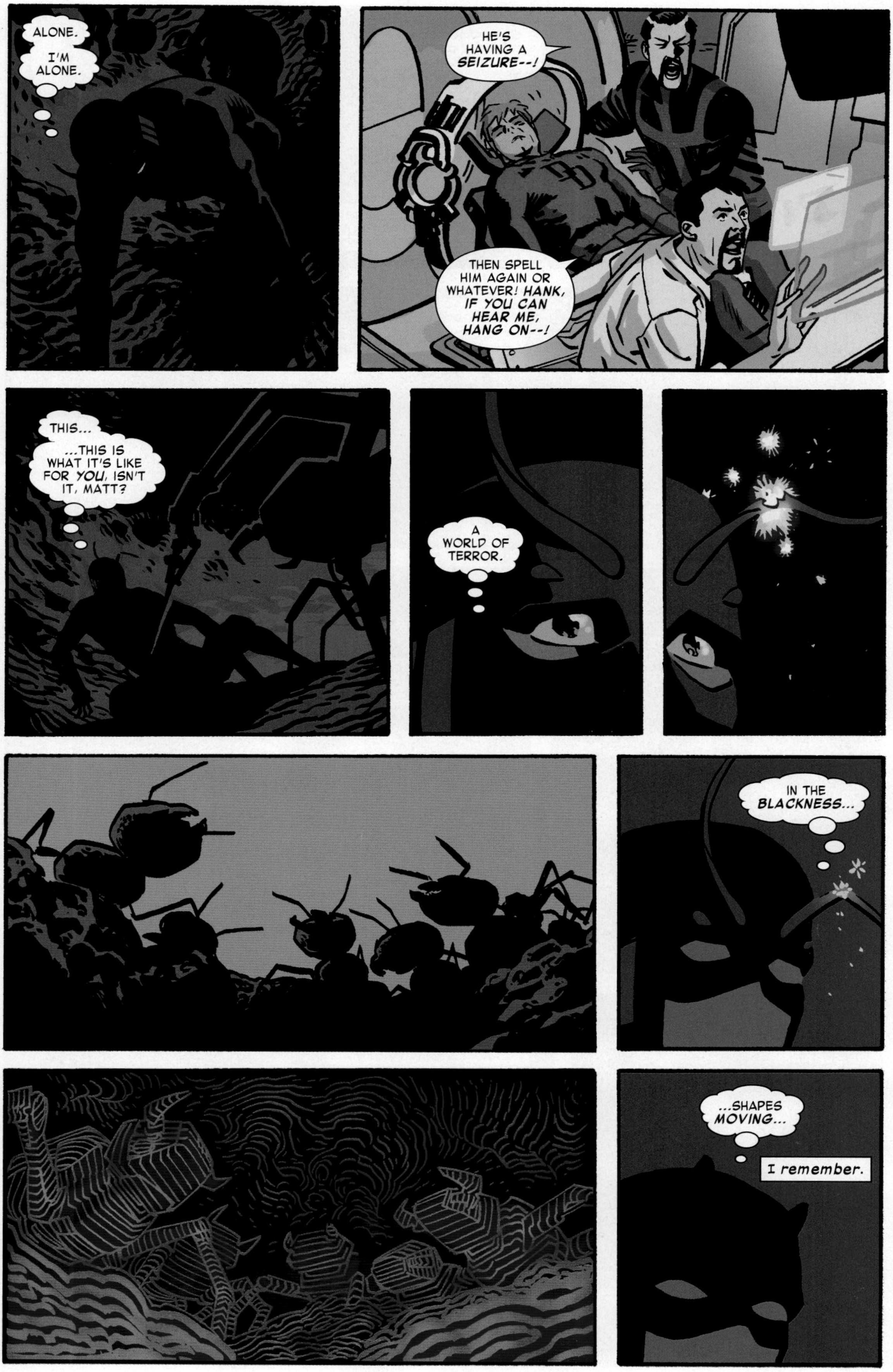

ALONE.
I'M ALONE.
HE'S HAVING A *SEIZURE--!*
THEN SPELL HIM AGAIN OR WHATEVER! *HANK, IF YOU CAN HEAR ME, HANG ON--!*
THIS...
...THIS IS WHAT IT'S LIKE FOR *YOU*, ISN'T IT, MATT?
A WORLD OF TERROR.
IN THE *BLACKNESS...*
...SHAPES *MOVING...*
I *remember.*

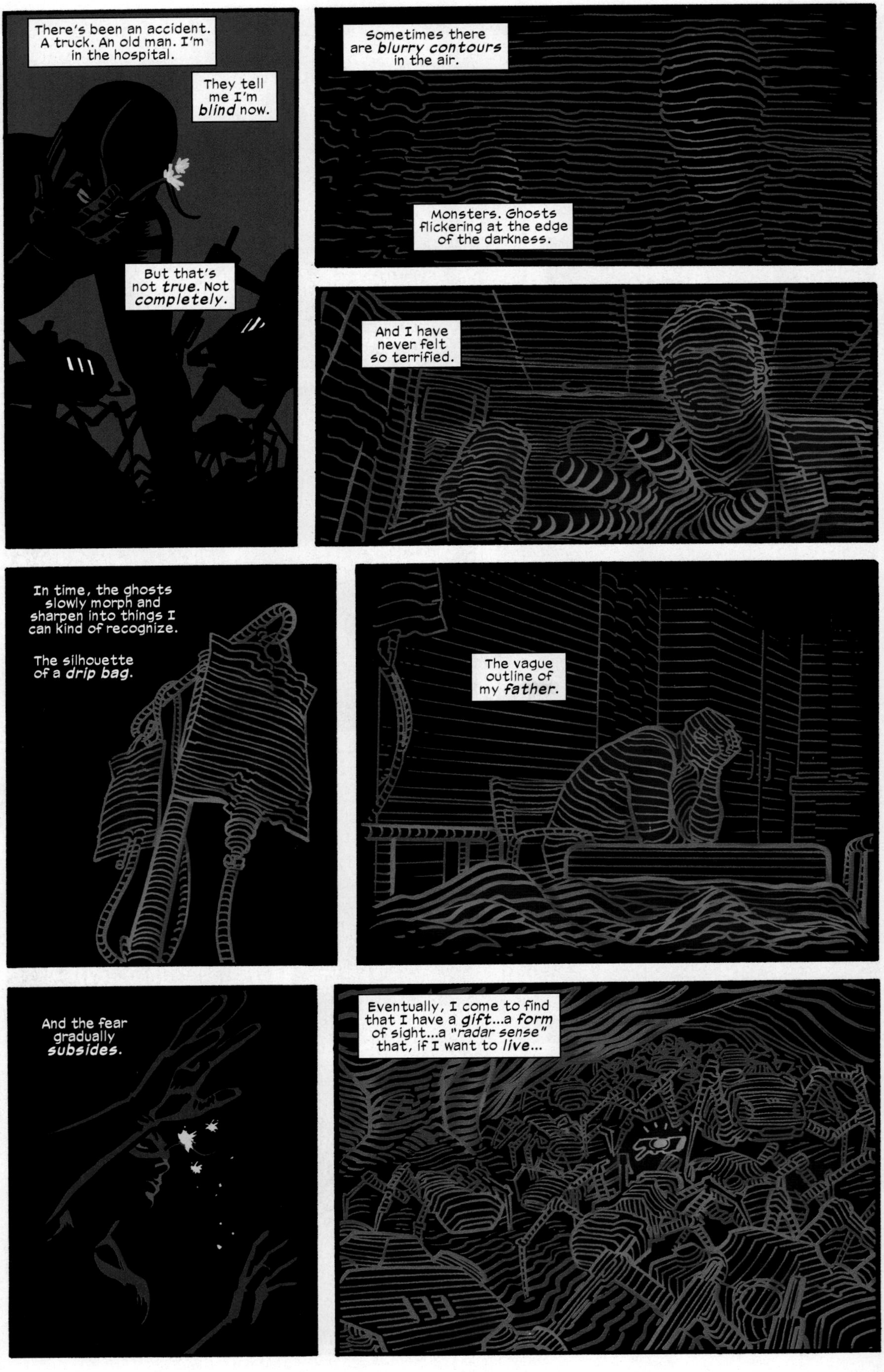
There's been an accident. A truck. An old man. I'm in the hospital.
They tell me I'm *blind* now.
But that's not *true*. Not *completely*.
Sometimes there are *blurry contours* in the air.
Monsters. Ghosts flickering at the edge of the darkness.
And I have never felt so terrified.
In time, the ghosts slowly morph and sharpen into things I can kind of recognize.
The silhouette of a *drip bag*.
The vague outline of my *father*.
And the fear gradually *subsides*.
Eventually, I come to find that I have a *gift*...a *form* of sight...a "*radar sense*" that, if I want to *live*...

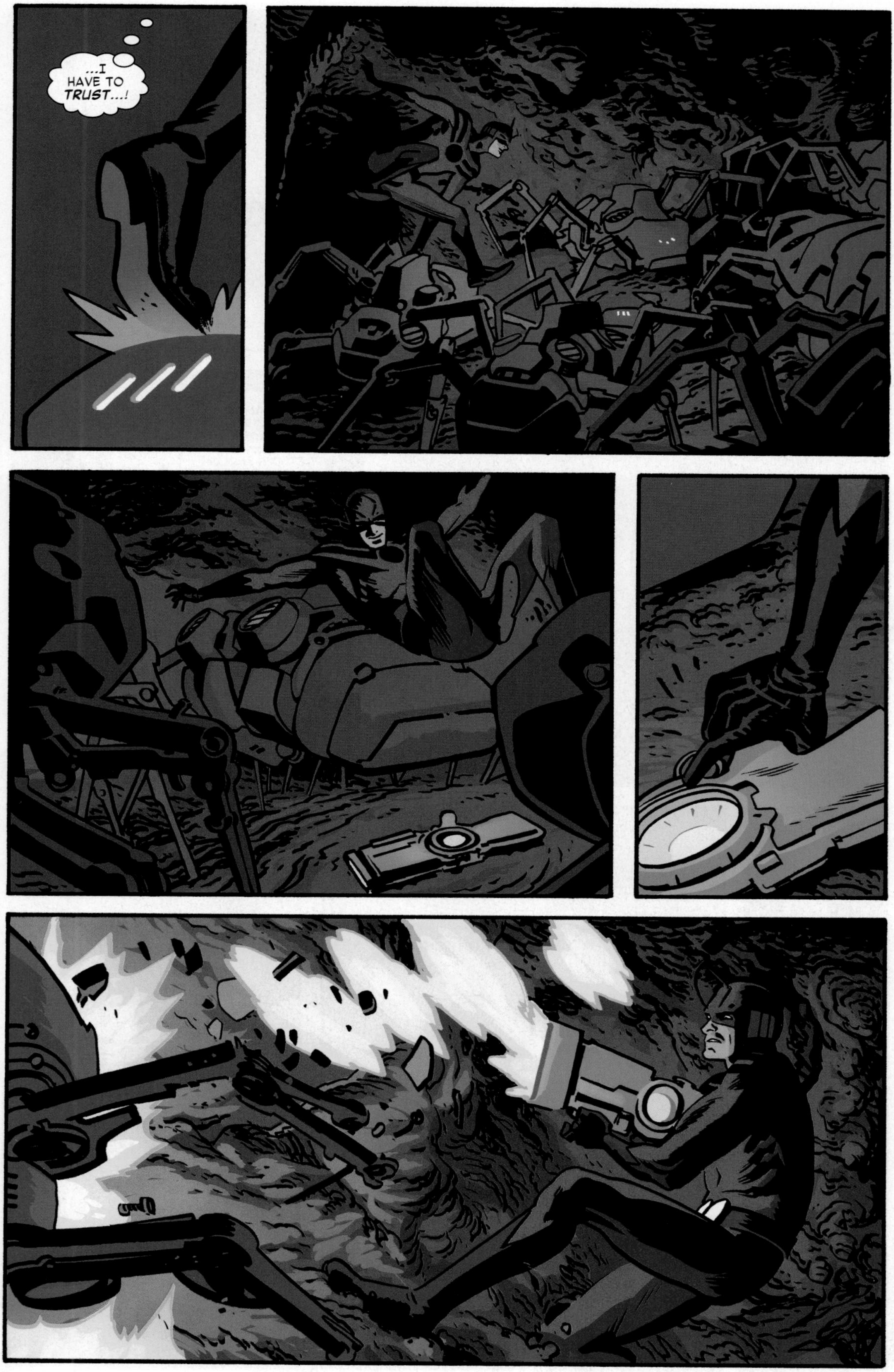
...I HAVE TO TRUST...!

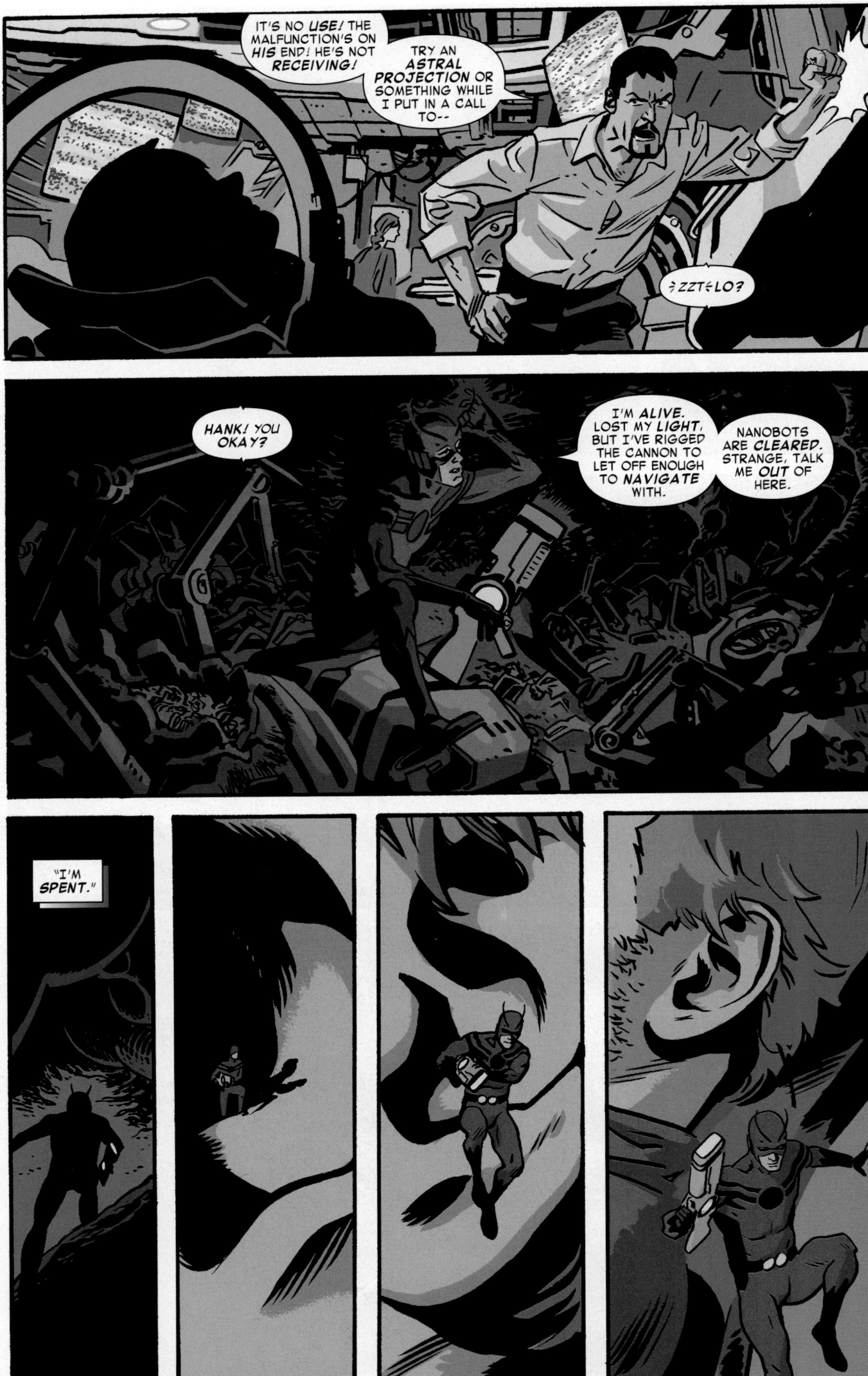
IT'S NO USE! THE MALFUNCTION'S ON HIS END! HE'S NOT RECEIVING!
TRY AN ASTRAL PROJECTION OR SOMETHING WHILE I PUT IN A CALL TO--
ZZT LO?
HANK! YOU OKAY?
I'M ALIVE. LOST MY LIGHT, BUT I'VE RIGGED THE CANNON TO LET OFF ENOUGH TO NAVIGATE WITH.
NANOBOTS ARE CLEARED. STRANGE, TALK ME OUT OF HERE.
"I'M SPENT."

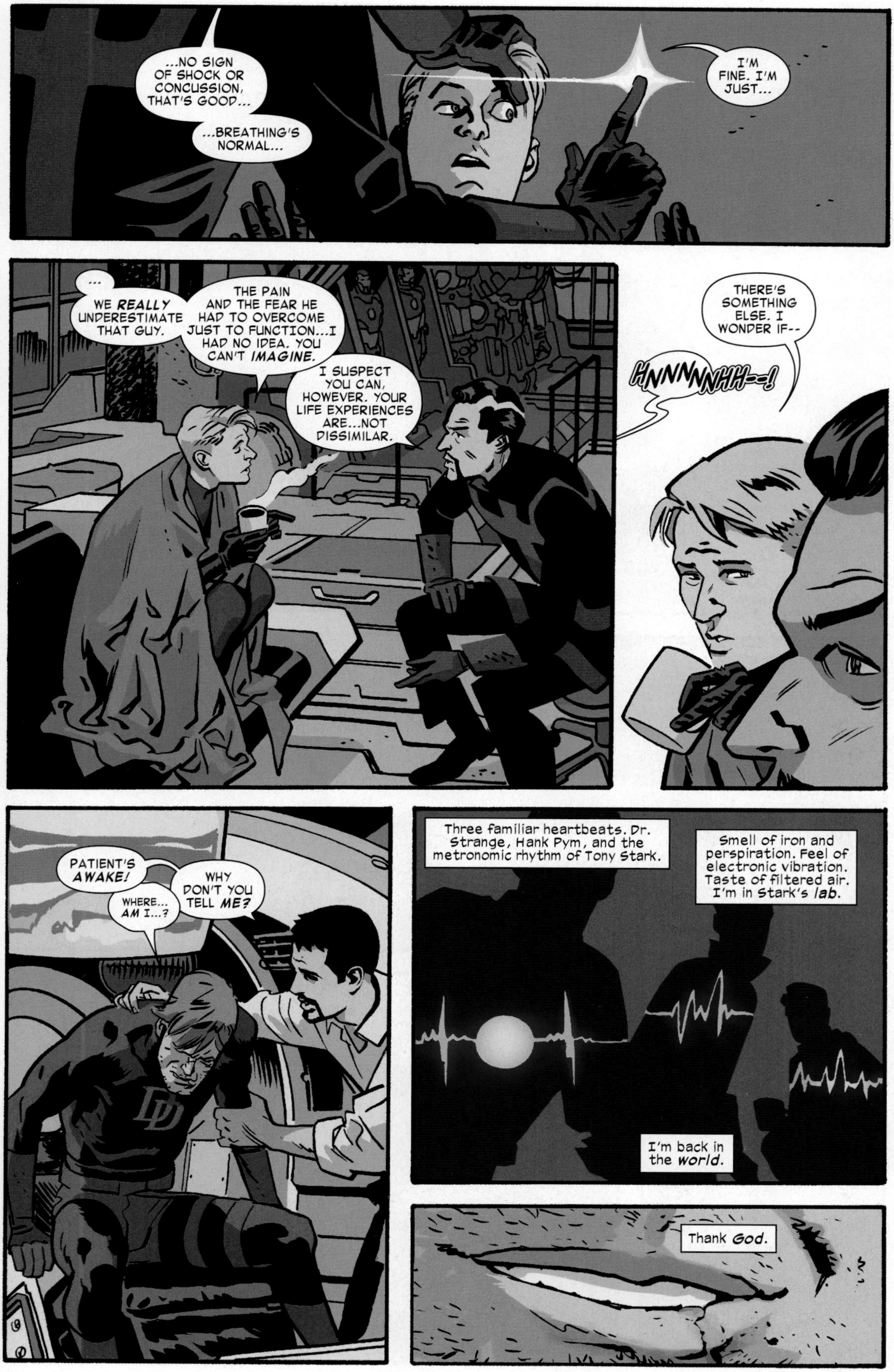

...NO SIGN OF SHOCK OR CONCUSSION, THAT'S GOOD...
...BREATHING'S NORMAL...
I'M FINE. I'M JUST...
...WE REALLY UNDERESTIMATE THAT GUY.
THE PAIN AND THE FEAR HE HAD TO OVERCOME JUST TO FUNCTION...I HAD NO IDEA. YOU CAN'T IMAGINE.
I SUSPECT YOU CAN, HOWEVER. YOUR LIFE EXPERIENCES ARE...NOT DISSIMILAR.
THERE'S SOMETHING ELSE. I WONDER IF--
HNNNNNHH--!
PATIENT'S AWAKE!
WHERE... AM I...?
WHY DON'T YOU TELL ME?
Three familiar heartbeats. Dr. Strange, Hank Pym, and the metronomic rhythm of Tony Stark.
Smell of iron and perspiration. Feel of electronic vibration. Taste of filtered air. I'm in Stark's lab.
I'm back in the world.
Thank God.

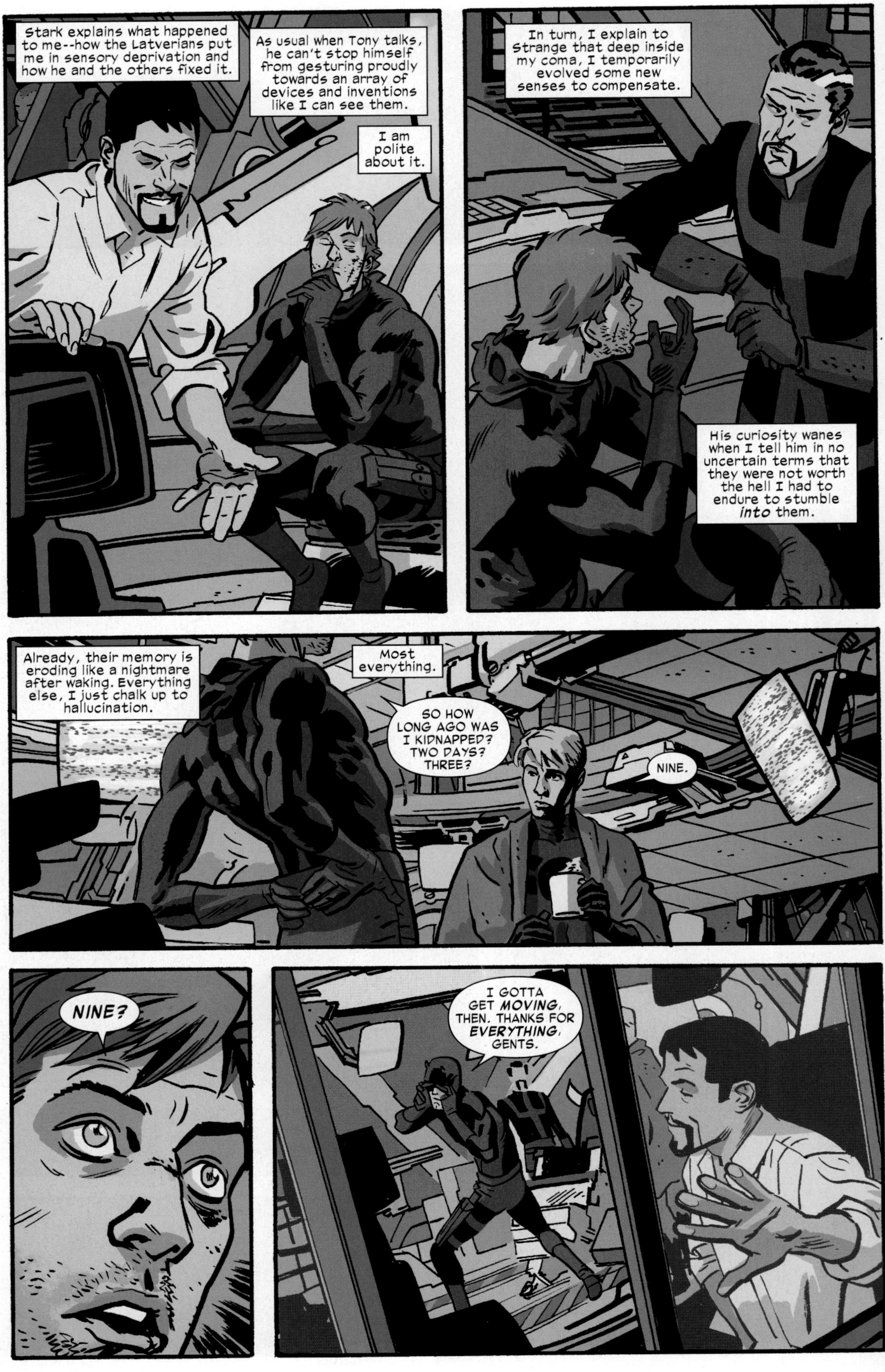
Stark explains what happened to me--how the Latverians put me in sensory deprivation and how he and the others fixed it.
As usual when Tony talks, he can't stop himself from gesturing proudly towards an array of devices and inventions like I can see them.
I am polite about it.
In turn, I explain to Strange that deep inside my coma, I temporarily evolved some new senses to compensate.
His curiosity wanes when I tell him in no uncertain terms that they were not worth the hell I had to endure to stumble *into* them.
Already, their memory is eroding like a nightmare after waking. Everything else, I just chalk up to hallucination.
Most everything.
SO HOW LONG AGO WAS I KIDNAPPED? TWO DAYS? THREE?
NINE.
NINE?
I GOTTA GET *MOVING*, THEN. THANKS FOR *EVERYTHING*, GENTS.

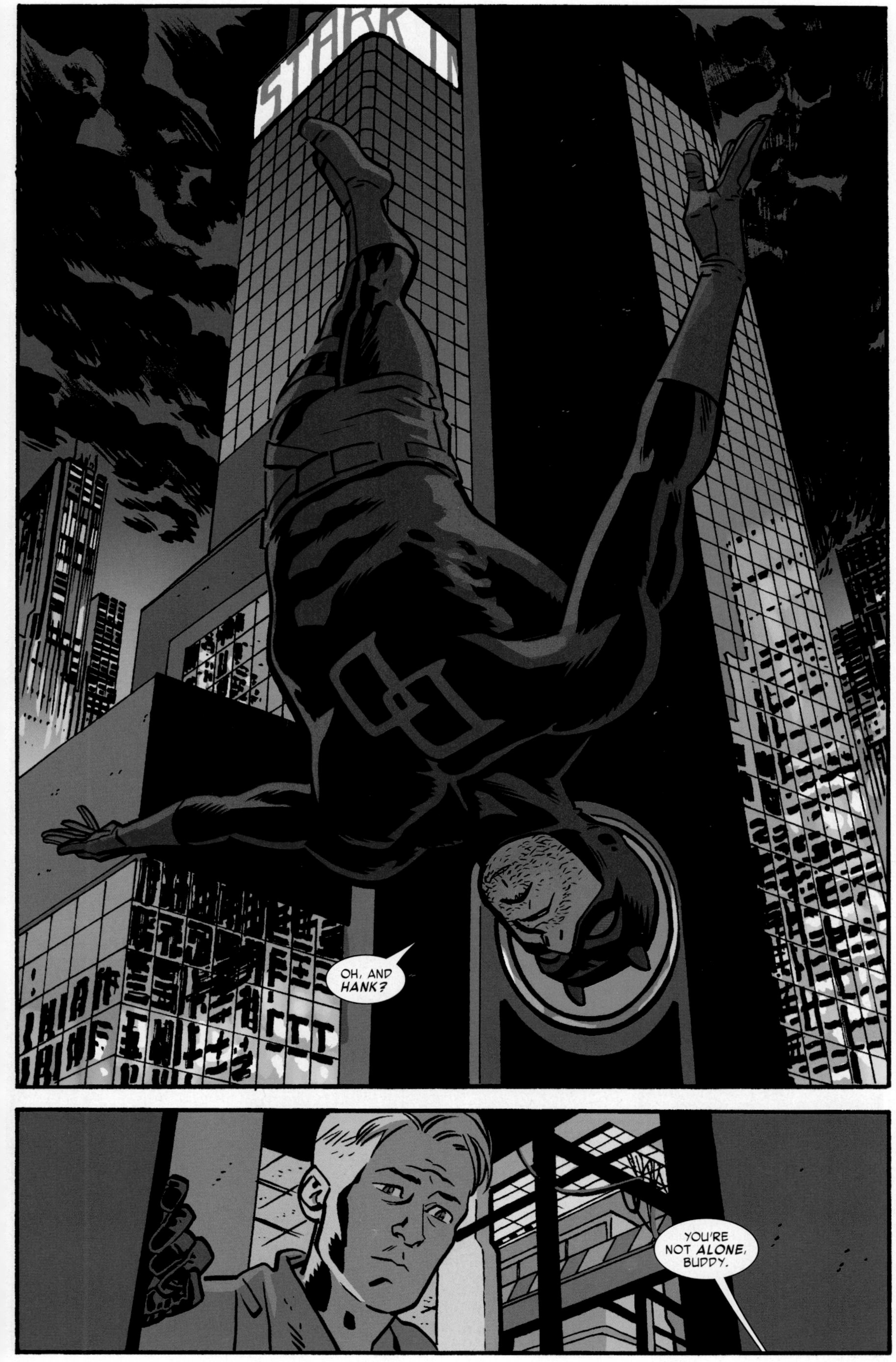
OH, AND HANK?
YOU'RE NOT ALONE, BUDDY.

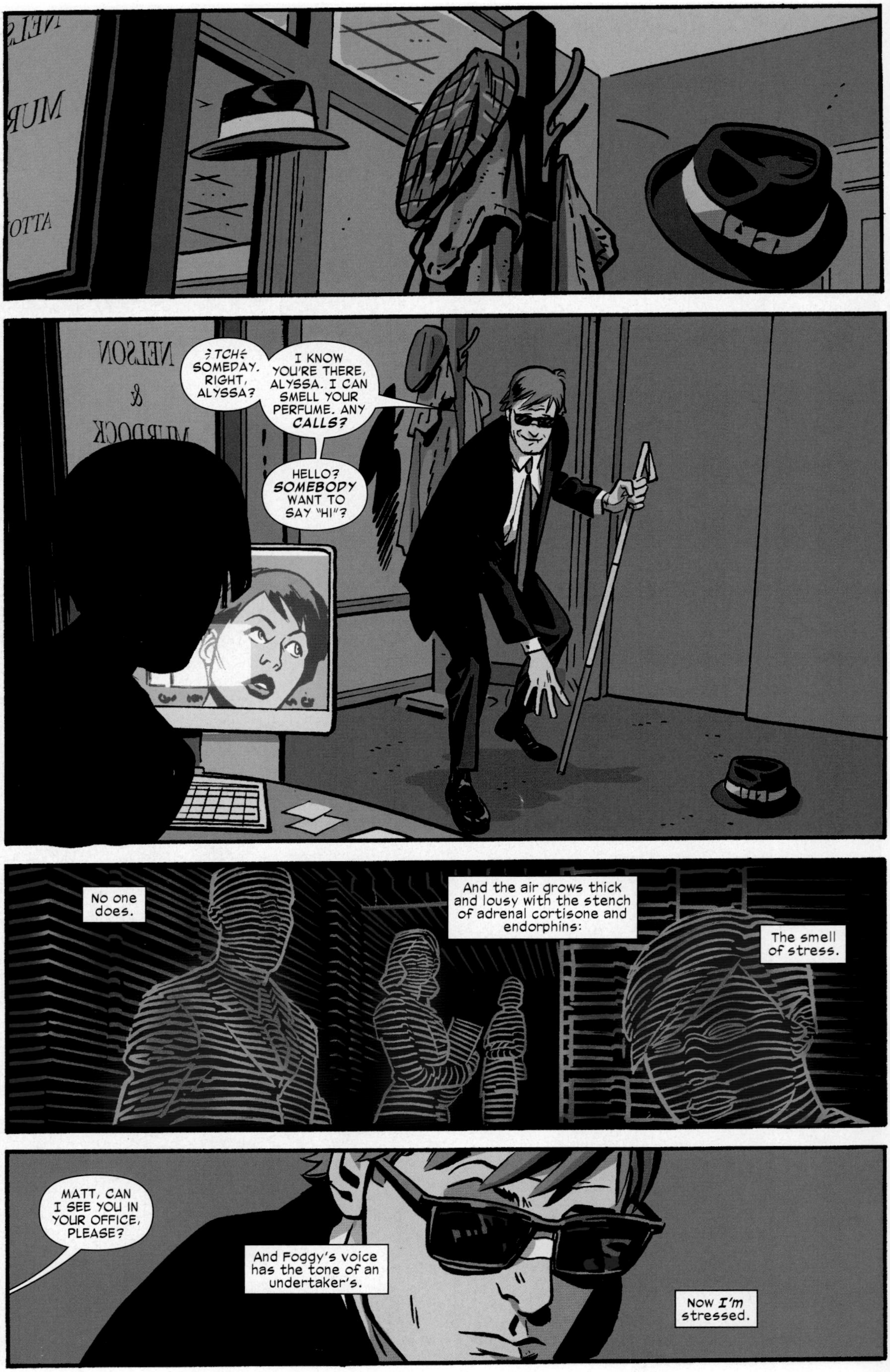

≷TCH≶ SOMEDAY. RIGHT, ALYSSA?
I KNOW YOU'RE THERE, ALYSSA. I CAN SMELL YOUR PERFUME. ANY *CALLS?*
HELLO? *SOMEBODY* WANT TO SAY "HI"?
No one does.
And the air grows thick and lousy with the stench of adrenal cortisone and endorphins:
The smell of stress.
MATT, CAN I SEE YOU IN YOUR OFFICE, PLEASE?
And Foggy's voice has the tone of an undertaker's.
Now *I'm* stressed.

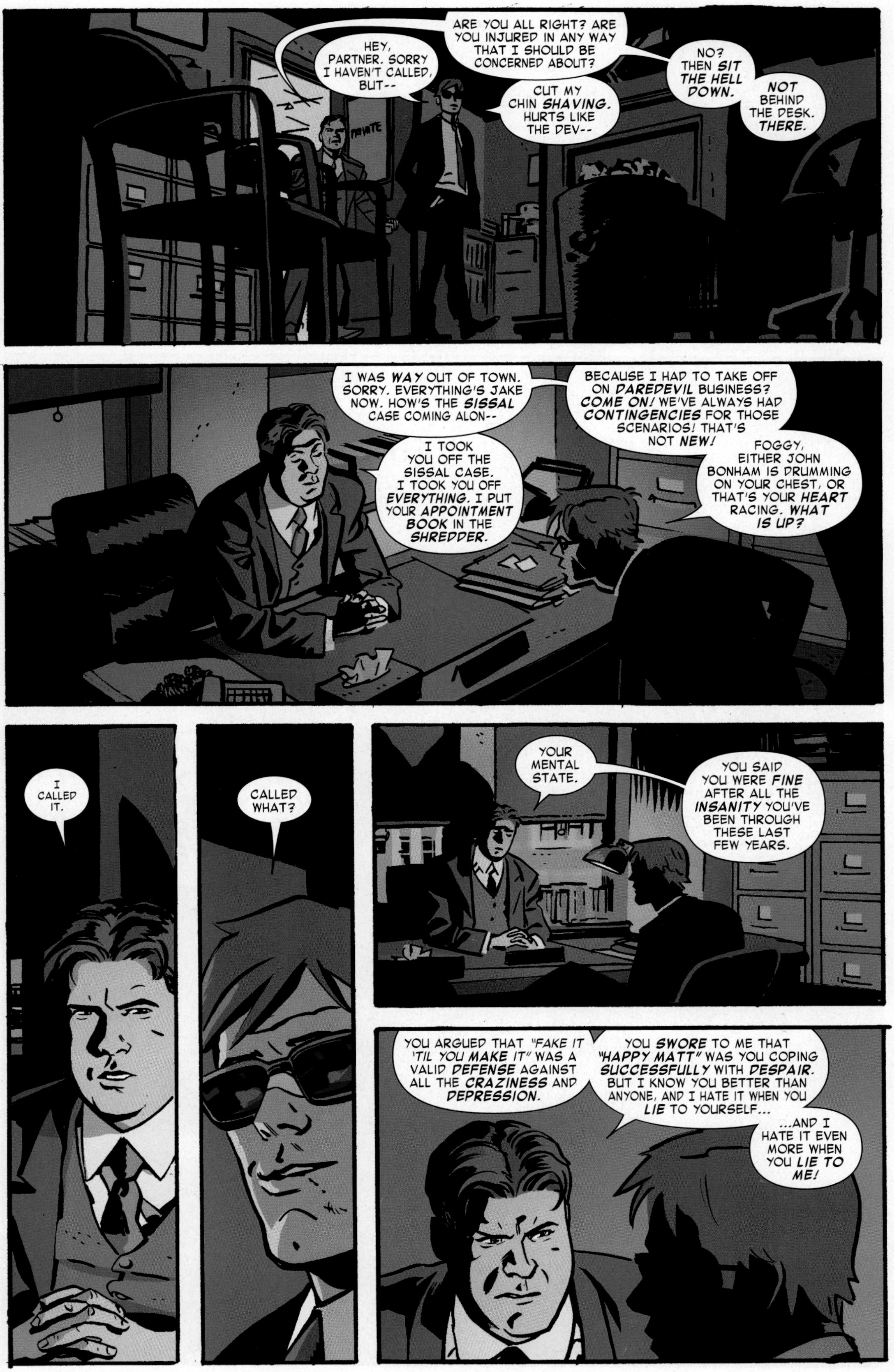
HEY, PARTNER. SORRY I HAVEN'T CALLED, BUT--
ARE YOU ALL RIGHT? ARE YOU INJURED IN ANY WAY THAT I SHOULD BE CONCERNED ABOUT?
CUT MY CHIN SHAVING. HURTS LIKE THE DEV--
NO? THEN SIT THE HELL DOWN.
NOT BEHIND THE DESK. THERE.
PRIVATE
I WAS WAY OUT OF TOWN. SORRY. EVERYTHING'S JAKE NOW. HOW'S THE SISSAL CASE COMING ALON--
I TOOK YOU OFF THE SISSAL CASE. I TOOK YOU OFF EVERYTHING. I PUT YOUR APPOINTMENT BOOK IN THE SHREDDER.
BECAUSE I HAD TO TAKE OFF ON DAREDEVIL BUSINESS? COME ON! WE'VE ALWAYS HAD CONTINGENCIES FOR THOSE SCENARIOS! THAT'S NOT NEW!
FOGGY, EITHER JOHN BONHAM IS DRUMMING ON YOUR CHEST, OR THAT'S YOUR HEART RACING. WHAT IS UP?
I CALLED IT.
CALLED WHAT?
YOUR MENTAL STATE.
YOU SAID YOU WERE FINE AFTER ALL THE INSANITY YOU'VE BEEN THROUGH THESE LAST FEW YEARS.
YOU ARGUED THAT "FAKE IT 'TIL YOU MAKE IT" WAS A VALID DEFENSE AGAINST ALL THE CRAZINESS AND DEPRESSION.
YOU SWORE TO ME THAT "HAPPY MATT" WAS YOU COPING SUCCESSFULLY WITH DESPAIR. BUT I KNOW YOU BETTER THAN ANYONE, AND I HATE IT WHEN YOU LIE TO YOURSELF...
...AND I HATE IT EVEN MORE WHEN YOU LIE TO ME!

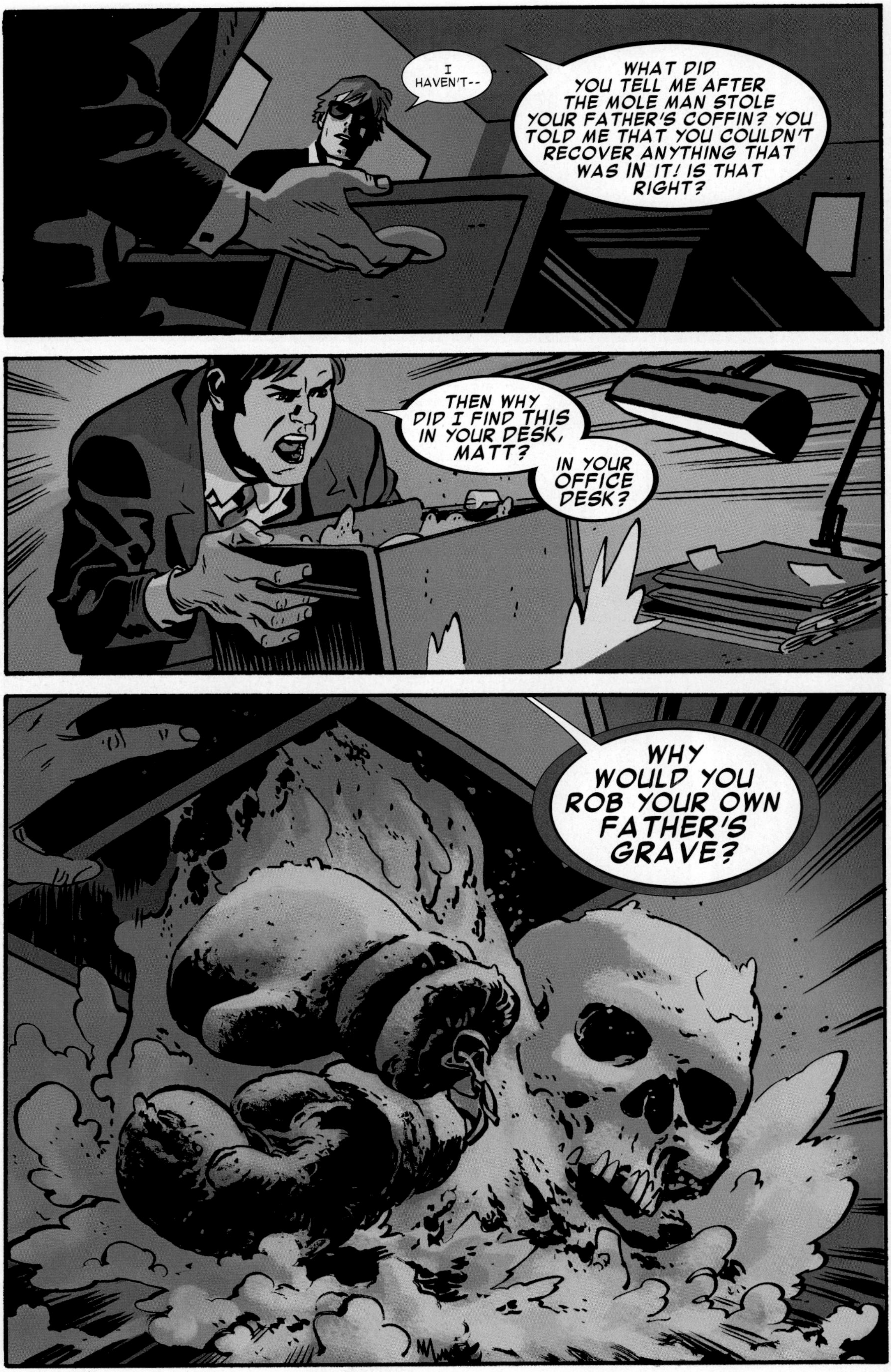
WHAT DID YOU TELL ME AFTER THE MOLE MAN STOLE YOUR FATHER'S COFFIN? YOU TOLD ME THAT YOU COULDN'T RECOVER ANYTHING THAT WAS IN IT! IS THAT RIGHT?
I HAVEN'T--
THEN WHY DID I FIND THIS IN YOUR DESK, MATT?
IN YOUR OFFICE DESK?
WHY WOULD YOU ROB YOUR OWN FATHER'S GRAVE?

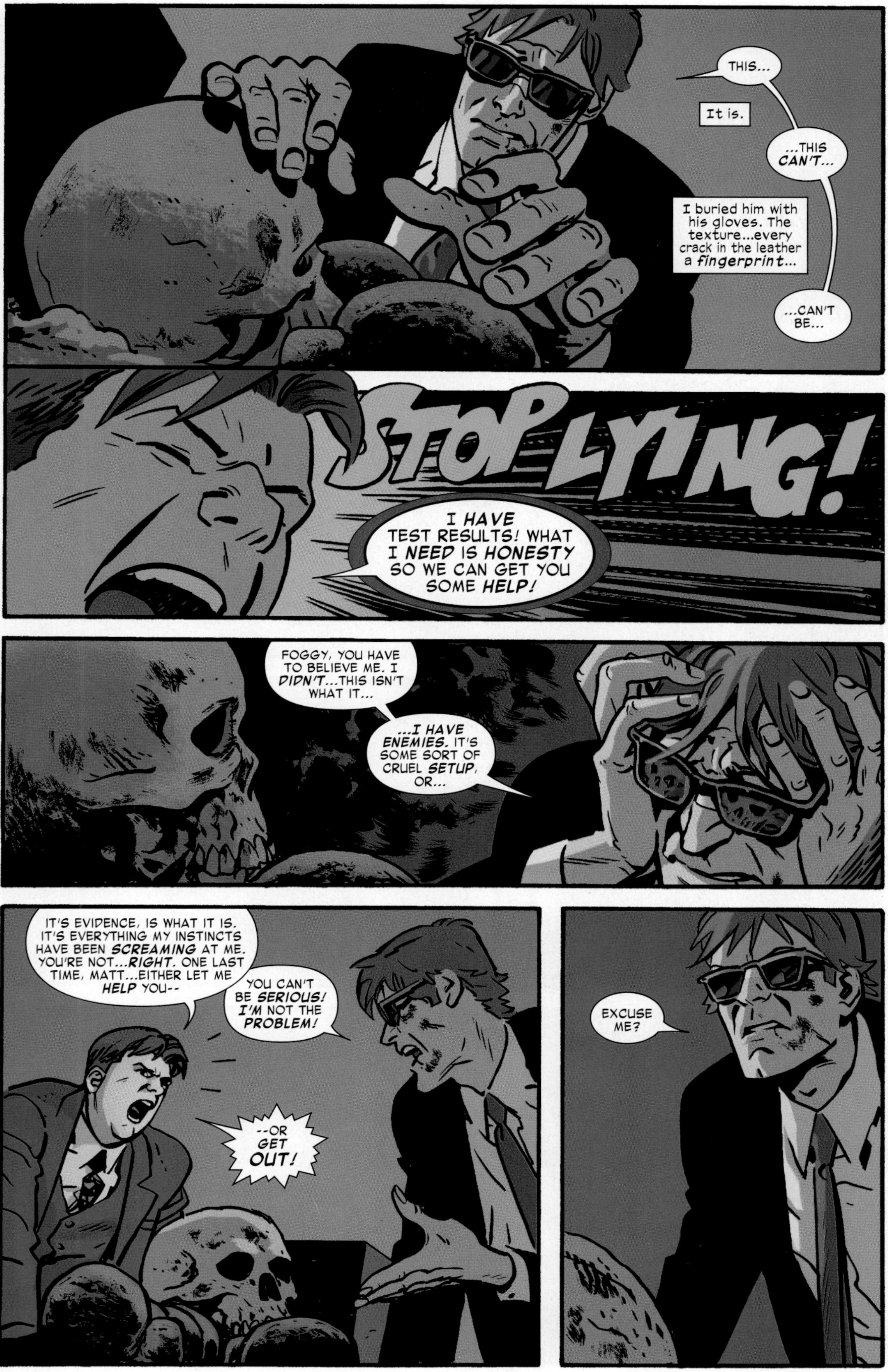
THIS...
It is.
...THIS CAN'T...
I buried him with his gloves. The texture...every crack in the leather a fingerprint...
...CAN'T BE...
STOP LYING!
I HAVE TEST RESULTS! WHAT I NEED IS HONESTY SO WE CAN GET YOU SOME HELP!
FOGGY, YOU HAVE TO BELIEVE ME. I DIDN'T...THIS ISN'T WHAT IT...
...I HAVE ENEMIES. IT'S SOME SORT OF CRUEL SETUP, OR...
IT'S EVIDENCE, IS WHAT IT IS. IT'S EVERYTHING MY INSTINCTS HAVE BEEN SCREAMING AT ME. YOU'RE NOT...RIGHT. ONE LAST TIME, MATT...EITHER LET ME HELP YOU--
YOU CAN'T BE SERIOUS! I'M NOT THE PROBLEM!
--OR GET OUT!
EXCUSE ME?

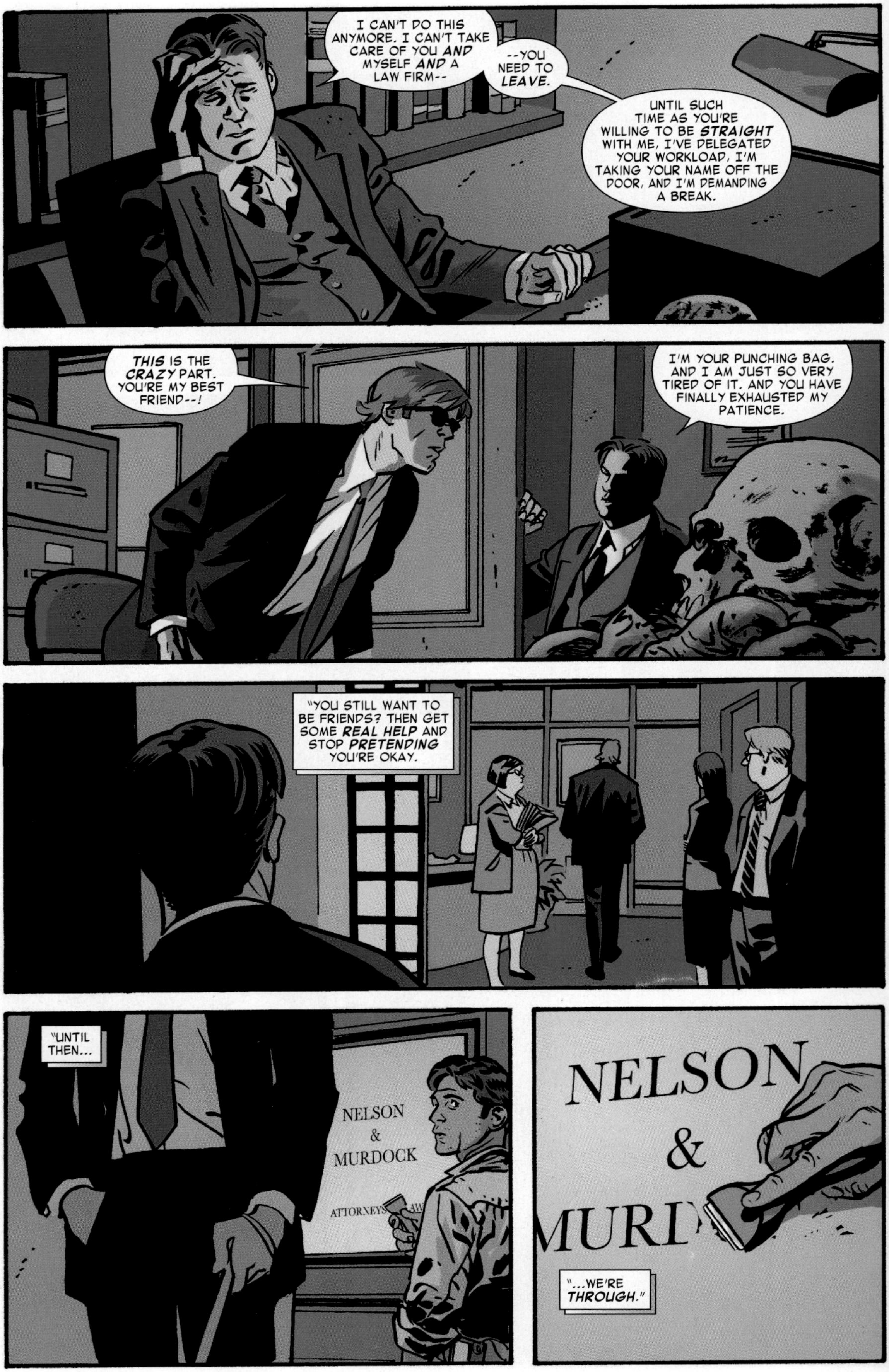
I CAN'T DO THIS ANYMORE. I CAN'T TAKE CARE OF YOU AND MYSELF AND A LAW FIRM--
--YOU NEED TO LEAVE.
UNTIL SUCH TIME AS YOU'RE WILLING TO BE STRAIGHT WITH ME, I'VE DELEGATED YOUR WORKLOAD, I'M TAKING YOUR NAME OFF THE DOOR, AND I'M DEMANDING A BREAK.
THIS IS THE CRAZY PART. YOU'RE MY BEST FRIEND--!
I'M YOUR PUNCHING BAG. AND I AM JUST SO VERY TIRED OF IT. AND YOU HAVE FINALLY EXHAUSTED MY PATIENCE.
"YOU STILL WANT TO BE FRIENDS? THEN GET SOME REAL HELP AND STOP PRETENDING YOU'RE OKAY.
"UNTIL THEN...
NELSON & MURDOCK
ATTORNEYS
NELSON & MURI
"...WE'RE THROUGH."

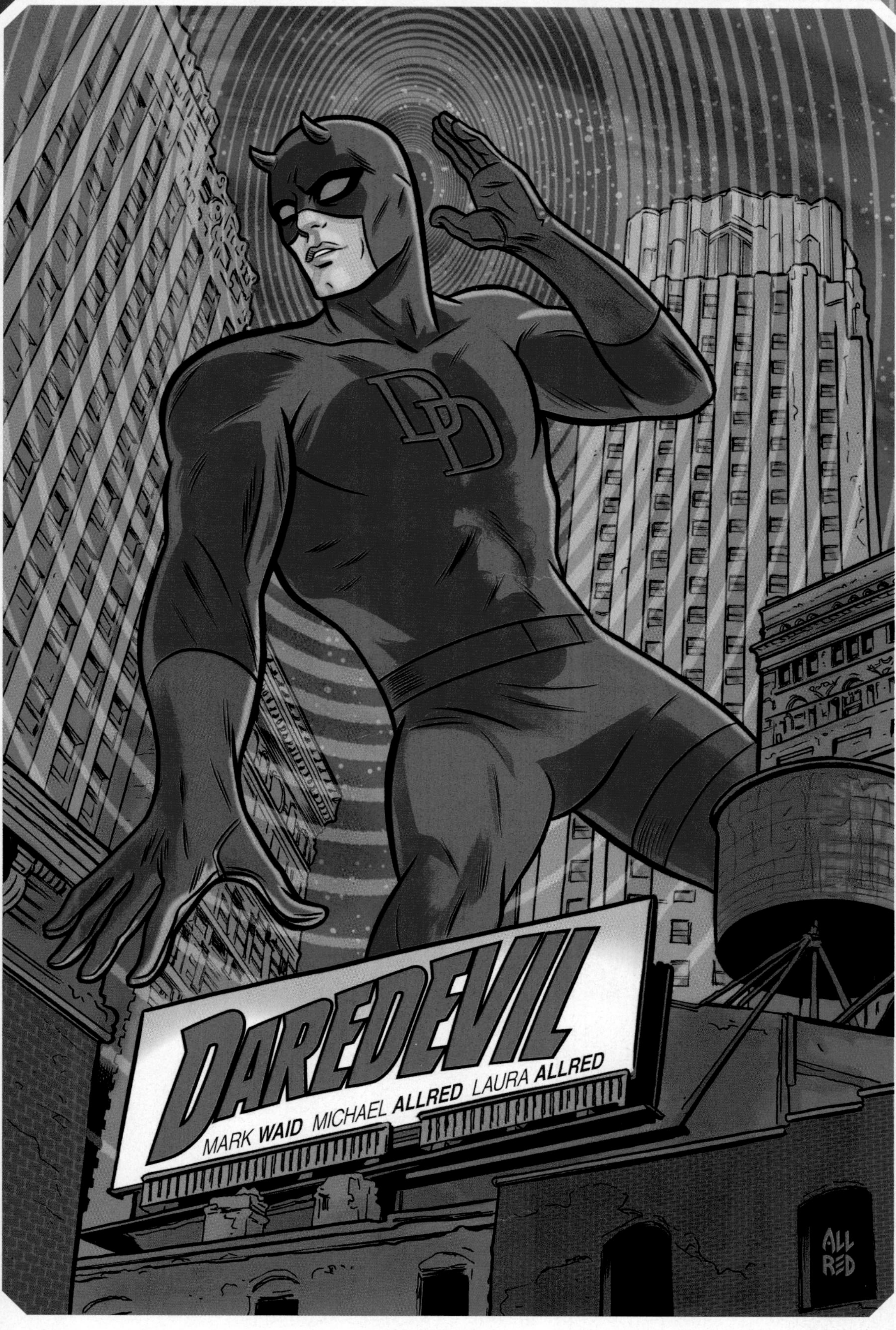
DAREDEVIL
MARK WAID MICHAEL ALLRED LAURA ALLRED
ALL RED

SEVENTEEN

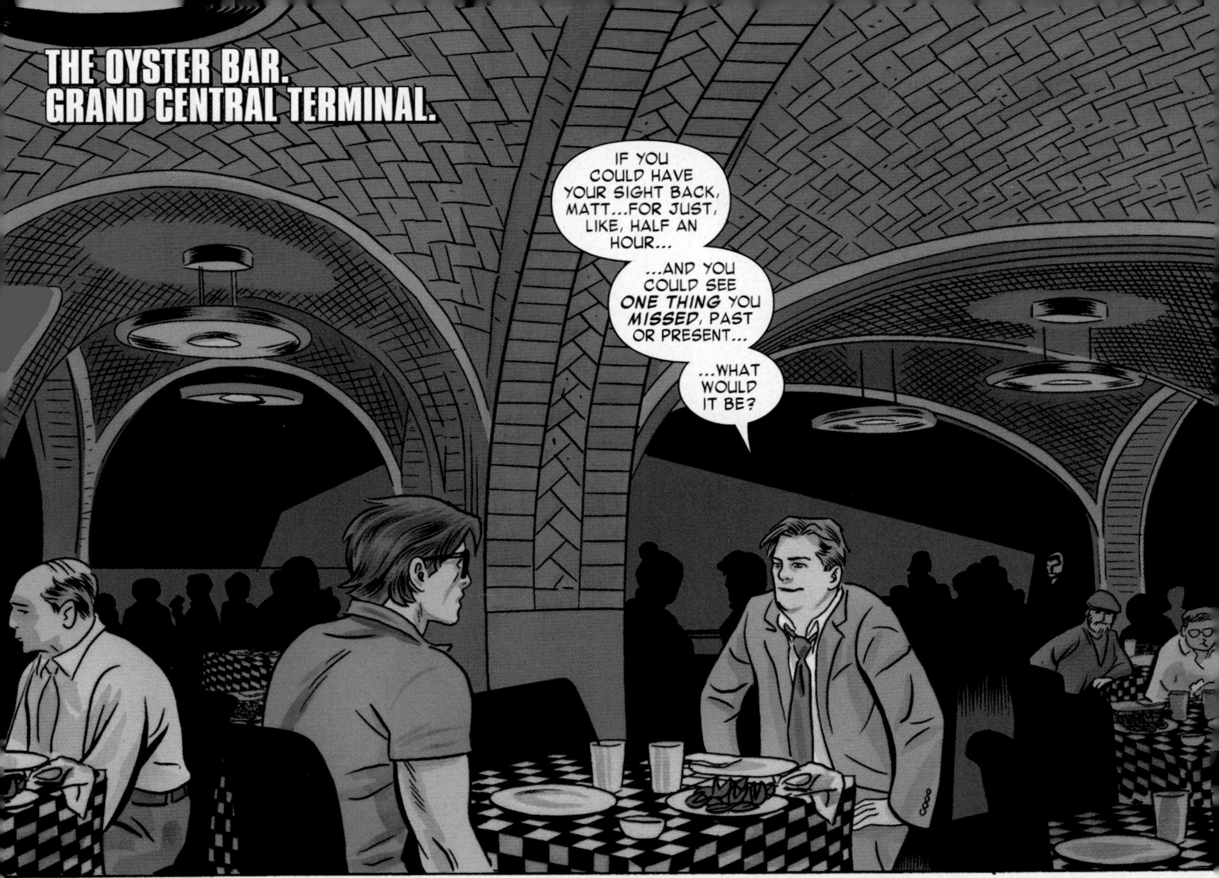
THE OYSTER BAR.
GRAND CENTRAL TERMINAL.
IF YOU COULD HAVE YOUR SIGHT BACK, MATT...FOR JUST, LIKE, HALF AN HOUR...
...AND YOU COULD SEE ONE THING YOU MISSED, PAST OR PRESENT...
...WHAT WOULD IT BE?

THE GREAT DIVIDE

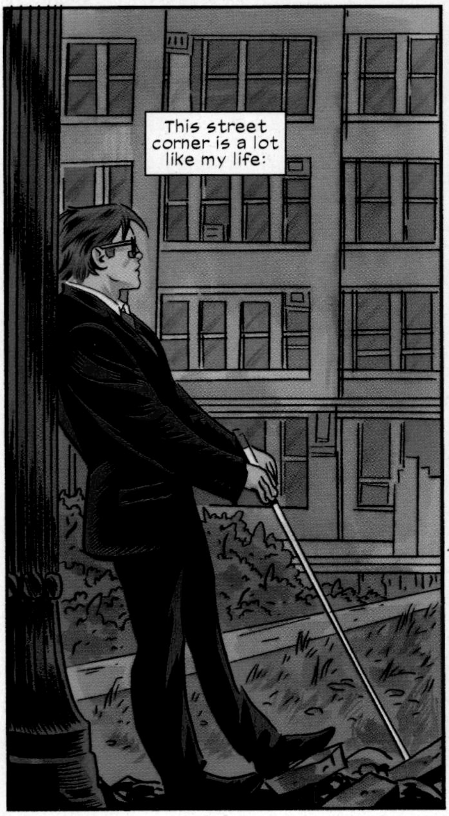
This street corner is a lot like my life:

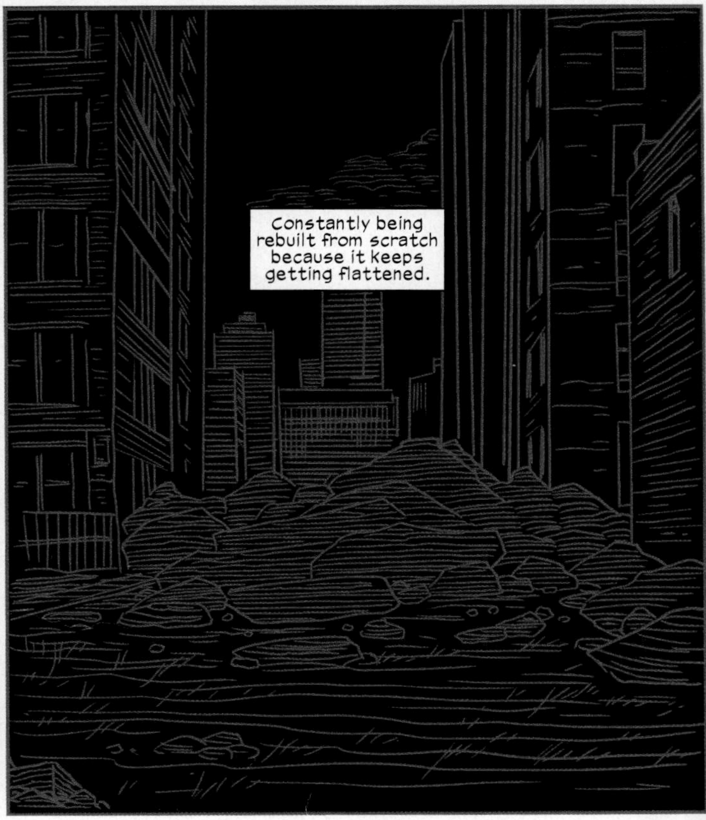
Constantly being rebuilt from scratch because it keeps getting flattened.

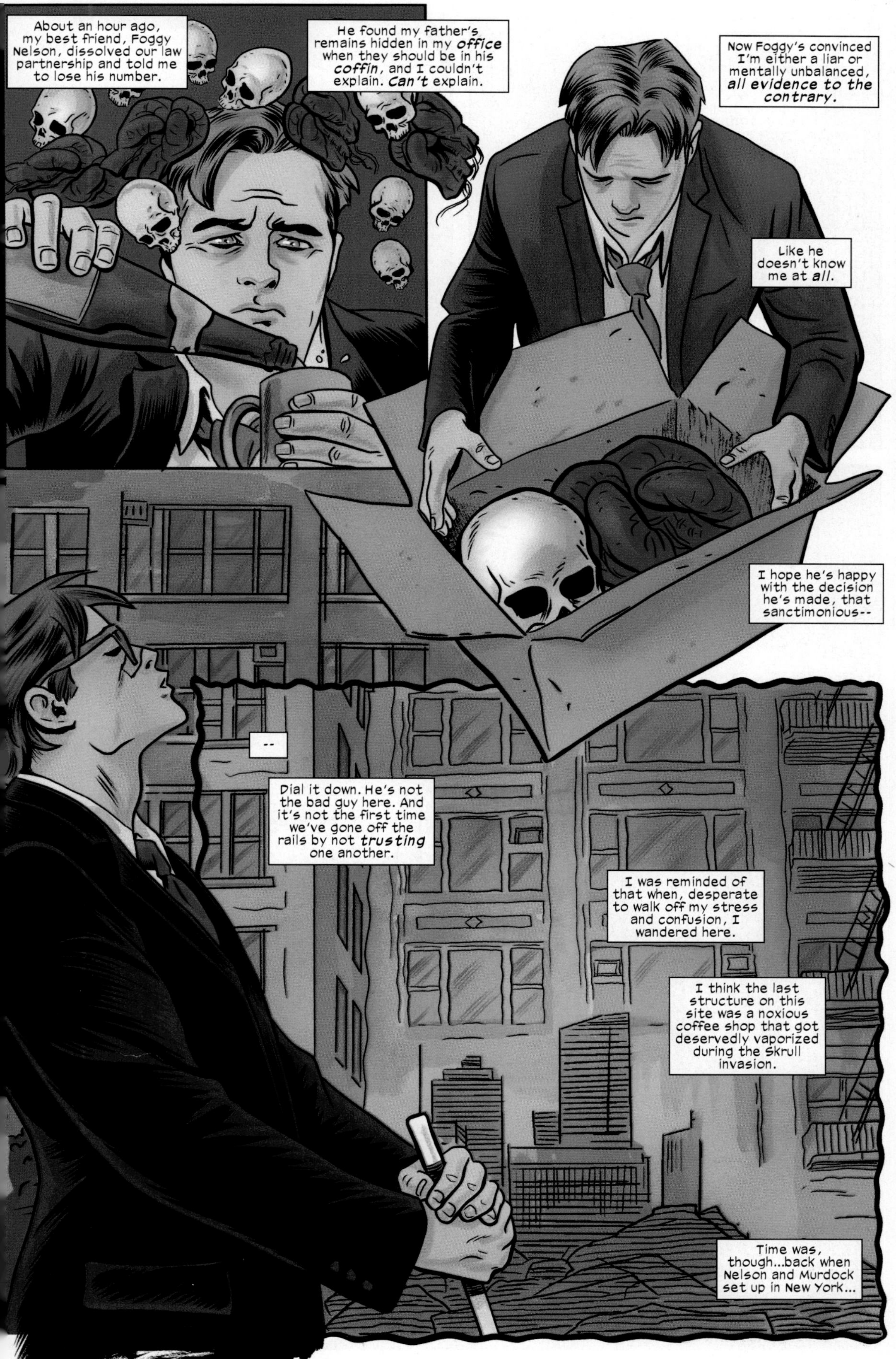
About an hour ago, my best friend, Foggy Nelson, dissolved our law partnership and told me to lose his number.
He found my father's remains hidden in my *office* when they should be in his *coffin*, and I couldn't explain. *Can't* explain.
Now Foggy's convinced I'm either a liar or mentally unbalanced, *all evidence to the contrary.*
Like he doesn't know me at *all*.
I hope he's happy with the decision he's made, that sanctimonious--
--
Dial it down. He's not the bad guy here. And it's not the first time we've gone off the rails by not *trusting* one another.
I was reminded of that when, desperate to walk off my stress and confusion, I wandered here.
I think the last structure on this site was a noxious coffee shop that got deservedly vaporized during the Skrull invasion.
Time was, though...back when Nelson and Murdock set up in New York...

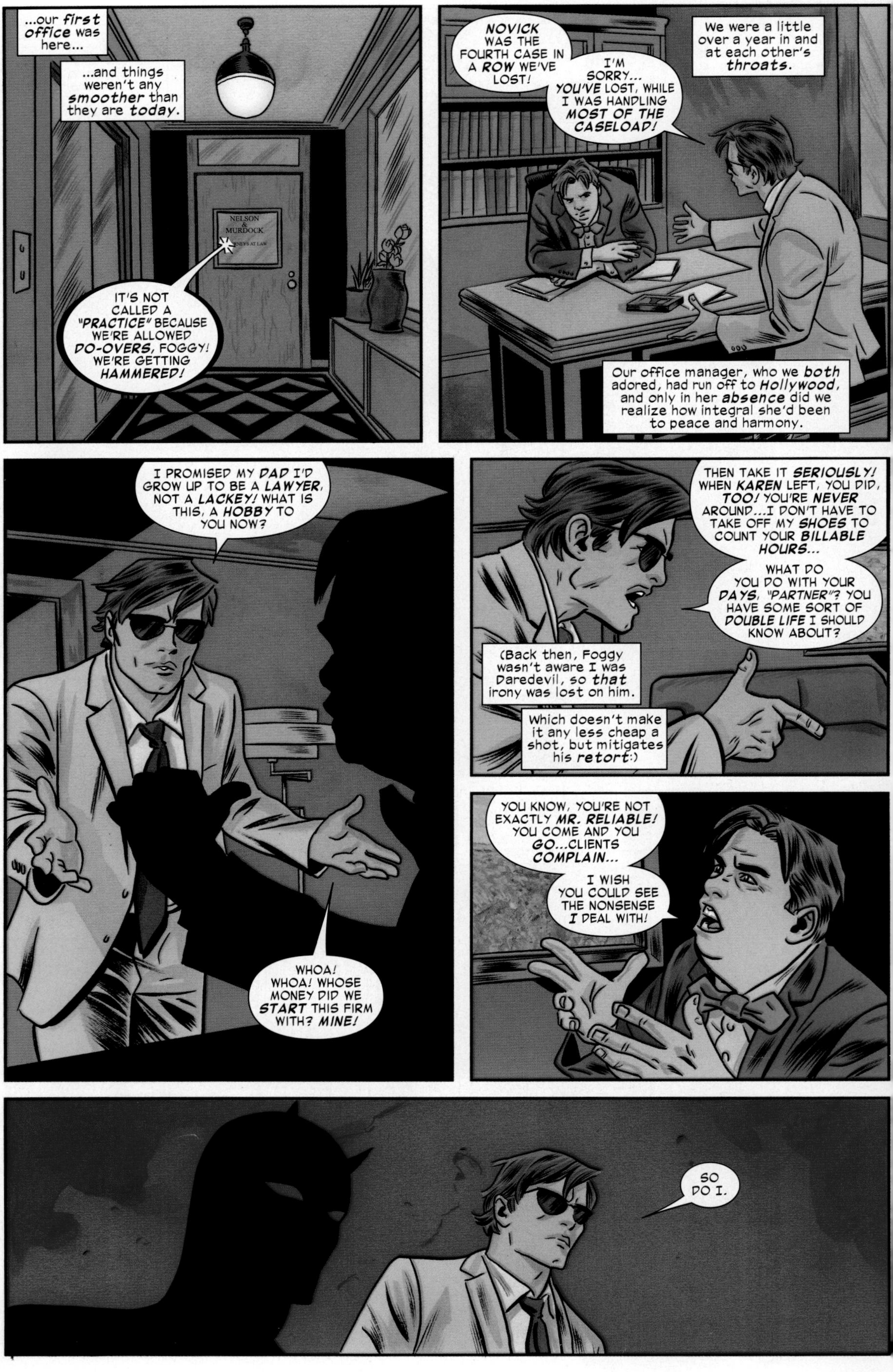
...our *first office* was here...
...and things weren't any *smoother* than they are *today*.
NELSON & MURDOCK
IT'S NOT CALLED A "*PRACTICE*" BECAUSE WE'RE ALLOWED *DO-OVERS*, FOGGY! WE'RE GETTING *HAMMERED!*
NOVICK WAS THE FOURTH CASE IN A *ROW* WE'VE LOST!
I'M SORRY... *YOU'VE* LOST, WHILE I WAS HANDLING *MOST OF THE CASELOAD!*
We were a little over a year in and at each other's *throats*.
Our office manager, who we *both* adored, had run off to *Hollywood*, and only in her *absence* did we realize how integral she'd been to peace and harmony.
I PROMISED MY *DAD* I'D GROW UP TO BE A *LAWYER*, NOT A *LACKEY!* WHAT IS THIS, A *HOBBY* TO YOU NOW?
WHOA! WHOA! WHOSE MONEY DID WE *START* THIS FIRM WITH? *MINE!*
THEN TAKE IT *SERIOUSLY!* WHEN *KAREN* LEFT, YOU DID, *TOO!* YOU'RE *NEVER* AROUND...I DON'T HAVE TO TAKE OFF MY *SHOES* TO COUNT YOUR *BILLABLE HOURS*...
WHAT DO YOU DO WITH YOUR *DAYS*, "*PARTNER*"? YOU HAVE SOME SORT OF *DOUBLE LIFE* I SHOULD KNOW ABOUT?
(Back then, Foggy wasn't aware I was Daredevil, so *that* irony was lost on him.
Which doesn't make it any less cheap a shot, but mitigates his *retort*:)
YOU KNOW, YOU'RE NOT EXACTLY *MR. RELIABLE!* YOU COME AND YOU *GO*...CLIENTS *COMPLAIN*...
I WISH YOU COULD SEE THE NONSENSE *I* DEAL WITH!
SO DO I.

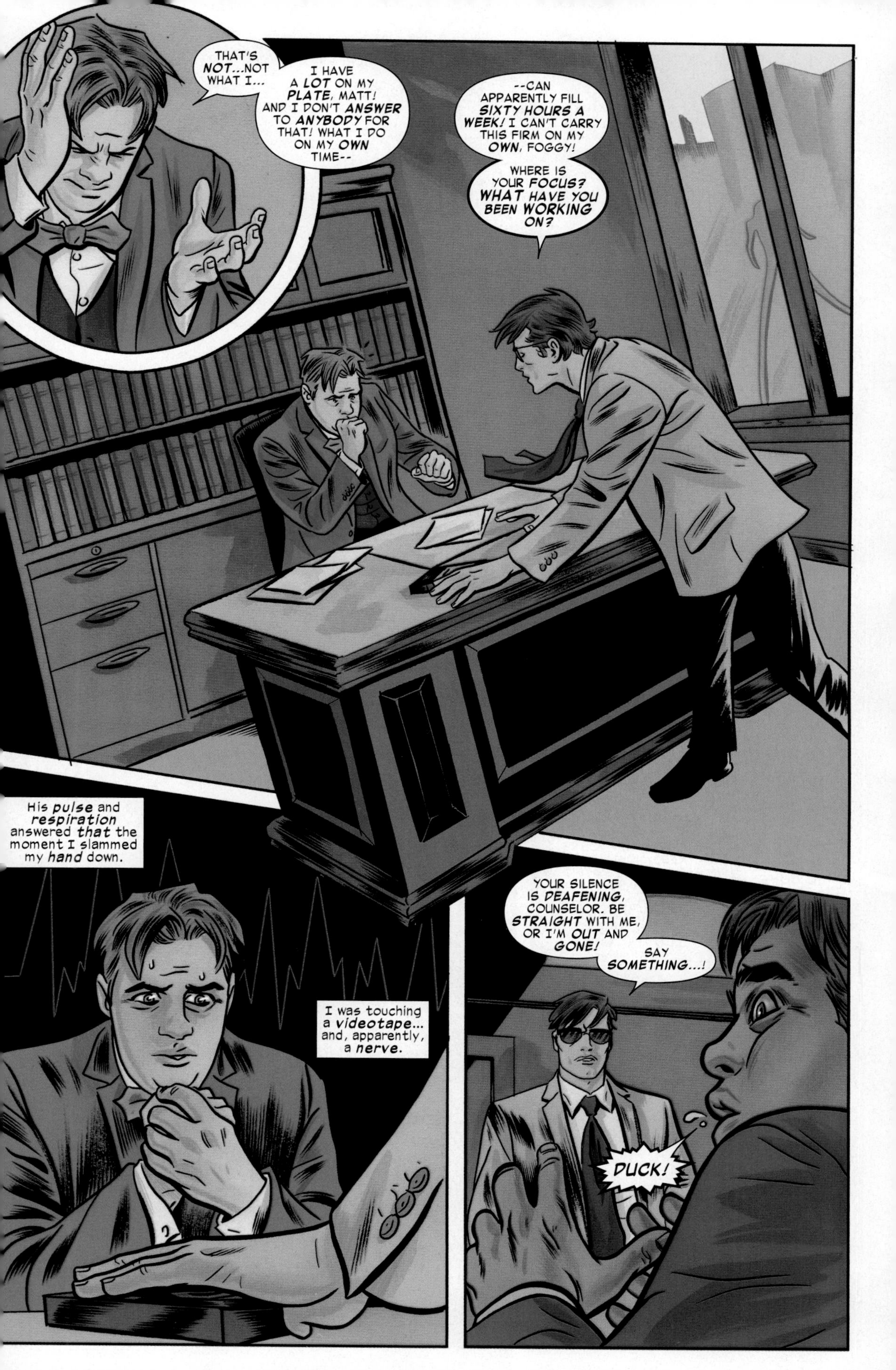
THAT'S NOT...NOT WHAT I...
I HAVE A LOT ON MY PLATE, MATT! AND I DON'T ANSWER TO ANYBODY FOR THAT! WHAT I DO ON MY OWN TIME--
--CAN APPARENTLY FILL SIXTY HOURS A WEEK! I CAN'T CARRY THIS FIRM ON MY OWN, FOGGY!
WHERE IS YOUR FOCUS? WHAT HAVE YOU BEEN WORKING ON?
His pulse and respiration answered that the moment I slammed my hand down.
I was touching a videotape... and, apparently, a nerve.
YOUR SILENCE IS DEAFENING, COUNSELOR. BE STRAIGHT WITH ME, OR I'M OUT AND GONE!
SAY SOMETHING...!
DUCK!

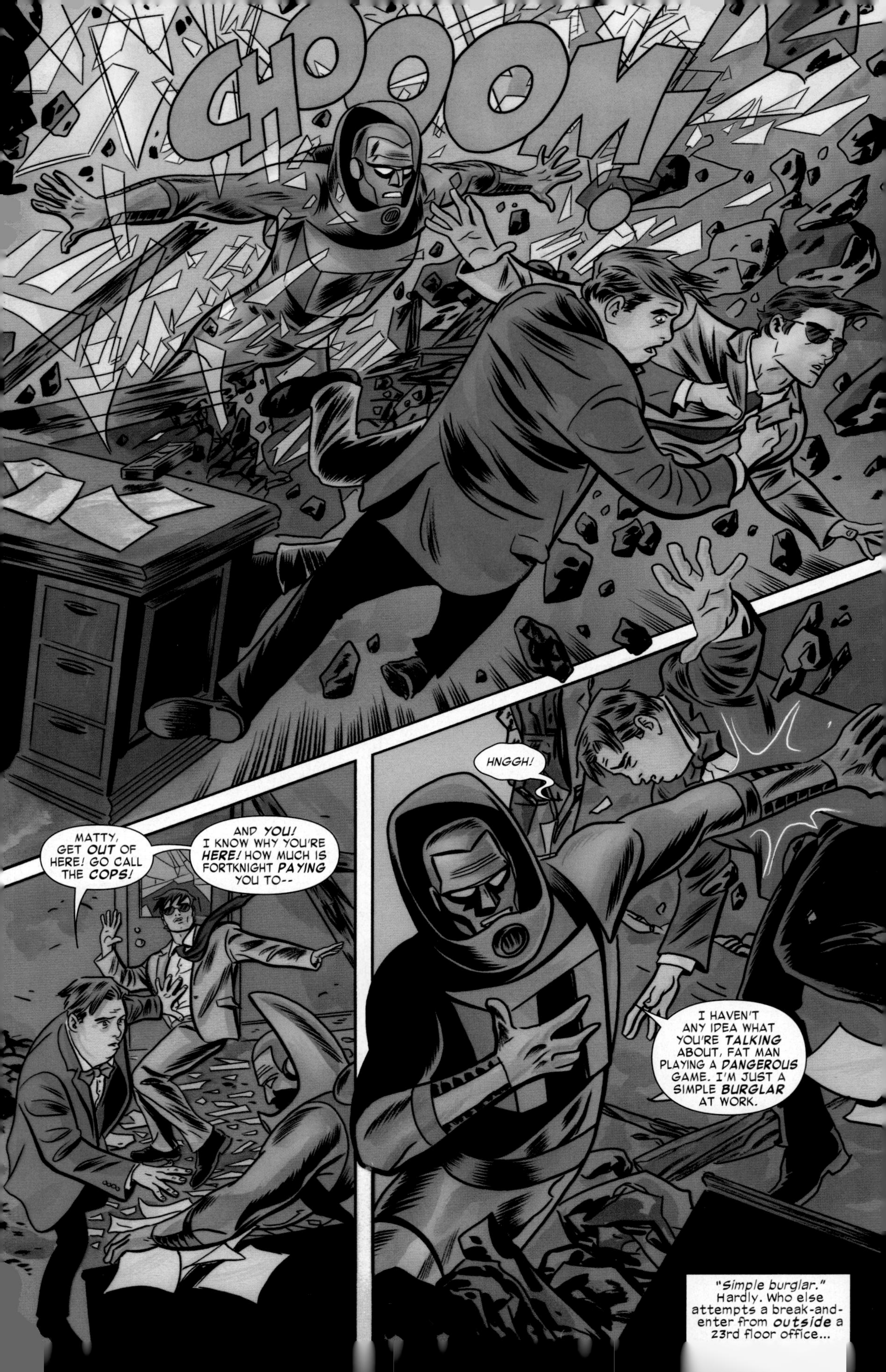
CHOOOM!
MATTY, GET OUT OF HERE! GO CALL THE COPS!
AND YOU! I KNOW WHY YOU'RE HERE! HOW MUCH IS FORTKNIGHT PAYING YOU TO--
HNGGH!
I HAVEN'T ANY IDEA WHAT YOU'RE TALKING ABOUT, FAT MAN PLAYING A DANGEROUS GAME. I'M JUST A SIMPLE BURGLAR AT WORK.
"Simple burglar." Hardly. Who else attempts a break-and-enter from outside a 23rd floor office...

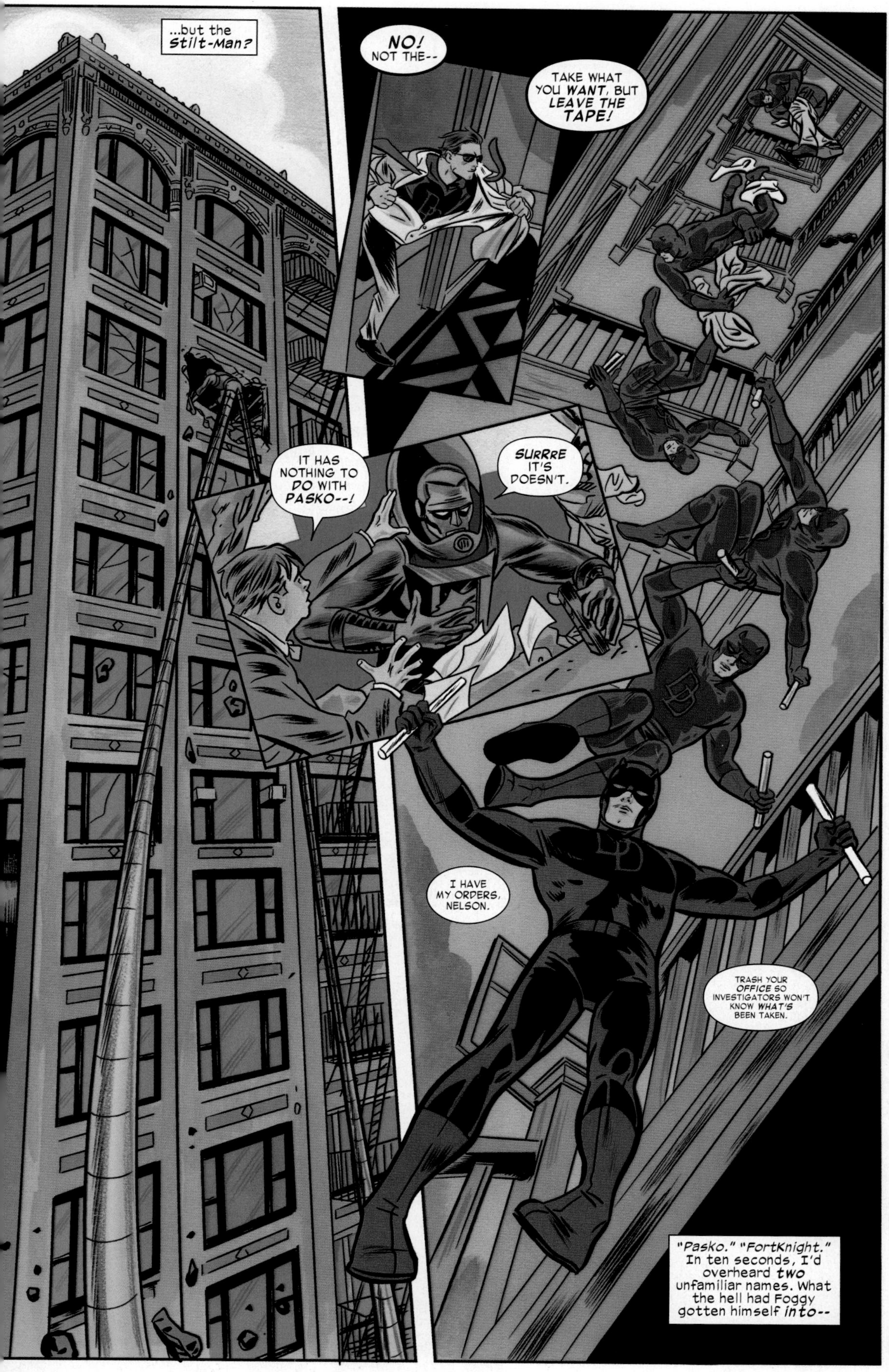
...but the Stilt-Man?
NO! NOT THE--
TAKE WHAT YOU WANT, BUT LEAVE THE TAPE!
IT HAS NOTHING TO DO WITH PASKO--!
SURRRE IT'S DOESN'T.
I HAVE MY ORDERS, NELSON.
TRASH YOUR OFFICE SO INVESTIGATORS WON'T KNOW WHAT'S BEEN TAKEN.
"Pasko." "FortKnight." In ten seconds, I'd overheard two unfamiliar names. What the hell had Foggy gotten himself into--

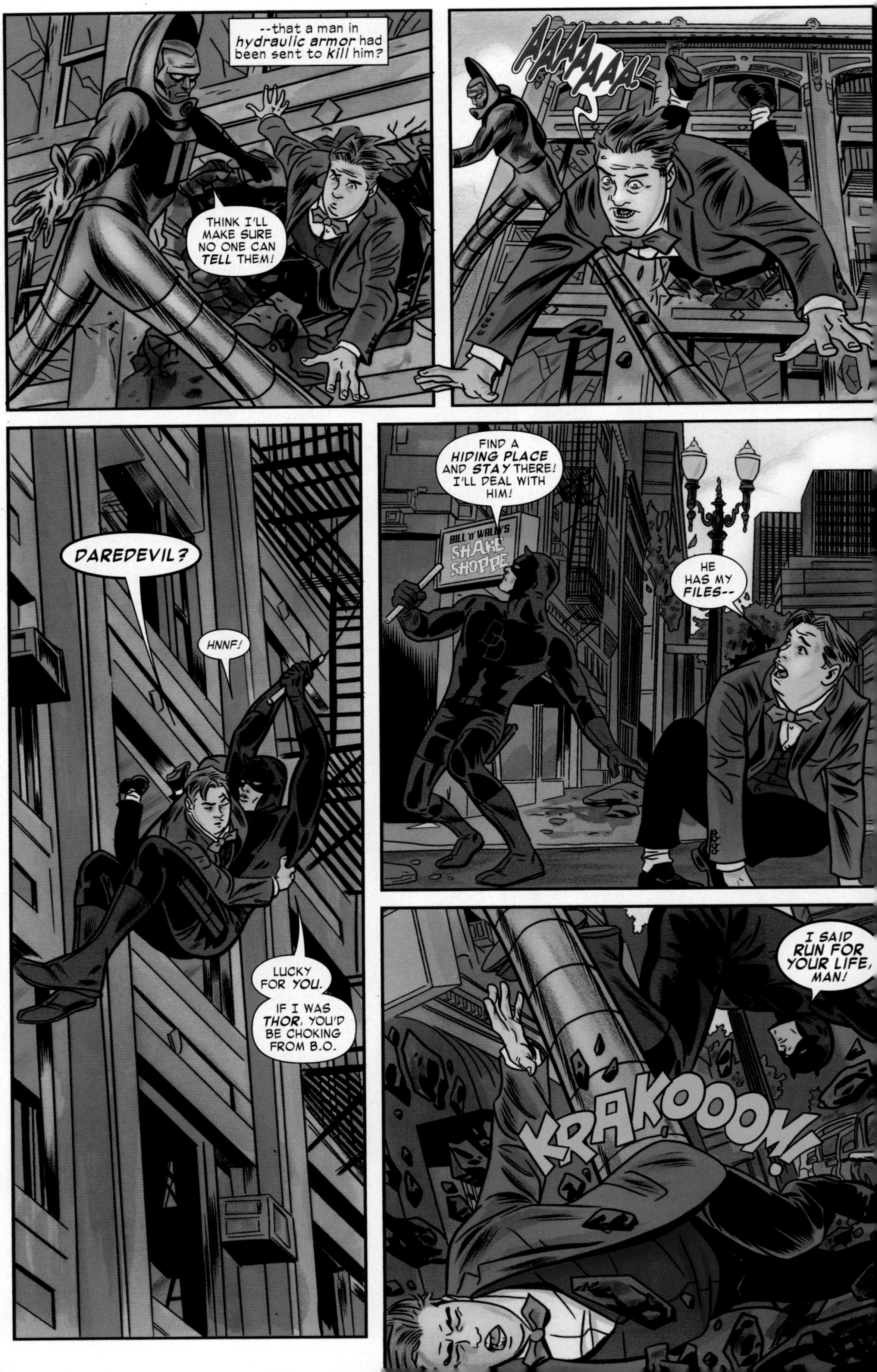
--that a man in *hydraulic armor* had been sent to *kill* him?
THINK I'LL MAKE SURE NO ONE CAN *TELL* THEM!
AAAAAAA!
DAREDEVIL?
HNNF!
LUCKY FOR *YOU*.
IF I WAS *THOR*, YOU'D BE CHOKING FROM B.O.
FIND A *HIDING PLACE* AND *STAY* THERE! I'LL DEAL WITH HIM!
BILL 'n' WALLY'S SHAKE SHOPPE
HE HAS MY *FILES*--
I SAID *RUN FOR YOUR LIFE*, MAN!
KRAKOOOM!

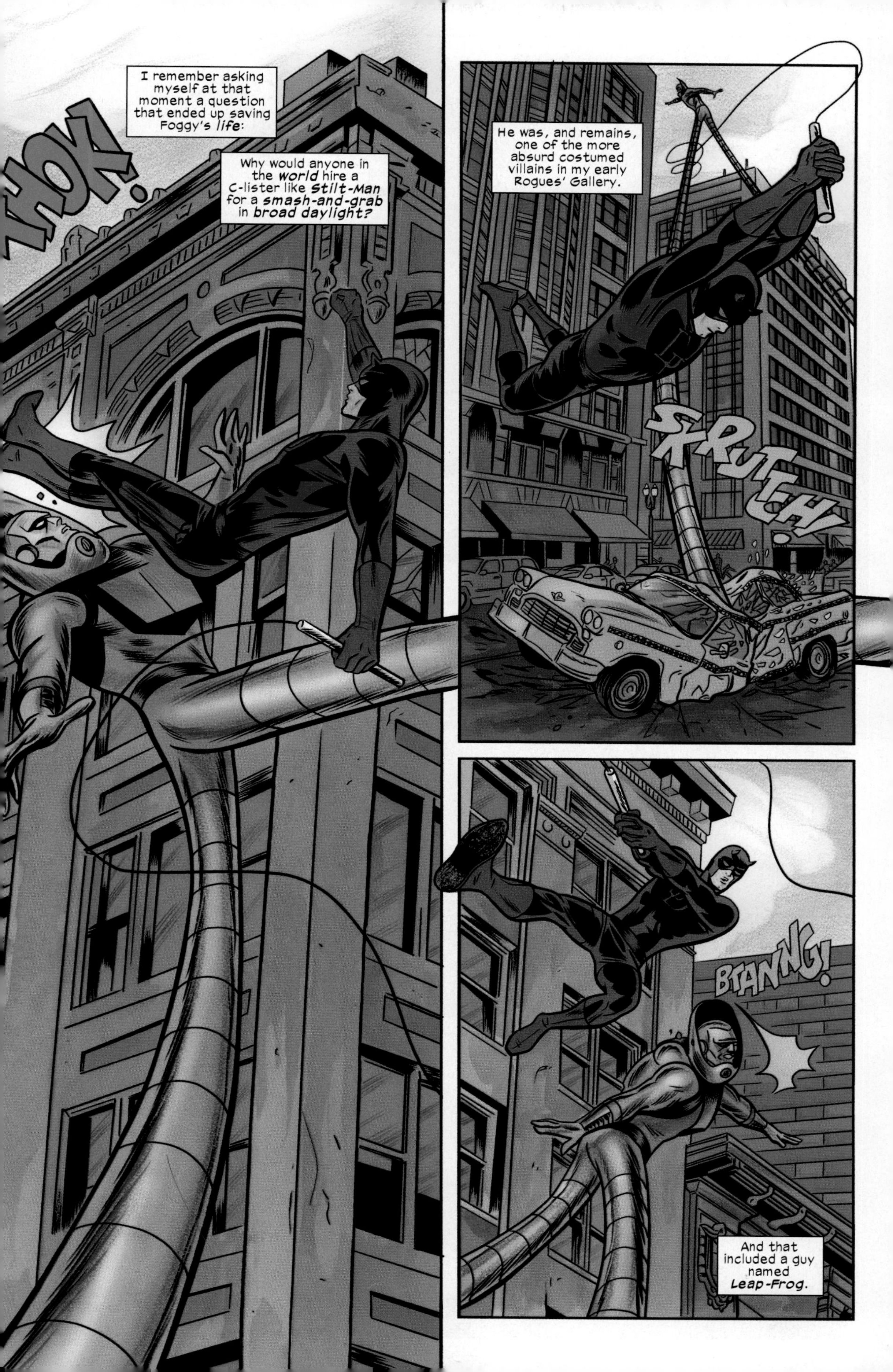
THOK!
I remember asking myself at that moment a question that ended up saving Foggy's *life*:
Why would anyone in the *world* hire a C-lister like *Stilt-Man* for a *smash-and-grab* in *broad daylight?*
He was, and remains, one of the more absurd costumed villains in my early Rogues' Gallery.
SKRUTCH!
BTANNG!
And that included a guy named *Leap-Frog*.

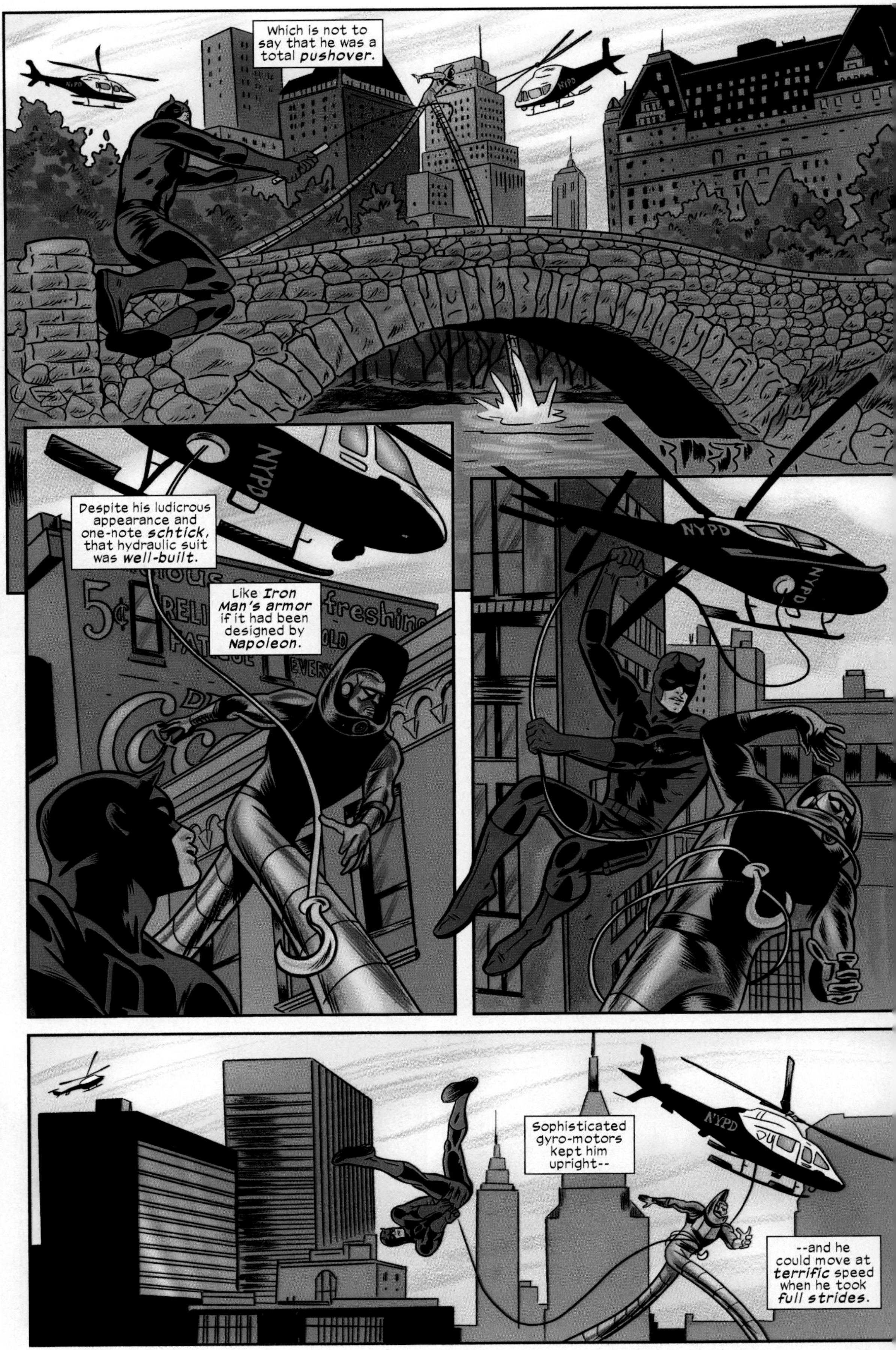

Which is not to say that he was a total *pushover*.
NYPD
NYPD
Despite his ludicrous appearance and one-note *schtick*, that hydraulic suit was *well-built*.
Like *Iron Man's armor* if it had been designed by *Napoleon*.
5¢
freshing
NYPD
Sophisticated gyro-motors kept him upright--
NYPD
--and he could move at *terrific* speed when he took *full strides*.

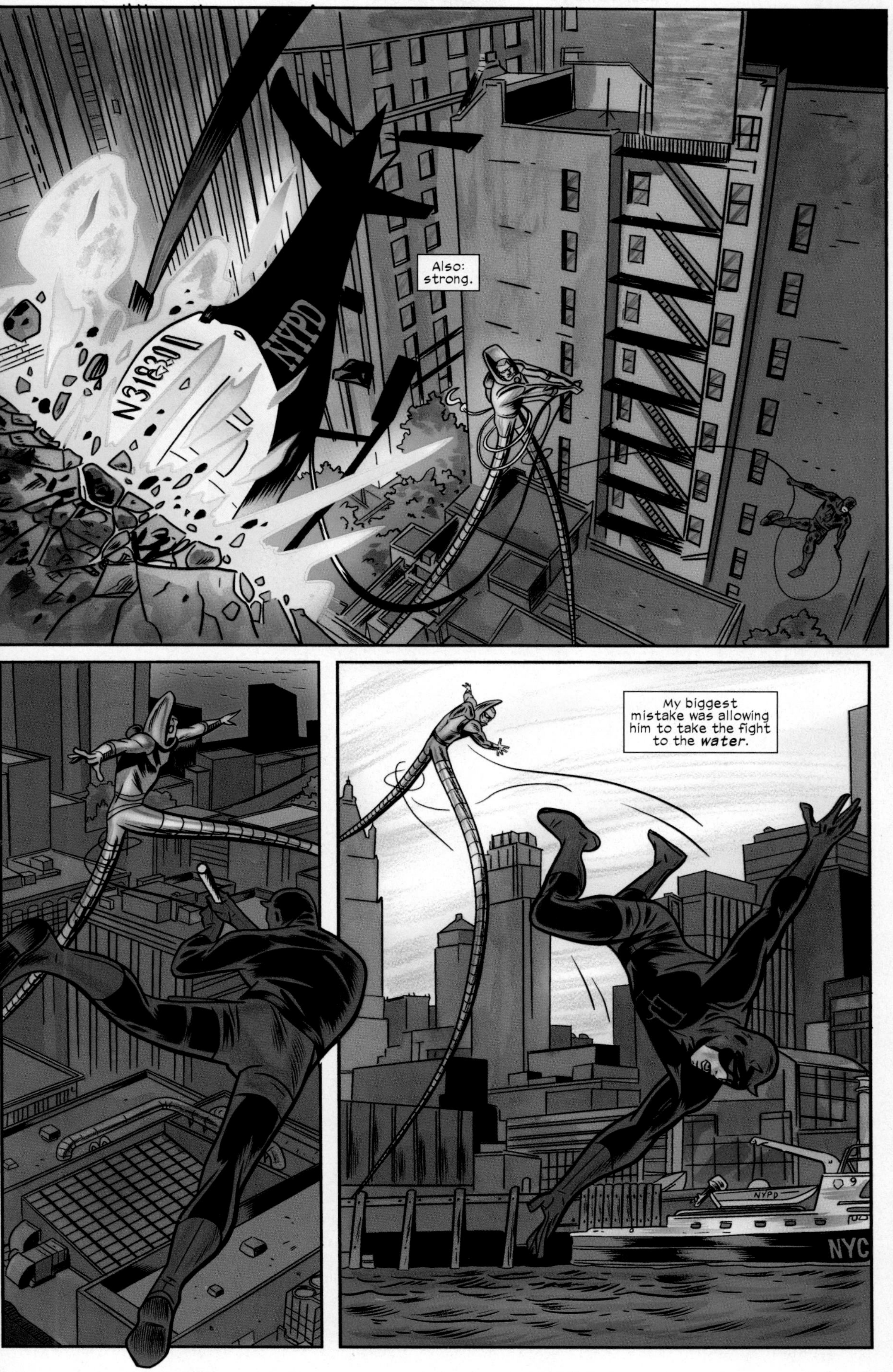
Also: strong.
NYPD
My biggest mistake was allowing him to take the fight to the *water*.
NYPD
NYC

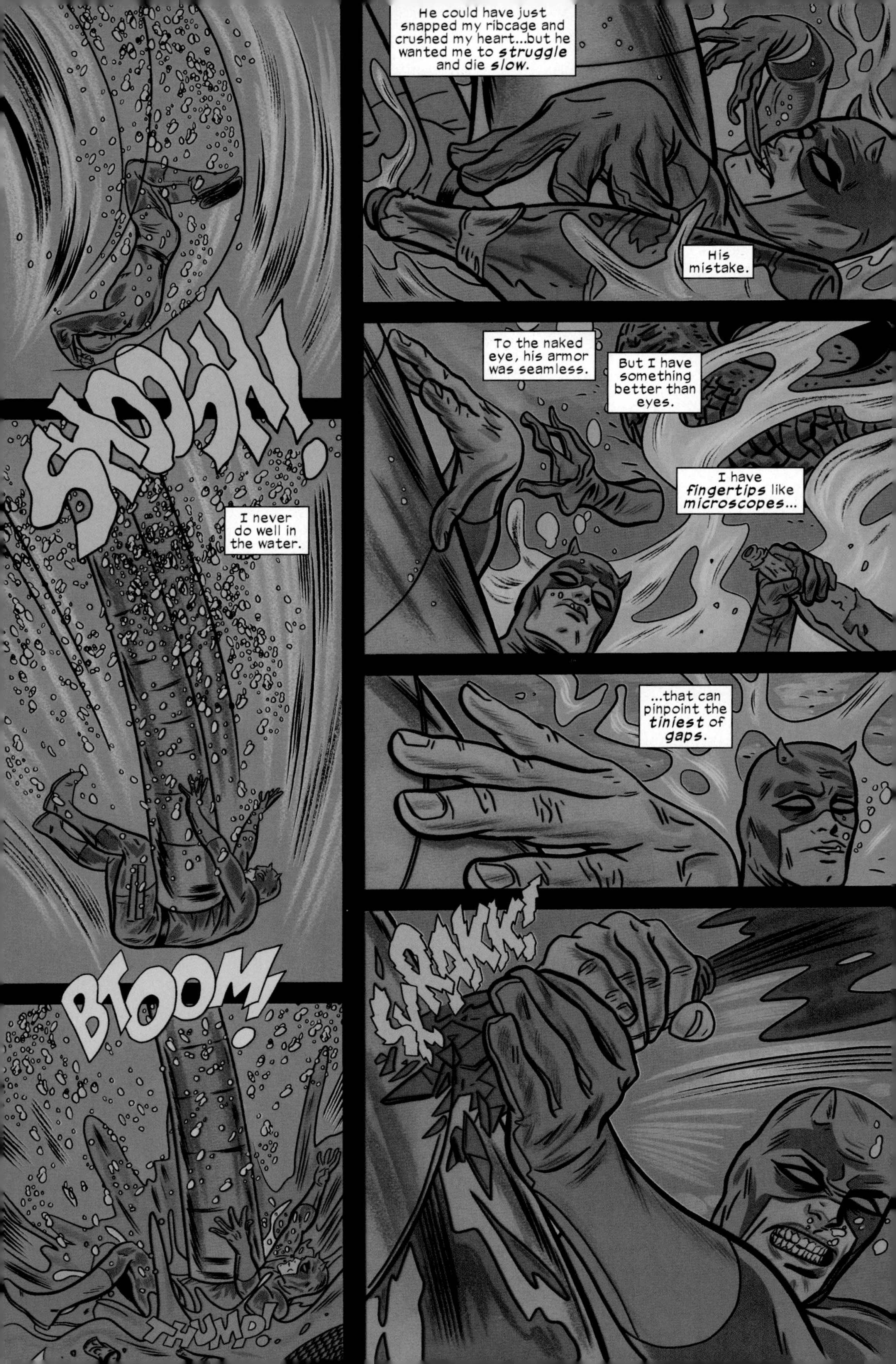

He could have just snapped my ribcage and crushed my heart...but he wanted me to *struggle* and die *slow*.
His mistake.
SPOOSH!
I never do well in the water.
To the naked eye, his armor was seamless.
But I have something better than eyes.
I have *fingertips* like *microscopes*...
...that can pinpoint the *tiniest* of *gaps*.
BLOOM!
SKRAKK!
THUMP!

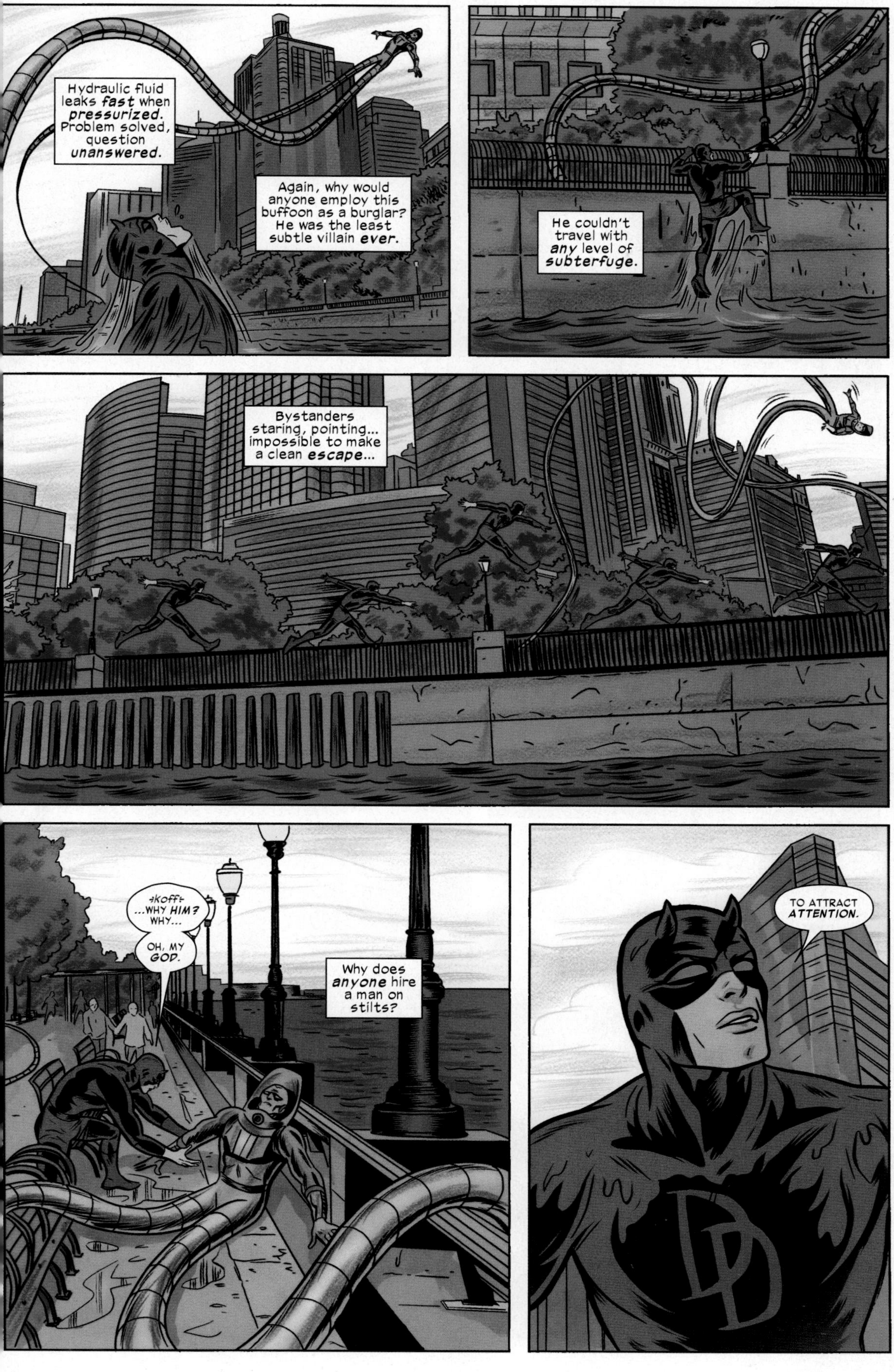

Hydraulic fluid leaks fast when pressurized. Problem solved, question unanswered.
Again, why would anyone employ this buffoon as a burglar? He was the least subtle villain ever.
He couldn't travel with any level of subterfuge.
Bystanders staring, pointing... impossible to make a clean escape...
KOFF ...WHY HIM? WHY...
OH, MY GOD.
Why does anyone hire a man on stilts?
TO ATTRACT ATTENTION.

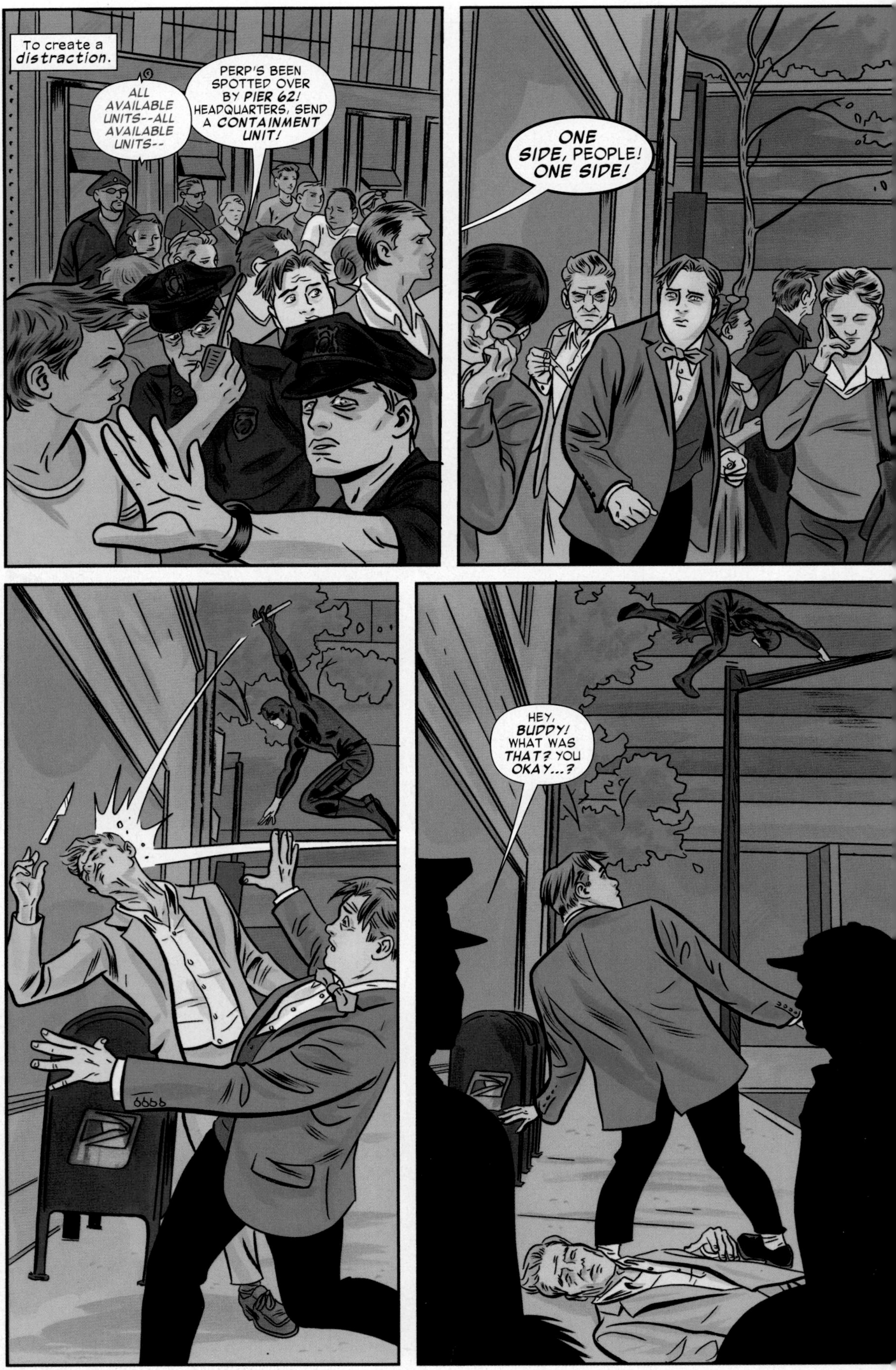
To create a distraction.
ALL AVAILABLE UNITS--ALL AVAILABLE UNITS--
PERP'S BEEN SPOTTED OVER BY PIER 62! HEADQUARTERS, SEND A CONTAINMENT UNIT!
ONE SIDE, PEOPLE! ONE SIDE!
HEY, BUDDY! WHAT WAS THAT? YOU OKAY...?

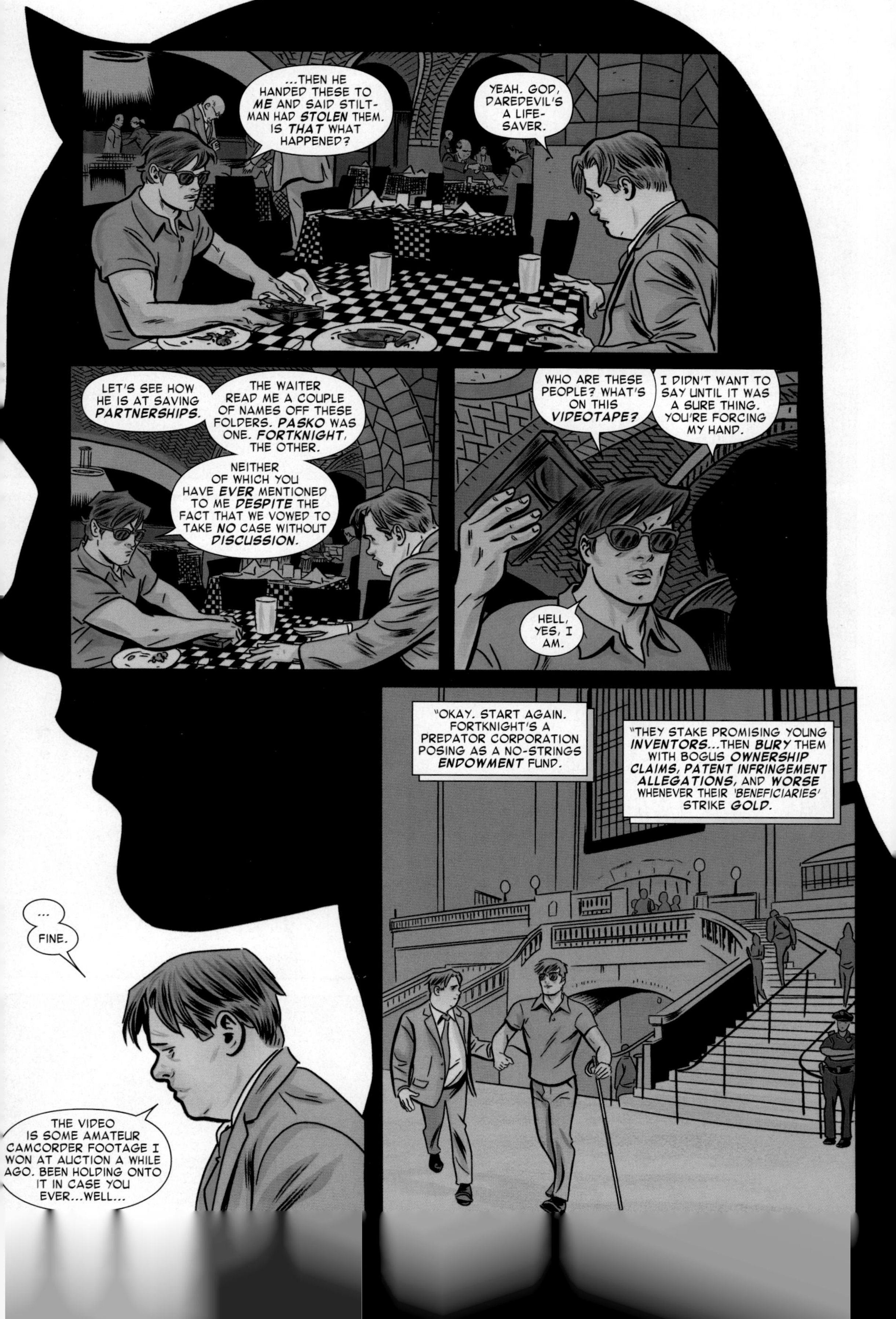

...THEN HE HANDED THESE TO ME AND SAID STILT-MAN HAD STOLEN THEM. IS THAT WHAT HAPPENED?
YEAH. GOD, DAREDEVIL'S A LIFE-SAVER.
LET'S SEE HOW HE IS AT SAVING PARTNERSHIPS.
THE WAITER READ ME A COUPLE OF NAMES OFF THESE FOLDERS. PASKO WAS ONE. FORTKNIGHT, THE OTHER.
NEITHER OF WHICH YOU HAVE EVER MENTIONED TO ME DESPITE THE FACT THAT WE VOWED TO TAKE NO CASE WITHOUT DISCUSSION.
WHO ARE THESE PEOPLE? WHAT'S ON THIS VIDEOTAPE?
I DIDN'T WANT TO SAY UNTIL IT WAS A SURE THING. YOU'RE FORCING MY HAND.
HELL, YES, I AM.
...
FINE.
THE VIDEO IS SOME AMATEUR CAMCORDER FOOTAGE I WON AT AUCTION A WHILE AGO. BEEN HOLDING ONTO IT IN CASE YOU EVER...WELL...
"OKAY. START AGAIN. FORTKNIGHT'S A PREDATOR CORPORATION POSING AS A NO-STRINGS ENDOWMENT FUND.
"THEY STAKE PROMISING YOUNG INVENTORS...THEN BURY THEM WITH BOGUS OWNERSHIP CLAIMS, PATENT INFRINGEMENT ALLEGATIONS, AND WORSE WHENEVER THEIR 'BENEFICIARIES' STRIKE GOLD.

"ELLIOT PASKO'S ONE OF THEIR *VICTIMS*. GOOD KID, FLAT BROKE. HE CAME TO US HAT IN HAND, AND WHEN I SAW HIS *WORK*, WE MADE A DEAL:

"ALL THE PRO BONO HE *REQUIRED* IN EXCHANGE FOR TEN PERCENT OF FUTURE PROFITS.

"IT'S STILL IN VERY EARLY *PROTOTYPE*, MATT, BUT SOMEDAY HIS INVENTION'S GOING TO CHANGE THE *WORLD*."

"IF IT'S WORTH KILLING PASKO'S *LAWYER* OVER, THEN I IMAGINE. YOU SHOULD HAVE TOLD ME, FOGGY. WHY DID YOU GO TO STUPID LENGTHS TO KEEP IT A SECRET?"

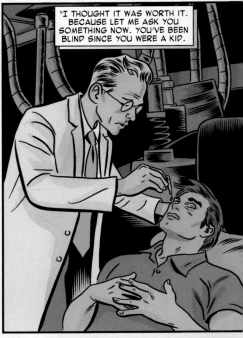

"I THOUGHT IT WAS WORTH IT. BECAUSE LET ME ASK YOU SOMETHING NOW. YOU'VE BEEN BLIND SINCE YOU WERE A KID.

"IF YOU COULD HAVE YOUR SIGHT BACK, MATT...FOR JUST, LIKE, HALF AN HOUR...

"...AND YOU COULD SEE *ONE THING* YOU *MISSED*, PAST OR PRESENT...WHAT WOULD IT BE?"

"I DON'T KNOW."

"I BET I DO."

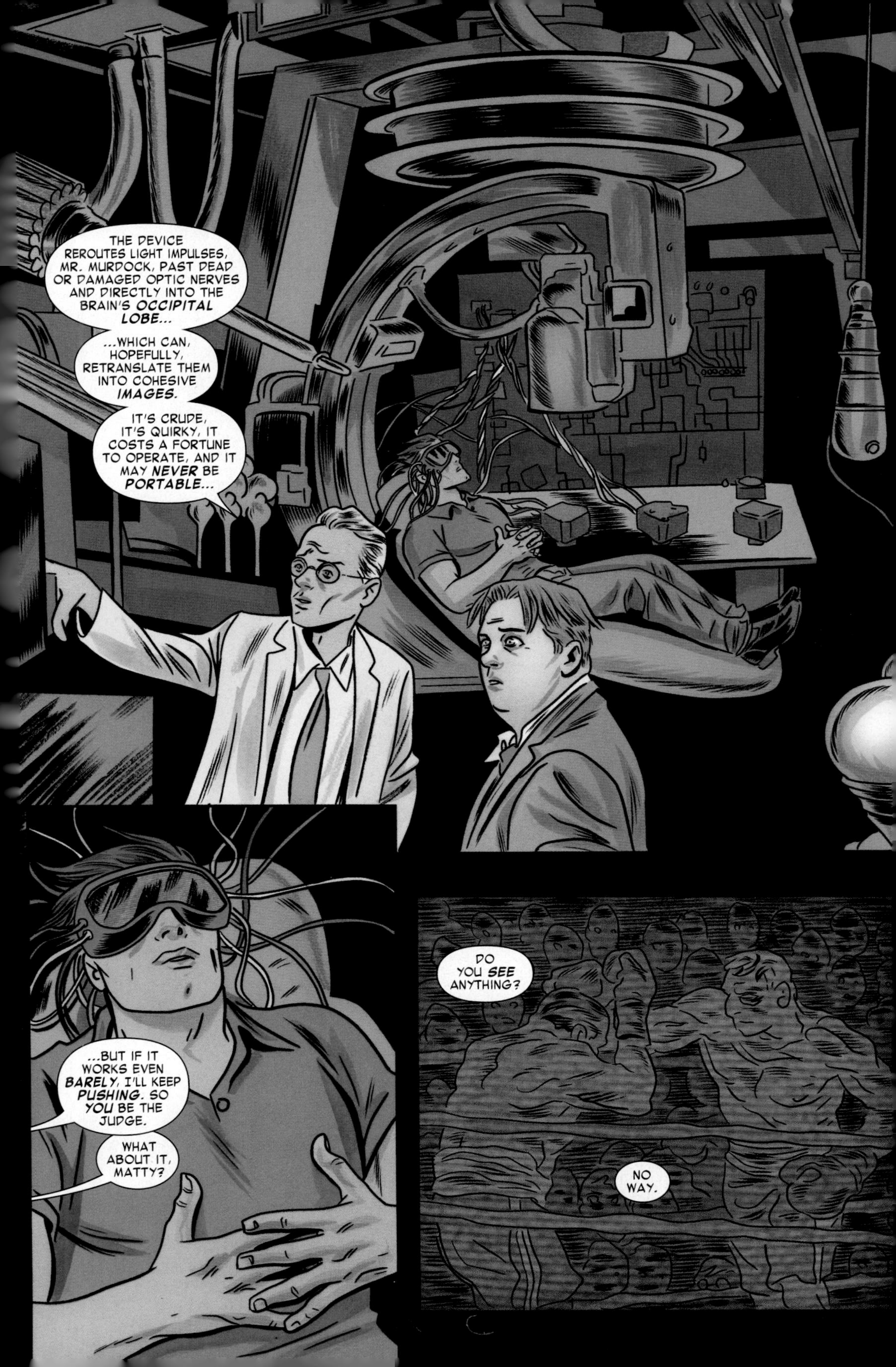
THE DEVICE REROUTES LIGHT IMPULSES, MR. MURDOCK, PAST DEAD OR DAMAGED OPTIC NERVES AND DIRECTLY INTO THE BRAIN'S OCCIPITAL LOBE...
...WHICH CAN, HOPEFULLY, RETRANSLATE THEM INTO COHESIVE IMAGES.
IT'S CRUDE, IT'S QUIRKY, IT COSTS A FORTUNE TO OPERATE, AND IT MAY NEVER BE PORTABLE...
...BUT IF IT WORKS EVEN BARELY, I'LL KEEP PUSHING. SO YOU BE THE JUDGE.
WHAT ABOUT IT, MATTY?
DO YOU SEE ANYTHING?
NO WAY.

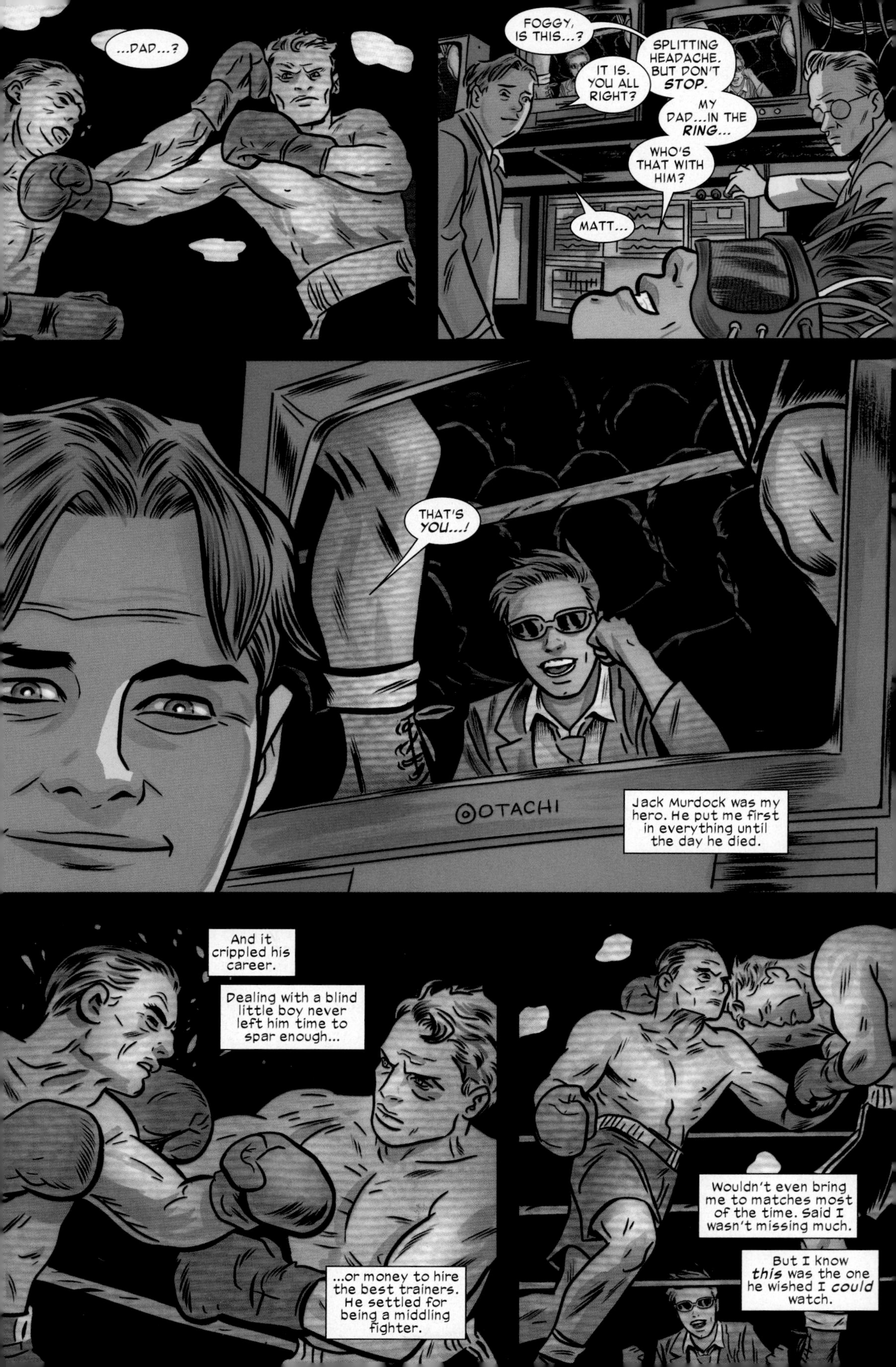

...DAD...?
FOGGY, IS THIS...?
IT IS. YOU ALL RIGHT?
SPLITTING HEADACHE. BUT DON'T STOP.
MY DAD...IN THE RING...
WHO'S THAT WITH HIM?
MATT...
THAT'S YOU...!
©OTACHI
Jack Murdock was my hero. He put me first in everything until the day he died.
And it crippled his career.
Dealing with a blind little boy never left him time to spar enough...
...or money to hire the best trainers. He settled for being a middling fighter.
Wouldn't even bring me to matches most of the time. Said I wasn't missing much.
But I know this was the one he wished I could watch.

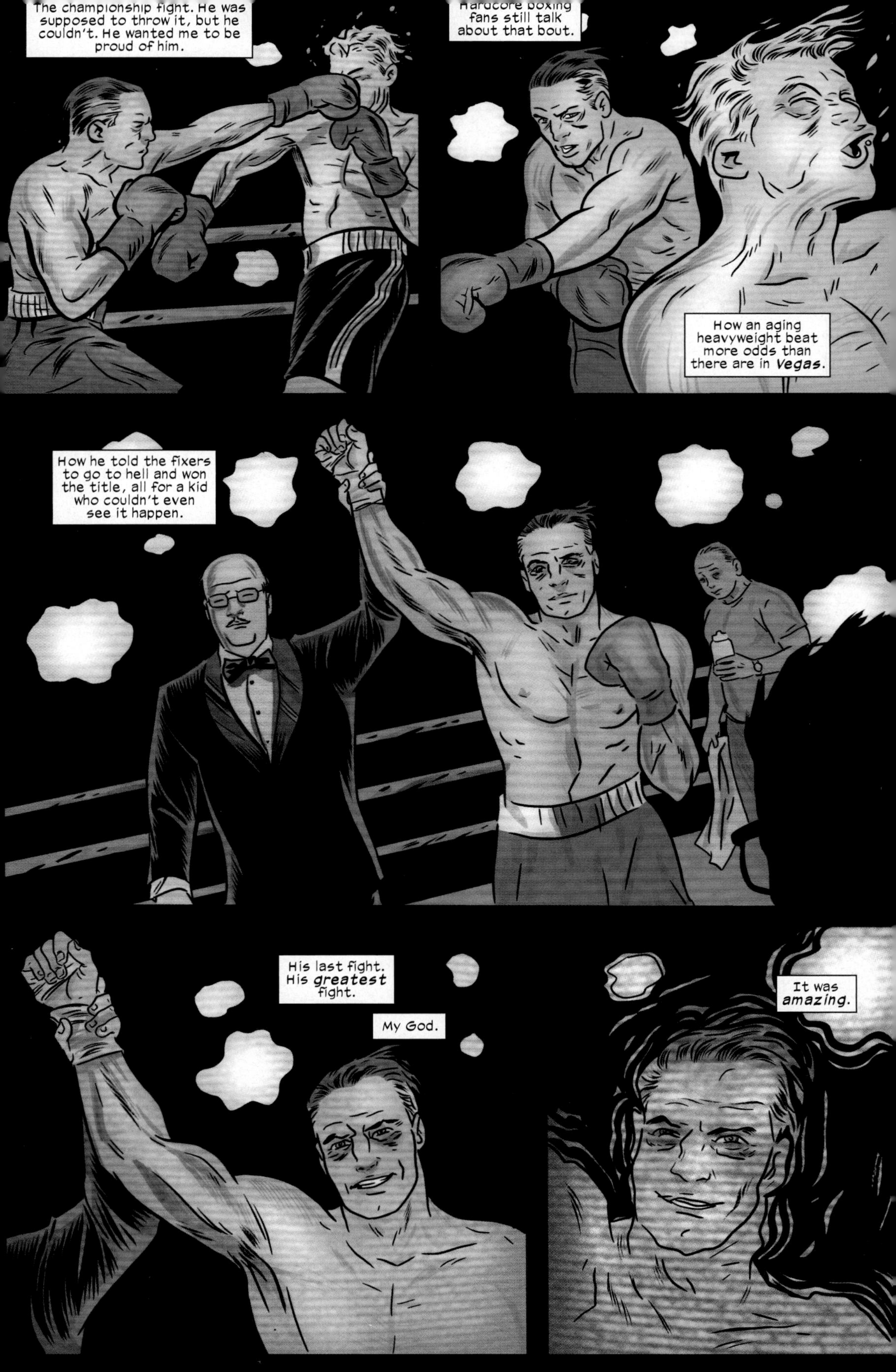
The championship fight. He was supposed to throw it, but he couldn't. He wanted me to be proud of him.
Hardcore boxing fans still talk about that bout.
How an aging heavyweight beat more odds than there are in Vegas.
How he told the fixers to go to hell and won the title, all for a kid who couldn't even see it happen.
His last fight. His greatest fight.
My God.
It was amazing.

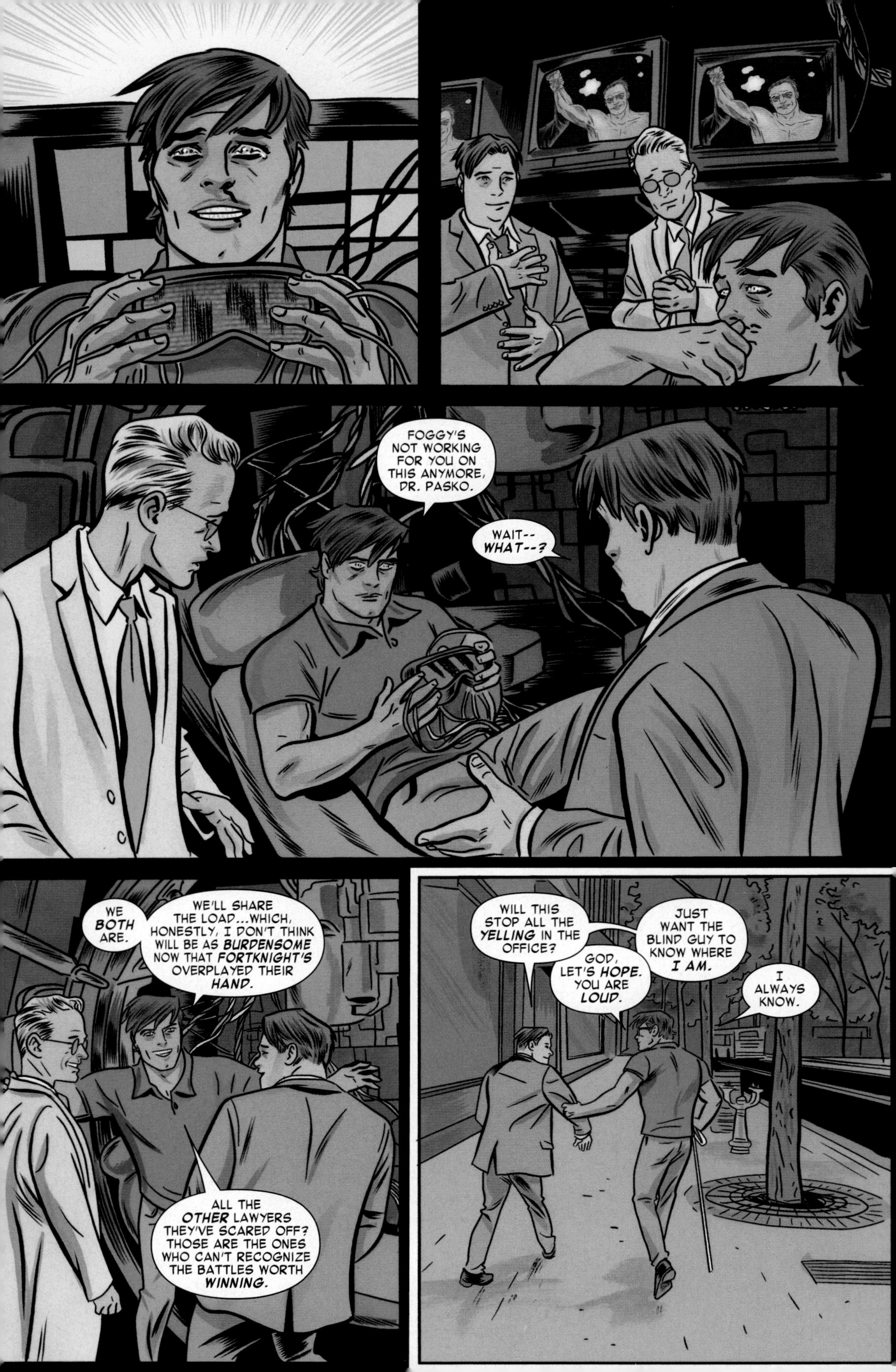

FOGGY'S NOT WORKING FOR YOU ON THIS ANYMORE, DR. PASKO.
WAIT-- WHAT--?
WE BOTH ARE.
WE'LL SHARE THE LOAD...WHICH, HONESTLY, I DON'T THINK WILL BE AS BURDENSOME NOW THAT FORTKNIGHT'S OVERPLAYED THEIR HAND.
ALL THE OTHER LAWYERS THEY'VE SCARED OFF? THOSE ARE THE ONES WHO CAN'T RECOGNIZE THE BATTLES WORTH WINNING.
WILL THIS STOP ALL THE YELLING IN THE OFFICE?
JUST WANT THE BLIND GUY TO KNOW WHERE I AM.
GOD, LET'S HOPE. YOU ARE LOUD.
I ALWAYS KNOW.

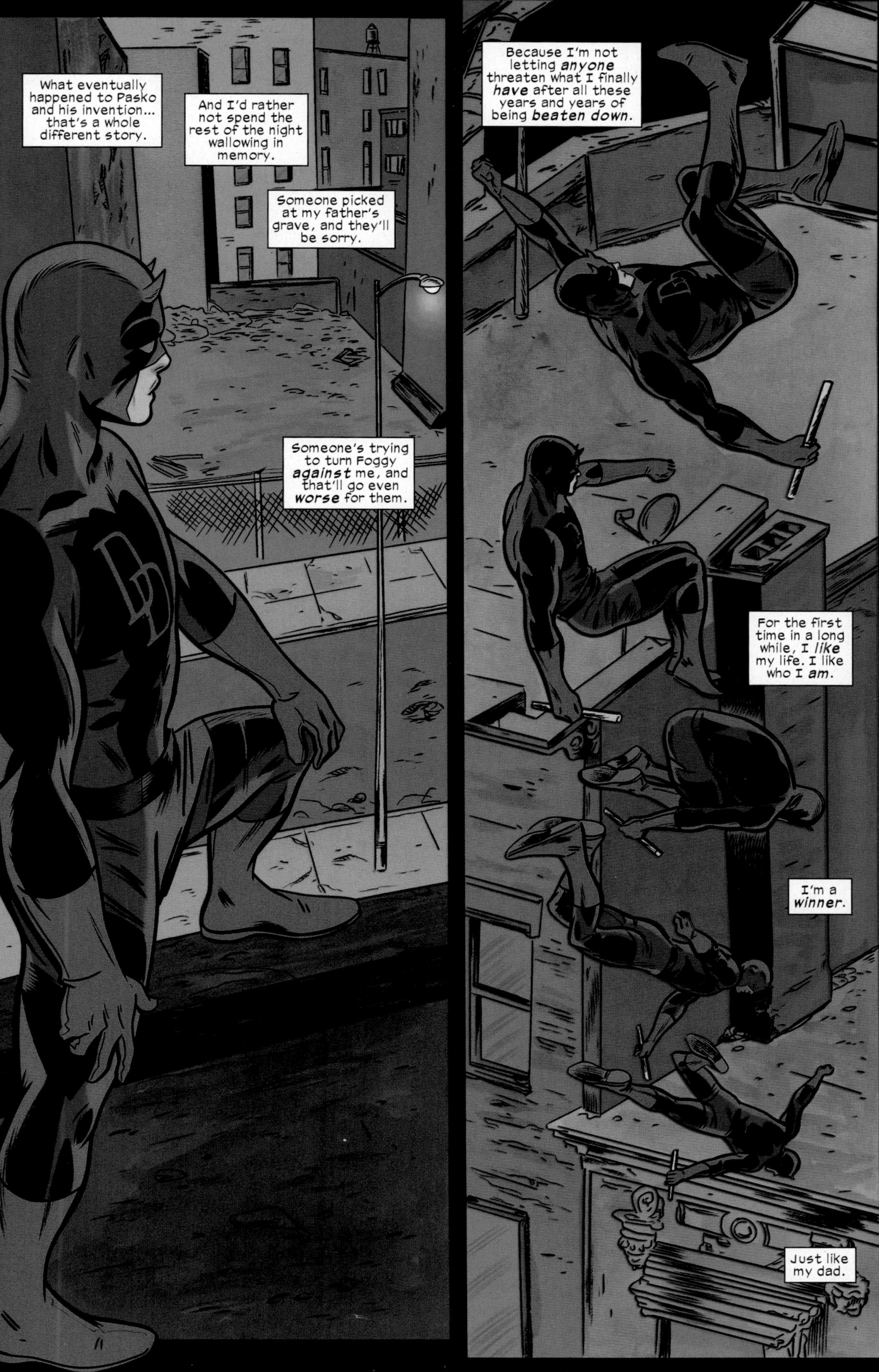
What eventually happened to Pasko and his invention... that's a whole different story.
And I'd rather not spend the rest of the night wallowing in memory.
Someone picked at my father's grave, and they'll be sorry.
Someone's trying to turn Foggy *against* me, and that'll go even *worse* for them.
Because I'm not letting *anyone* threaten what I finally *have* after all these years and years of being *beaten down*.
For the first time in a long while, I *like* my life. I like who I *am*.
I'm a *winner*.
Just like my dad.

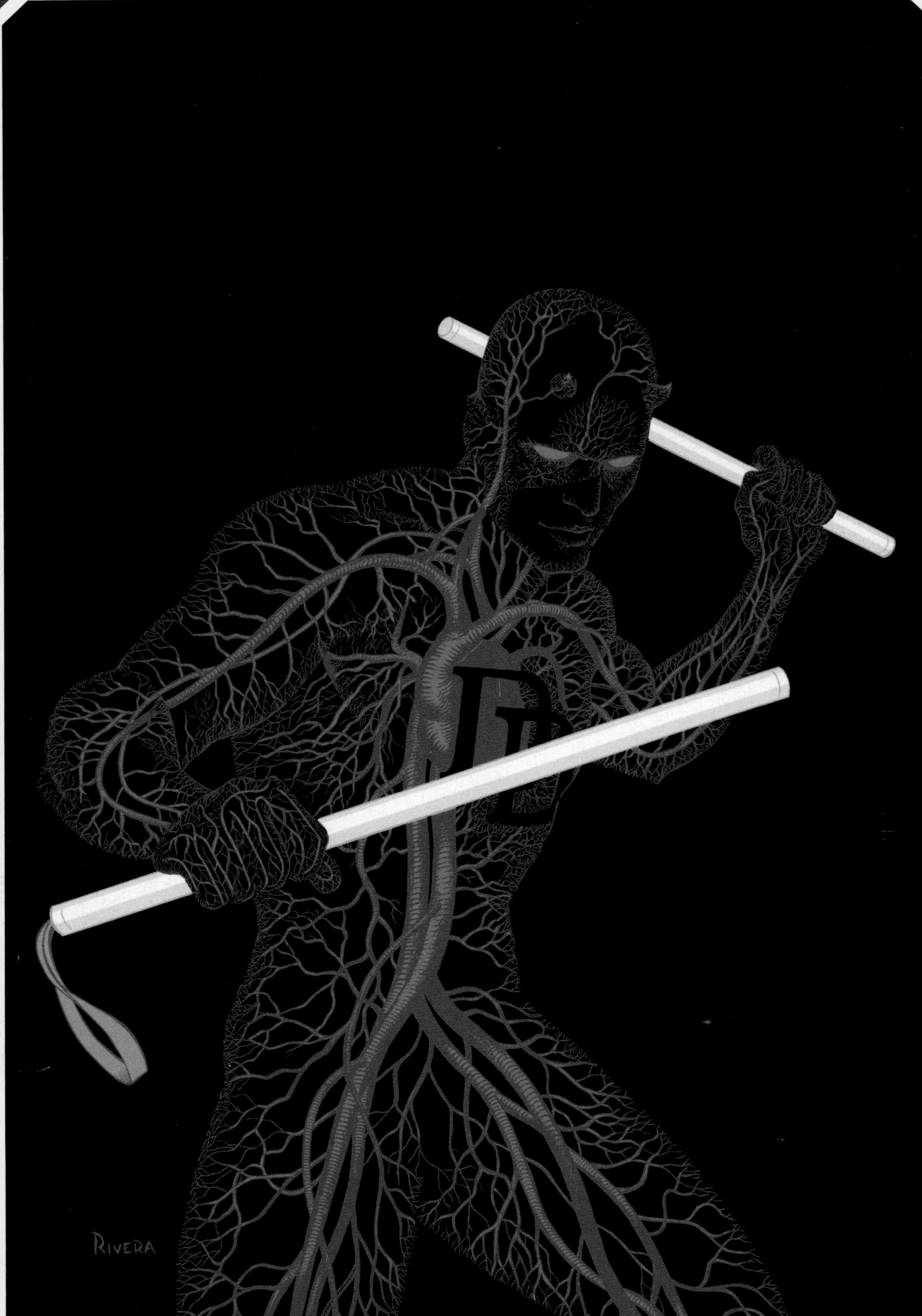
RIVERA

EIGHTEEN

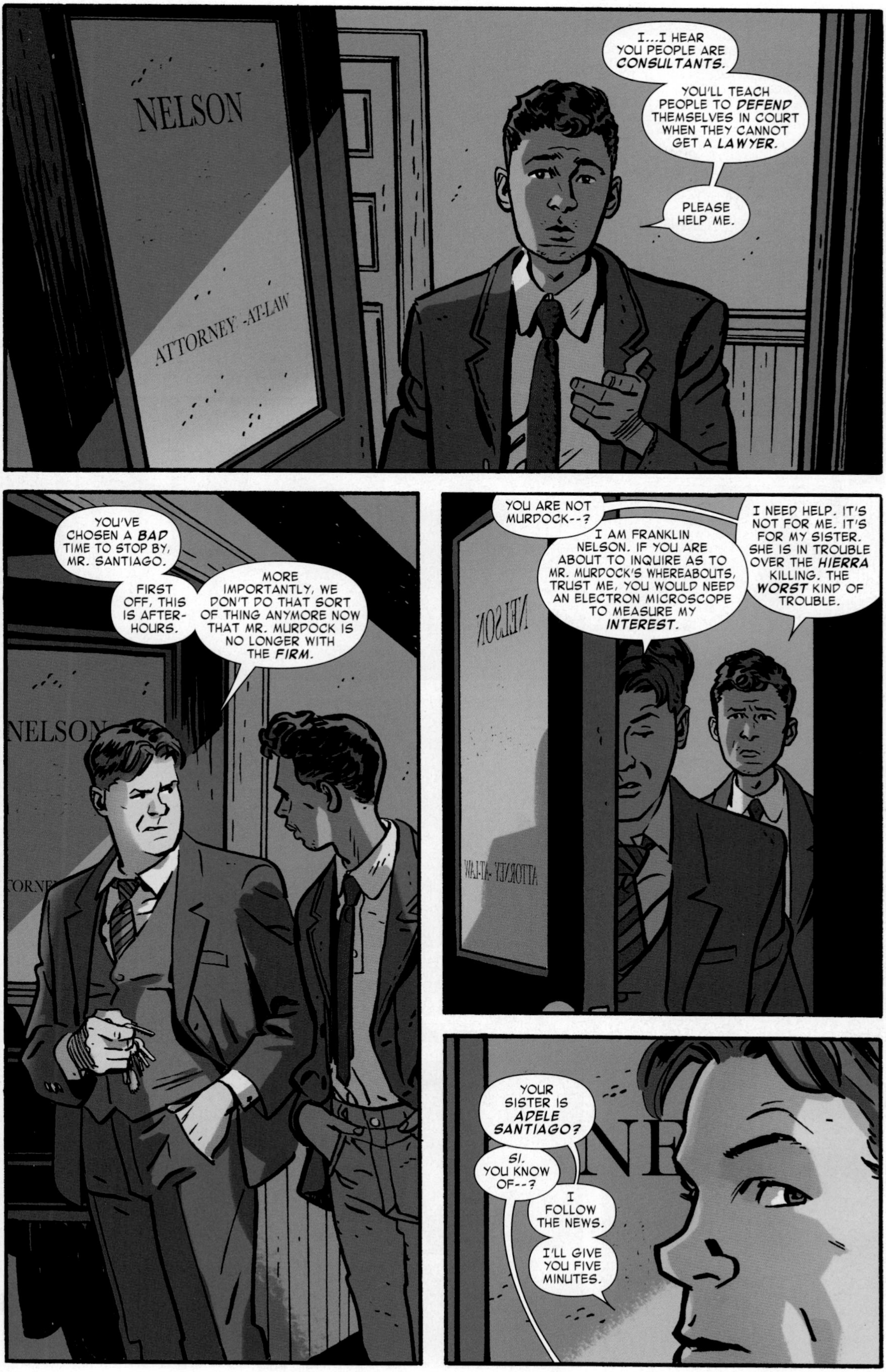
NELSON
ATTORNEY -AT-LAW
I...I HEAR YOU PEOPLE ARE CONSULTANTS.
YOU'LL TEACH PEOPLE TO DEFEND THEMSELVES IN COURT WHEN THEY CANNOT GET A LAWYER.
PLEASE HELP ME.
YOU'VE CHOSEN A BAD TIME TO STOP BY, MR. SANTIAGO.
FIRST OFF, THIS IS AFTER-HOURS.
MORE IMPORTANTLY, WE DON'T DO THAT SORT OF THING ANYMORE NOW THAT MR. MURDOCK IS NO LONGER WITH THE FIRM.
YOU ARE NOT MURDOCK--?
I AM FRANKLIN NELSON. IF YOU ARE ABOUT TO INQUIRE AS TO MR. MURDOCK'S WHEREABOUTS, TRUST ME, YOU WOULD NEED AN ELECTRON MICROSCOPE TO MEASURE MY INTEREST.
I NEED HELP. IT'S NOT FOR ME. IT'S FOR MY SISTER. SHE IS IN TROUBLE OVER THE HIERRA KILLING. THE WORST KIND OF TROUBLE.
YOUR SISTER IS ADELE SANTIAGO?
SI. YOU KNOW OF--?
I FOLLOW THE NEWS.
I'LL GIVE YOU FIVE MINUTES.

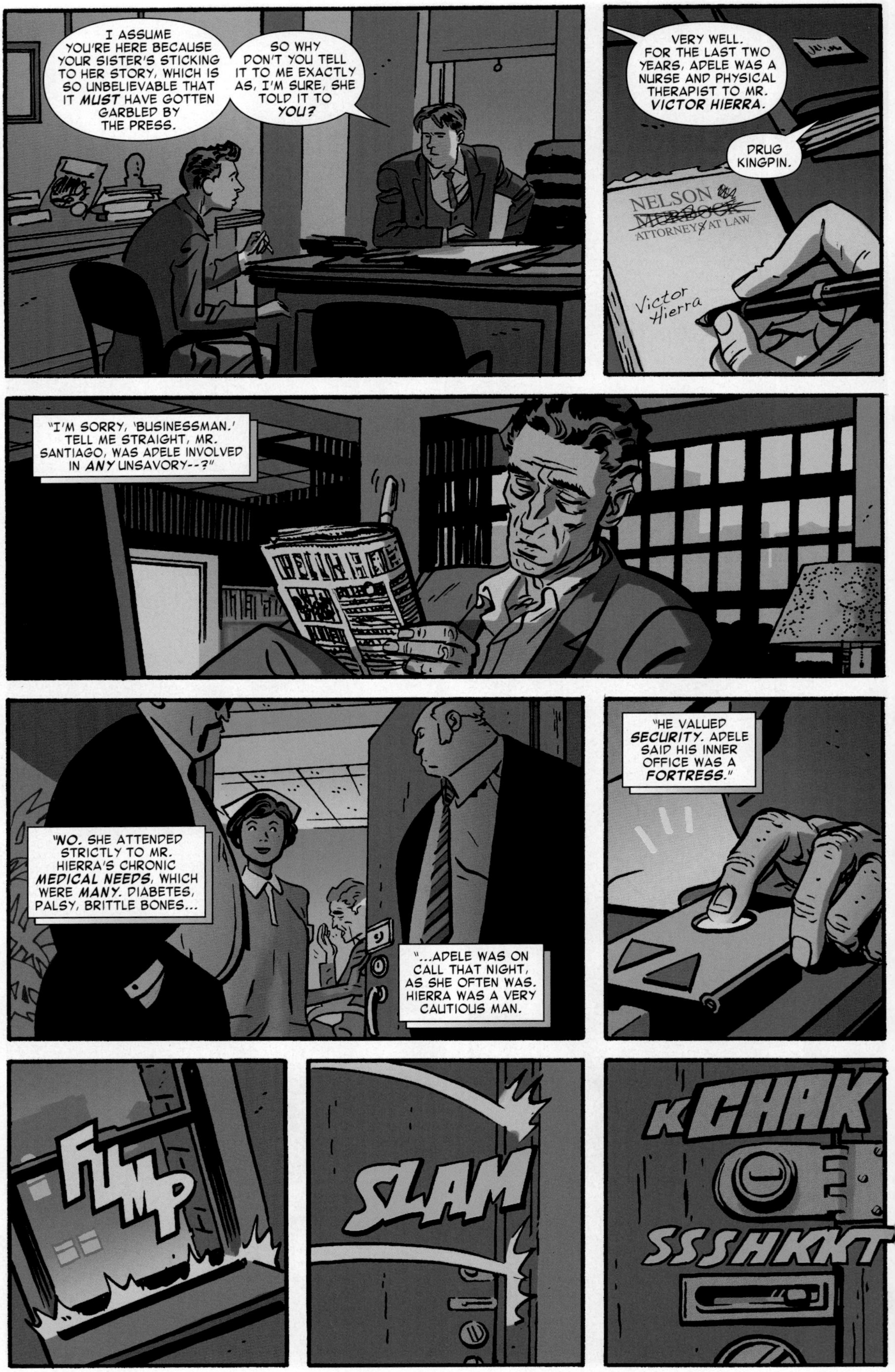
I ASSUME YOU'RE HERE BECAUSE YOUR SISTER'S STICKING TO HER STORY, WHICH IS SO UNBELIEVABLE THAT IT *MUST* HAVE GOTTEN GARBLED BY THE PRESS.
SO WHY DON'T YOU TELL IT TO ME EXACTLY AS, I'M SURE, SHE TOLD IT TO *YOU?*
VERY WELL. FOR THE LAST TWO YEARS, ADELE WAS A NURSE AND PHYSICAL THERAPIST TO MR. *VICTOR HIERRA.*
DRUG KINGPIN.
NELSON
MURDOCK
ATTORNEYS AT LAW
Victor Hierra
"I'M SORRY, 'BUSINESSMAN.' TELL ME STRAIGHT, MR. SANTIAGO, WAS ADELE INVOLVED IN *ANY* UNSAVORY--?"
"*NO.* SHE ATTENDED STRICTLY TO MR. HIERRA'S CHRONIC *MEDICAL NEEDS*, WHICH WERE *MANY.* DIABETES, PALSY, BRITTLE BONES...
"...ADELE WAS ON CALL THAT NIGHT, AS SHE OFTEN WAS. HIERRA WAS A VERY CAUTIOUS MAN.
"HE VALUED *SECURITY.* ADELE SAID HIS INNER OFFICE WAS A *FORTRESS.*"
FUMP
SLAM
KCHAK
SSSHKKT

LOCKED FROM THE *INSIDE*. JUST THE *TWO* OF THEM, ADELE AND HIERRA. FOR HOW LONG?

ABOUT AN HOUR.

DURING WHICH?

ADELE SIMPLY TENDED TO HER *DUTIES*...

"...SORTING PILLS, CHARTING DOSAGES, RECORDING CALORIE COUNTS AND OTHER SUCH THINGS.

"IT WAS HER JOB TO KEEP HIERRA IN THE PINK OF HEALTH, AND SHE TOOK HER RESPONSIBILITIES *SERIOUSLY*.

"SHE SAW NOTHING. THIS I KNOW, BECAUSE I WAS ON THE PHONE WITH HER AT THE TIME IT *HAPPENED*. SHE SIMPLY HEARD THE OLD MAN *FALL*.

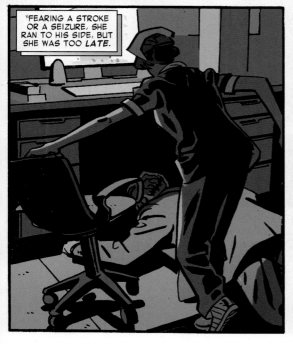

"FEARING A STROKE OR A SEIZURE, SHE RAN TO HIS SIDE, BUT SHE WAS TOO *LATE*.

"HIERRA WAS LYING *DEAD* ON A *DRY* AND *SPOTLESS CARPET*--

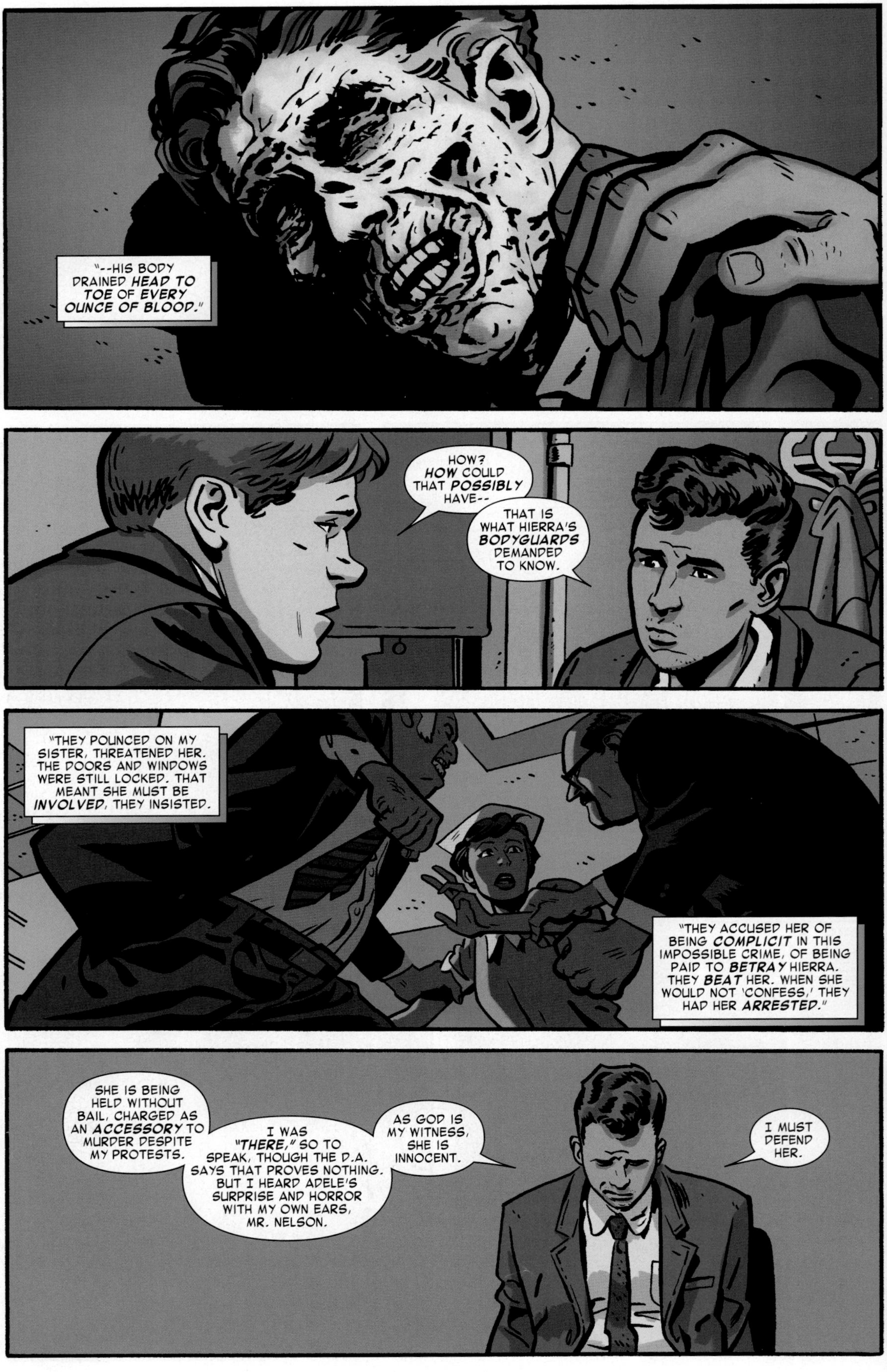
"--HIS BODY DRAINED HEAD TO TOE OF EVERY OUNCE OF BLOOD."
HOW? HOW COULD THAT POSSIBLY HAVE--
THAT IS WHAT HIERRA'S BODYGUARDS DEMANDED TO KNOW.
"THEY POUNCED ON MY SISTER, THREATENED HER. THE DOORS AND WINDOWS WERE STILL LOCKED. THAT MEANT SHE MUST BE INVOLVED, THEY INSISTED.
"THEY ACCUSED HER OF BEING COMPLICIT IN THIS IMPOSSIBLE CRIME, OF BEING PAID TO BETRAY HIERRA. THEY BEAT HER. WHEN SHE WOULD NOT 'CONFESS,' THEY HAD HER ARRESTED."
SHE IS BEING HELD WITHOUT BAIL, CHARGED AS AN ACCESSORY TO MURDER DESPITE MY PROTESTS.
I WAS "THERE," SO TO SPEAK, THOUGH THE D.A. SAYS THAT PROVES NOTHING. BUT I HEARD ADELE'S SURPRISE AND HORROR WITH MY OWN EARS, MR. NELSON.
AS GOD IS MY WITNESS, SHE IS INNOCENT.
I MUST DEFEND HER.

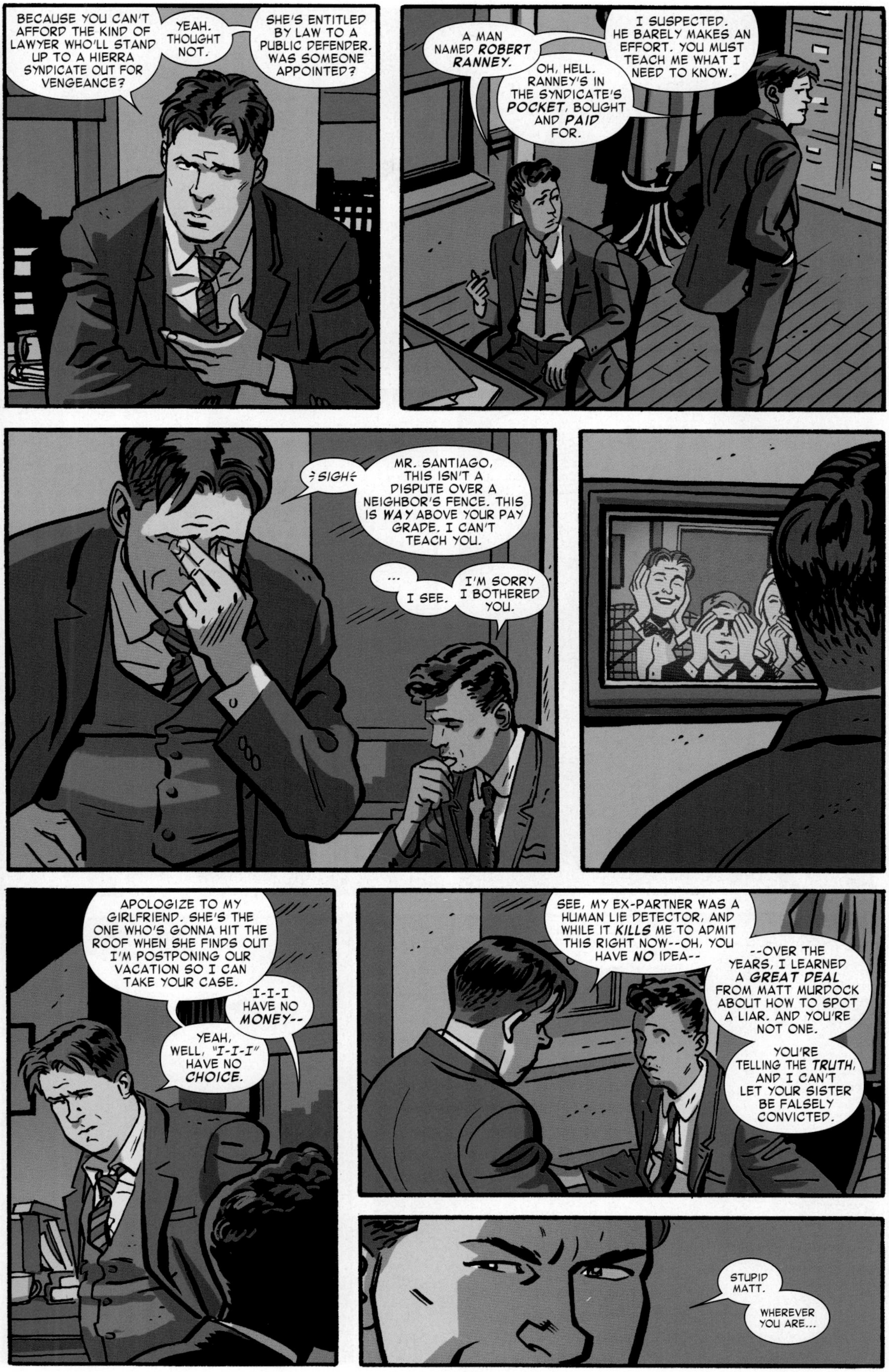
BECAUSE YOU CAN'T AFFORD THE KIND OF LAWYER WHO'LL STAND UP TO A HIERRA SYNDICATE OUT FOR VENGEANCE?
YEAH. THOUGHT NOT.
SHE'S ENTITLED BY LAW TO A PUBLIC DEFENDER. WAS SOMEONE APPOINTED?
A MAN NAMED ROBERT RANNEY.
OH, HELL. RANNEY'S IN THE SYNDICATE'S POCKET, BOUGHT AND PAID FOR.
I SUSPECTED. HE BARELY MAKES AN EFFORT. YOU MUST TEACH ME WHAT I NEED TO KNOW.
SIGH
MR. SANTIAGO, THIS ISN'T A DISPUTE OVER A NEIGHBOR'S FENCE. THIS IS WAY ABOVE YOUR PAY GRADE. I CAN'T TEACH YOU.
... I SEE.
I'M SORRY I BOTHERED YOU.
APOLOGIZE TO MY GIRLFRIEND. SHE'S THE ONE WHO'S GONNA HIT THE ROOF WHEN SHE FINDS OUT I'M POSTPONING OUR VACATION SO I CAN TAKE YOUR CASE.
I-I-I HAVE NO MONEY--
YEAH, WELL, "I-I-I" HAVE NO CHOICE.
SEE, MY EX-PARTNER WAS A HUMAN LIE DETECTOR, AND WHILE IT KILLS ME TO ADMIT THIS RIGHT NOW--OH, YOU HAVE NO IDEA--
--OVER THE YEARS, I LEARNED A GREAT DEAL FROM MATT MURDOCK ABOUT HOW TO SPOT A LIAR. AND YOU'RE NOT ONE.
YOU'RE TELLING THE TRUTH, AND I CAN'T LET YOUR SISTER BE FALSELY CONVICTED.
STUPID MATT.
WHEREVER YOU ARE...

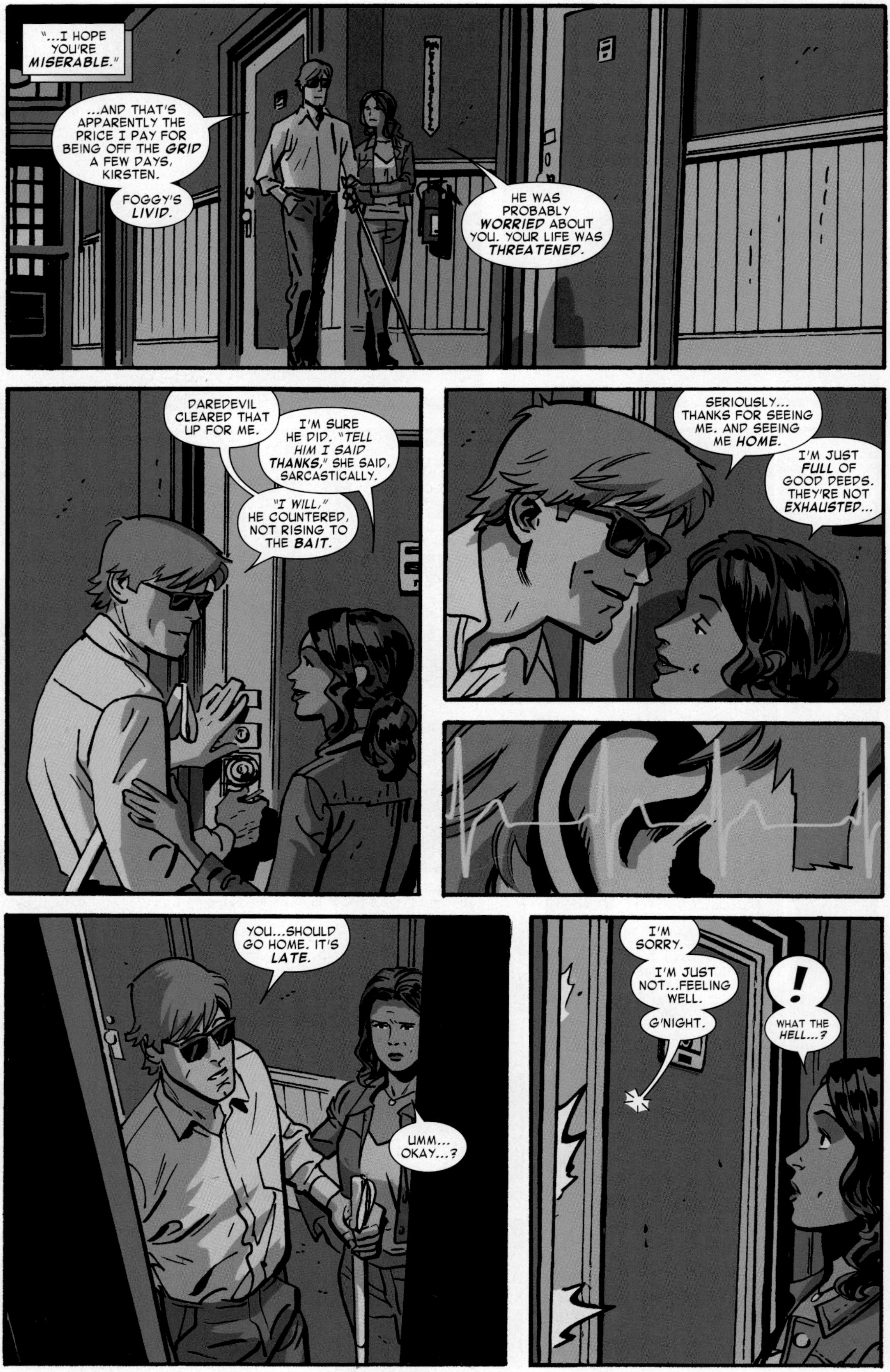
"...I HOPE YOU'RE *MISERABLE.*"
...AND THAT'S APPARENTLY THE PRICE I PAY FOR BEING OFF THE *GRID* A FEW DAYS, KIRSTEN.
FOGGY'S *LIVID.*
HE WAS PROBABLY *WORRIED* ABOUT YOU. YOUR LIFE WAS *THREATENED.*
DAREDEVIL CLEARED THAT UP FOR ME.
I'M SURE HE DID. "*TELL HIM I SAID THANKS,*" SHE SAID, SARCASTICALLY.
"*I WILL,*" HE COUNTERED, NOT RISING TO THE *BAIT.*
SERIOUSLY... THANKS FOR SEEING ME. AND SEEING ME *HOME.*
I'M JUST *FULL* OF GOOD DEEDS. THEY'RE NOT *EXHAUSTED...*
YOU...SHOULD GO HOME. IT'S *LATE.*
UMM... OKAY...?
I'M SORRY.
I'M JUST NOT...FEELING WELL.
G'NIGHT.
!
WHAT THE *HELL...?*

MATT?

MATT, IS THAT YOU...?

She can't...

...*be* here...

...this isn't *happening*...

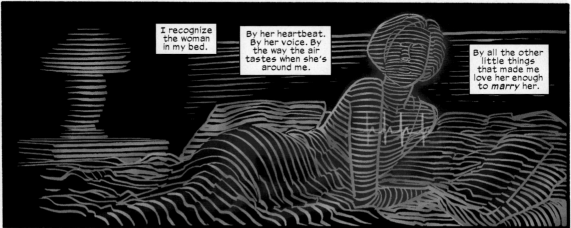

I recognize the woman in my bed.

By her heartbeat. By her voice. By the way the air tastes when she's around me.

By all the other little things that made me love her enough to *marry* her.

MATT, YOU'RE *SCARING* ME. WHAT'S *WRONG*...?

What's wrong is that you're supposed to be upstate in a *mental institution*, Milla.

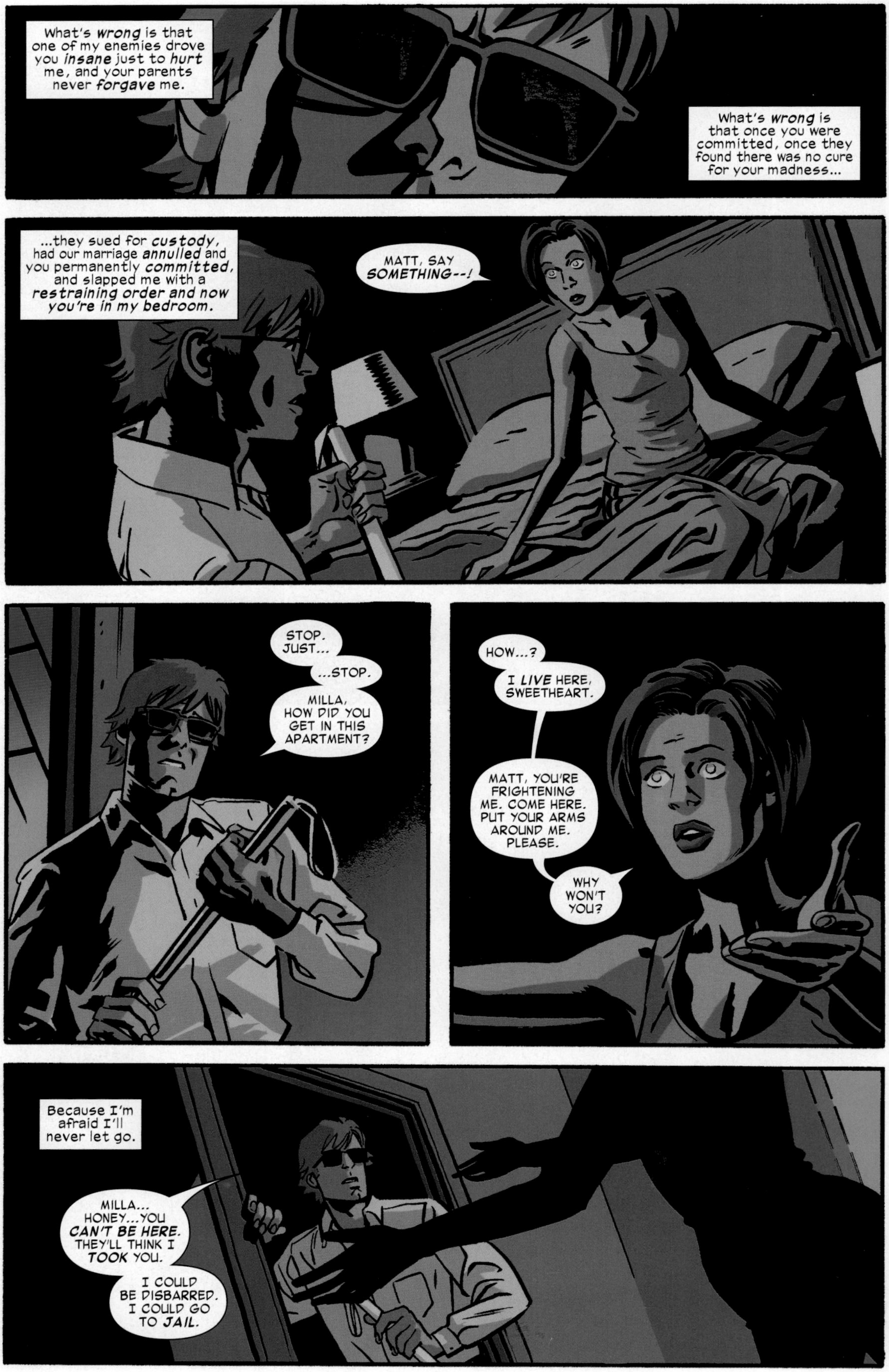
What's wrong is that one of my enemies drove you insane just to hurt me, and your parents never forgave me.
What's wrong is that once you were committed, once they found there was no cure for your madness...
...they sued for custody, had our marriage annulled and you permanently committed, and slapped me with a restraining order and now you're in my bedroom.
MATT, SAY SOMETHING--!
STOP. JUST...
...STOP.
MILLA, HOW DID YOU GET IN THIS APARTMENT?
HOW...?
I LIVE HERE, SWEETHEART.
MATT, YOU'RE FRIGHTENING ME. COME HERE. PUT YOUR ARMS AROUND ME. PLEASE.
WHY WON'T YOU?
Because I'm afraid I'll never let go.
MILLA... HONEY...YOU CAN'T BE HERE. THEY'LL THINK I TOOK YOU.
I COULD BE DISBARRED. I COULD GO TO JAIL.

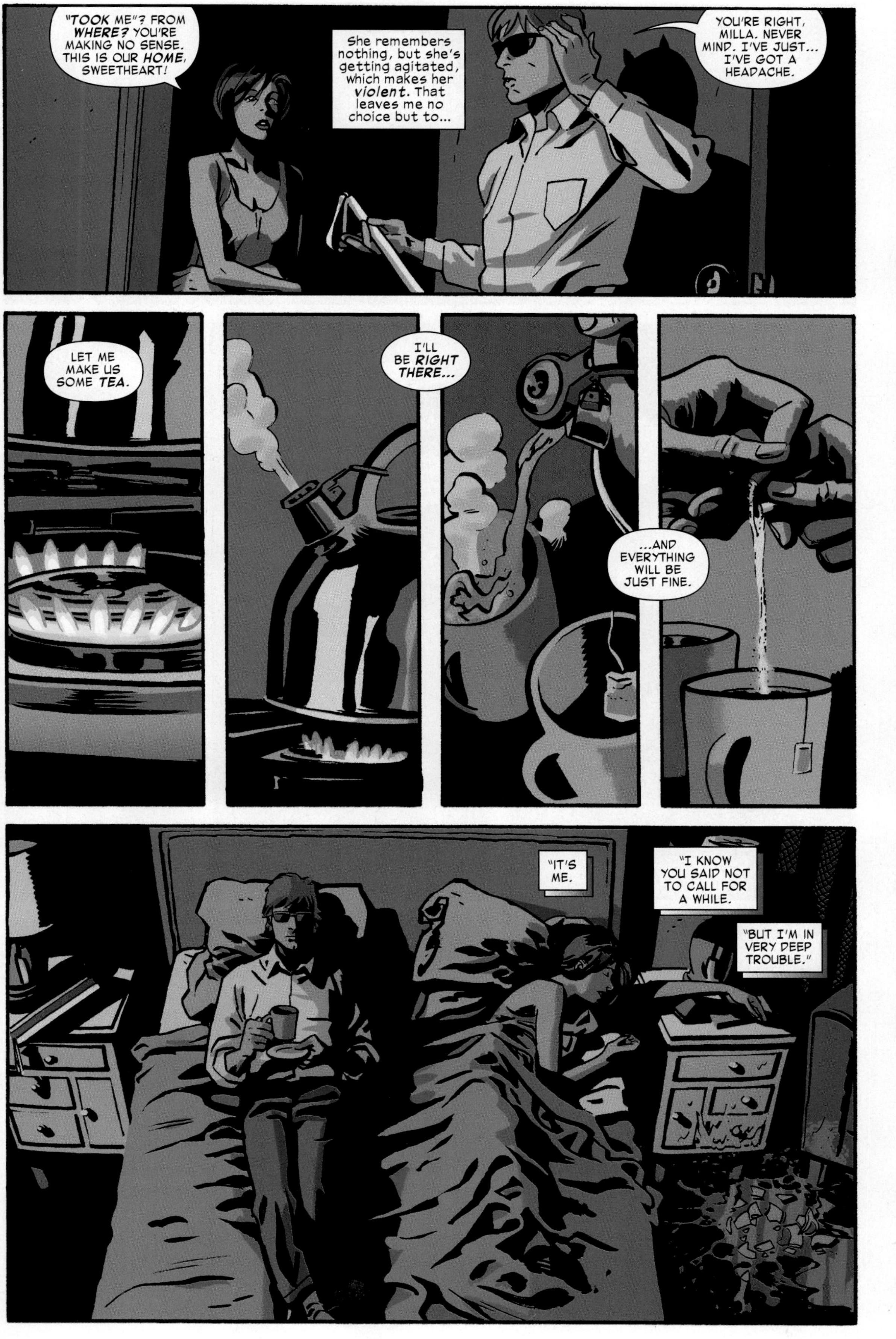
"TOOK ME"? FROM WHERE? YOU'RE MAKING NO SENSE. THIS IS OUR HOME, SWEETHEART!
She remembers nothing, but she's getting agitated, which makes her violent. That leaves me no choice but to...
YOU'RE RIGHT, MILLA. NEVER MIND. I'VE JUST... I'VE GOT A HEADACHE.
LET ME MAKE US SOME TEA.
I'LL BE RIGHT THERE...
...AND EVERYTHING WILL BE JUST FINE.
"IT'S ME.
"I KNOW YOU SAID NOT TO CALL FOR A WHILE.
"BUT I'M IN VERY DEEP TROUBLE."

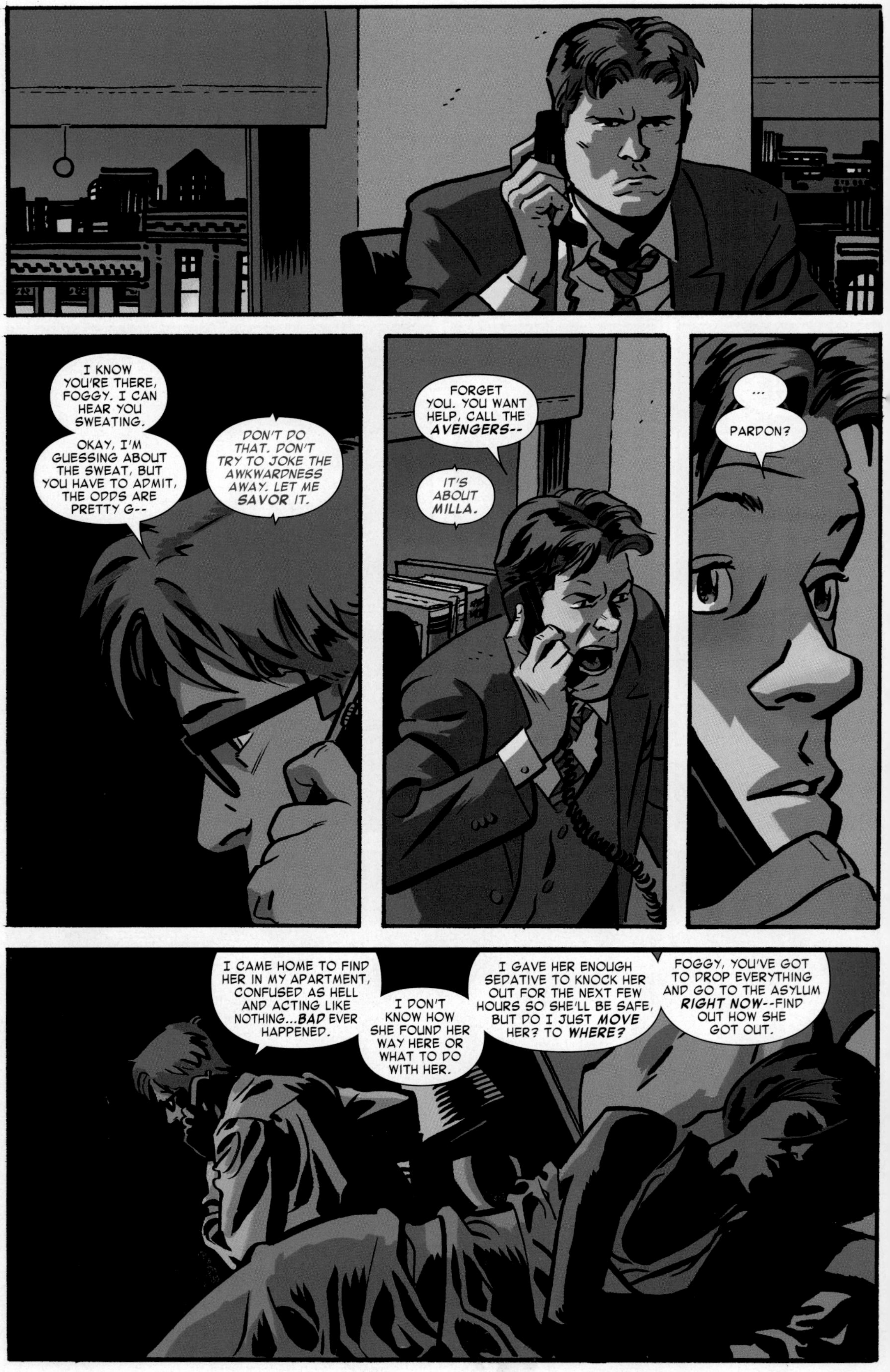
I KNOW YOU'RE THERE, FOGGY. I CAN HEAR YOU SWEATING.
OKAY, I'M GUESSING ABOUT THE SWEAT, BUT YOU HAVE TO ADMIT, THE ODDS ARE PRETTY G--
DON'T DO THAT. DON'T TRY TO JOKE THE AWKWARDNESS AWAY. LET ME SAVOR IT.
FORGET YOU. YOU WANT HELP, CALL THE AVENGERS--
IT'S ABOUT MILLA.
...
PARDON?
I CAME HOME TO FIND HER IN MY APARTMENT, CONFUSED AS HELL AND ACTING LIKE NOTHING...BAD EVER HAPPENED.
I DON'T KNOW HOW SHE FOUND HER WAY HERE OR WHAT TO DO WITH HER.
I GAVE HER ENOUGH SEDATIVE TO KNOCK HER OUT FOR THE NEXT FEW HOURS SO SHE'LL BE SAFE, BUT DO I JUST MOVE HER? TO WHERE?
FOGGY, YOU'VE GOT TO DROP EVERYTHING AND GO TO THE ASYLUM RIGHT NOW--FIND OUT HOW SHE GOT OUT.

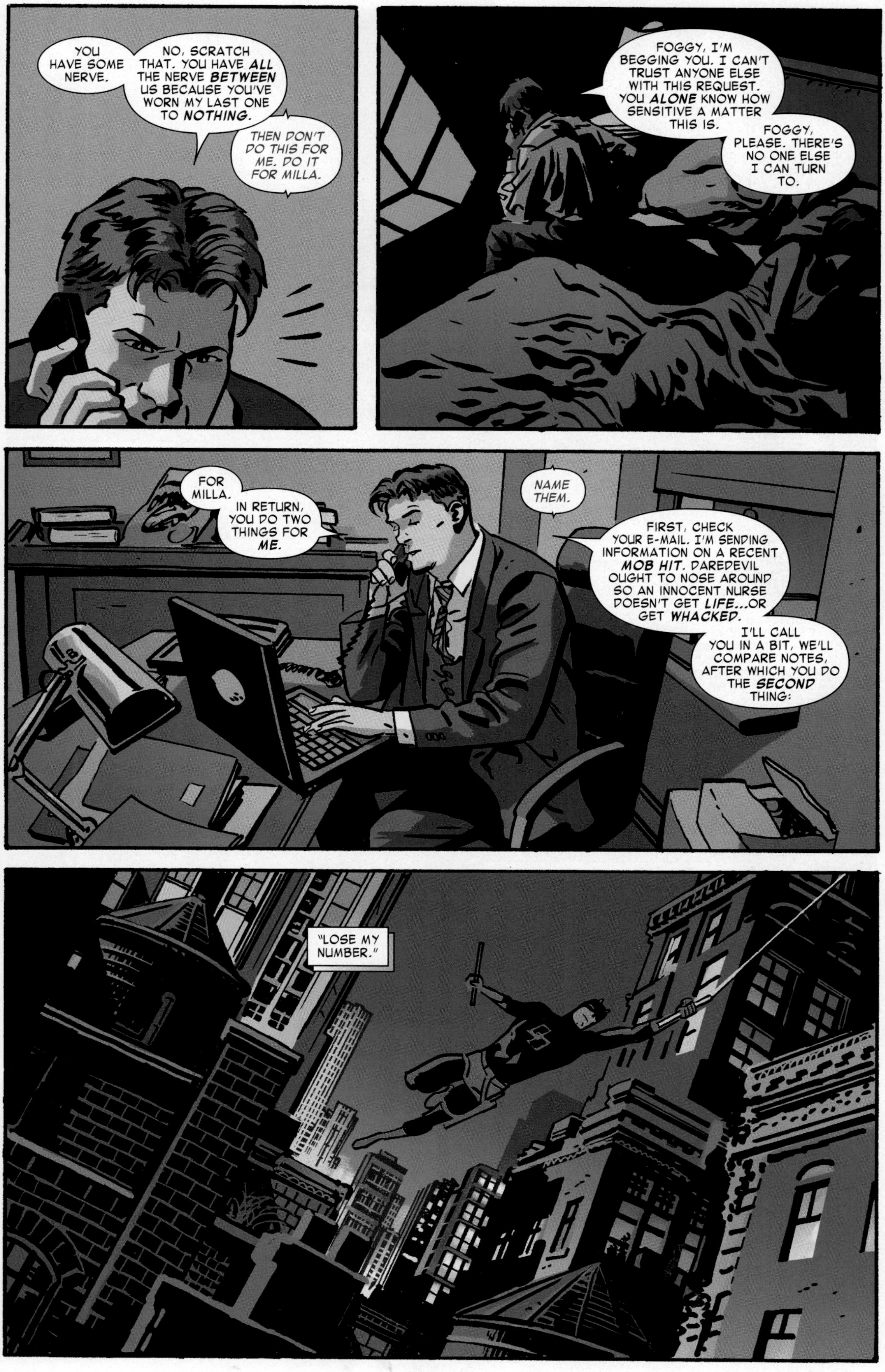
YOU HAVE SOME NERVE.
NO, SCRATCH THAT. YOU HAVE ALL THE NERVE BETWEEN US BECAUSE YOU'VE WORN MY LAST ONE TO NOTHING.
THEN DON'T DO THIS FOR ME. DO IT FOR MILLA.
FOGGY, I'M BEGGING YOU. I CAN'T TRUST ANYONE ELSE WITH THIS REQUEST. YOU ALONE KNOW HOW SENSITIVE A MATTER THIS IS.
FOGGY, PLEASE. THERE'S NO ONE ELSE I CAN TURN TO.
FOR MILLA.
IN RETURN, YOU DO TWO THINGS FOR ME.
NAME THEM.
FIRST, CHECK YOUR E-MAIL. I'M SENDING INFORMATION ON A RECENT MOB HIT. DAREDEVIL OUGHT TO NOSE AROUND SO AN INNOCENT NURSE DOESN'T GET LIFE...OR GET WHACKED.
I'LL CALL YOU IN A BIT, WE'LL COMPARE NOTES, AFTER WHICH YOU DO THE SECOND THING:
"LOSE MY NUMBER."

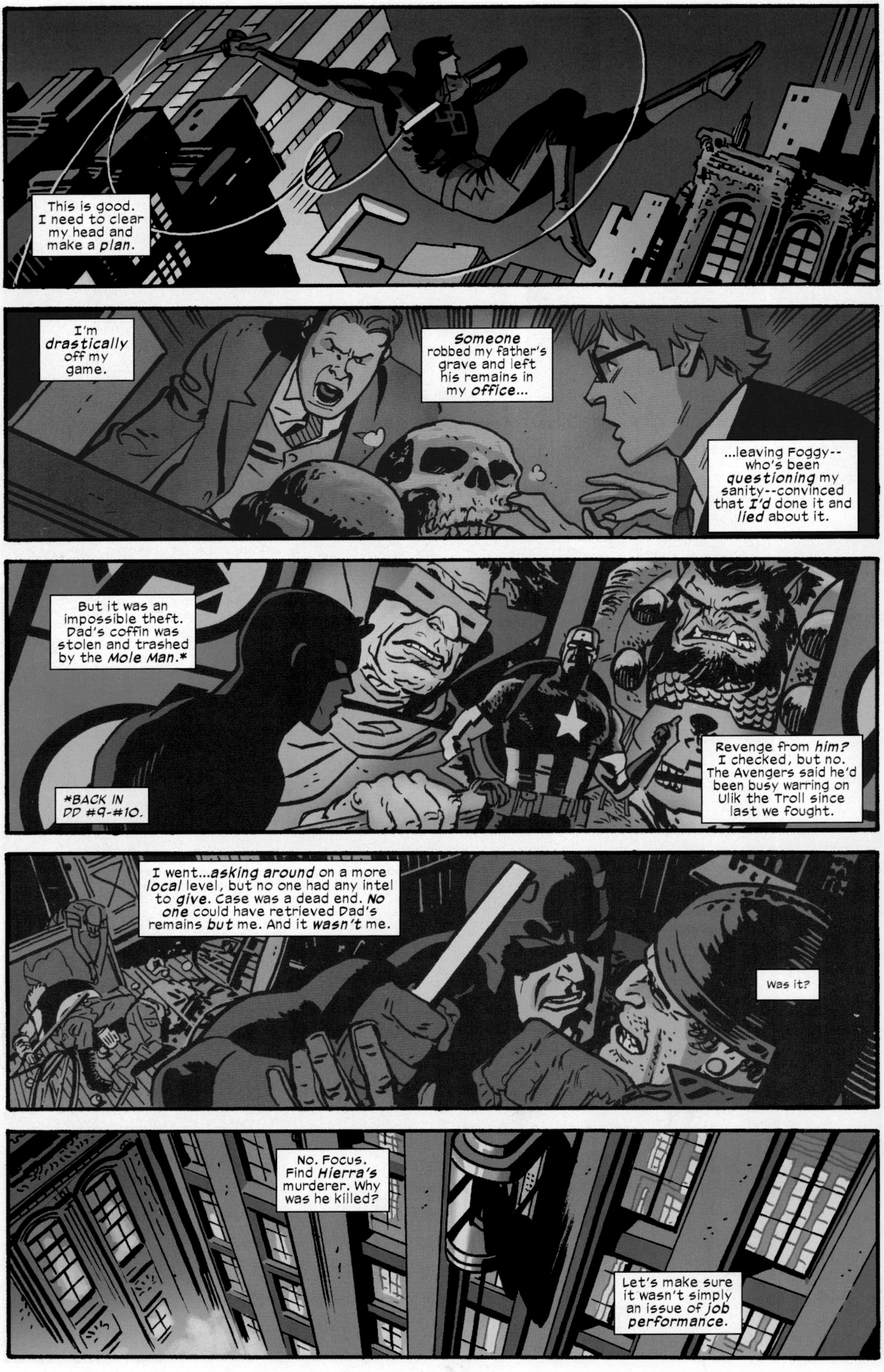
This is good. I need to clear my head and make a *plan.*
I'm *drastically* off my game.
Someone robbed my father's grave and left his remains in my *office*...
...leaving Foggy--who's been *questioning* my sanity--convinced that *I'd* done it and *lied* about it.
But it was an impossible theft. Dad's coffin was stolen and trashed by the *Mole Man.**
*BACK IN DD #9-#10.
Revenge from *him?* I checked, but no. The Avengers said he'd been busy warring on Ulik the Troll since last we fought.
I went...*asking around* on a more *local* level, but no one had any intel to *give*. Case was a dead end. *No one* could have retrieved Dad's remains *but* me. And it *wasn't* me.
Was it?
No. Focus. Find *Hierra's* murderer. Why was he killed?
Let's make sure it wasn't simply an issue of *job performance*.

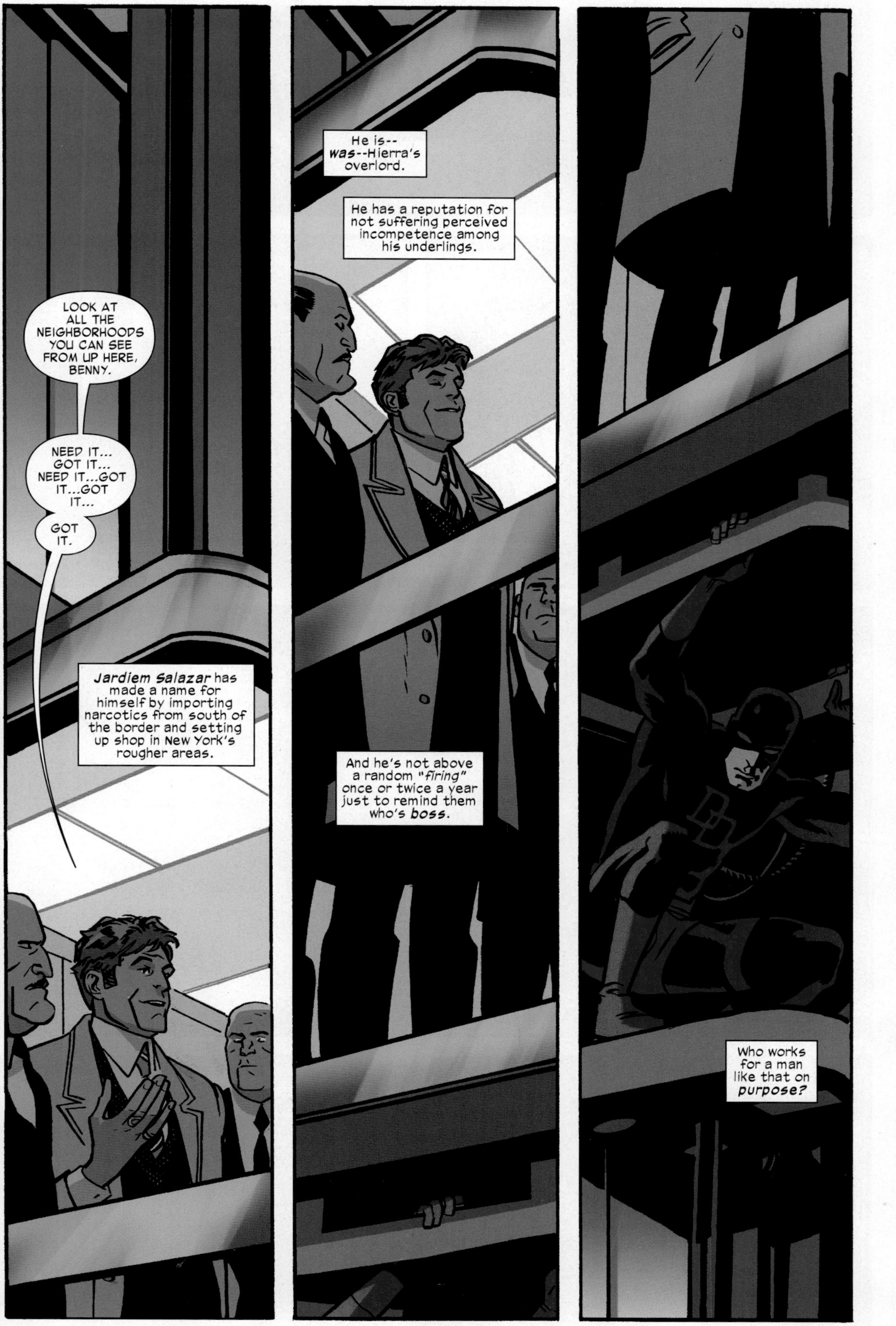

LOOK AT ALL THE NEIGHBORHOODS YOU CAN SEE FROM UP HERE, BENNY.
NEED IT... GOT IT... NEED IT...GOT IT...GOT IT...
GOT IT.
Jardiem Salazar has made a name for himself by importing narcotics from south of the border and setting up shop in New York's rougher areas.
He is--was--Hierra's overlord.
He has a reputation for not suffering perceived incompetence among his underlings.
And he's not above a random "firing" once or twice a year just to remind them who's boss.
Who works for a man like that on purpose?

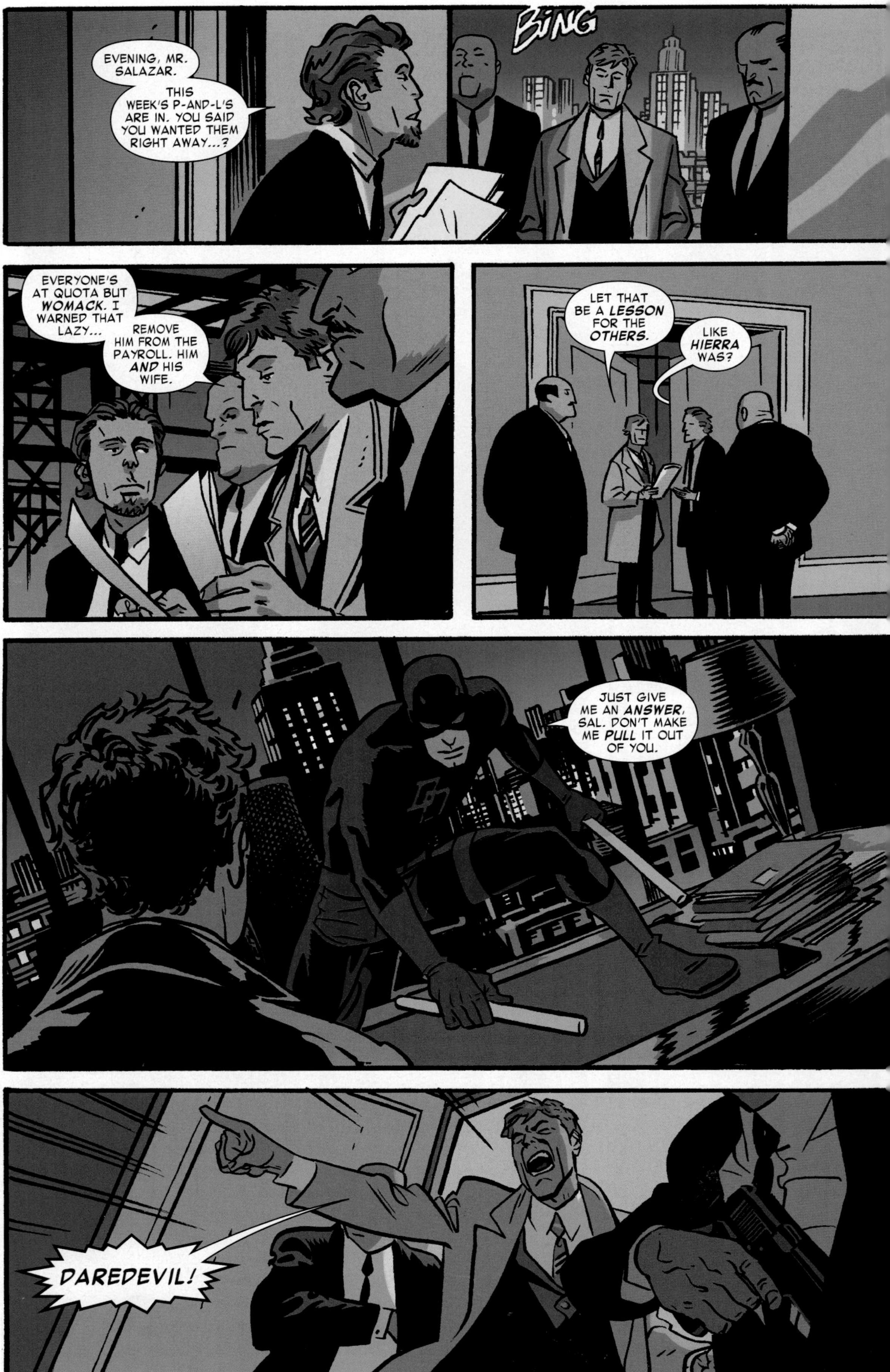
BING
EVENING, MR. SALAZAR.
THIS WEEK'S P-AND-L'S ARE IN. YOU SAID YOU WANTED THEM RIGHT AWAY...?
EVERYONE'S AT QUOTA BUT WOMACK. I WARNED THAT LAZY...
REMOVE HIM FROM THE PAYROLL. HIM AND HIS WIFE.
LET THAT BE A LESSON FOR THE OTHERS.
LIKE HIERRA WAS?
JUST GIVE ME AN ANSWER, SAL. DON'T MAKE ME PULL IT OUT OF YOU.
DAREDEVIL!

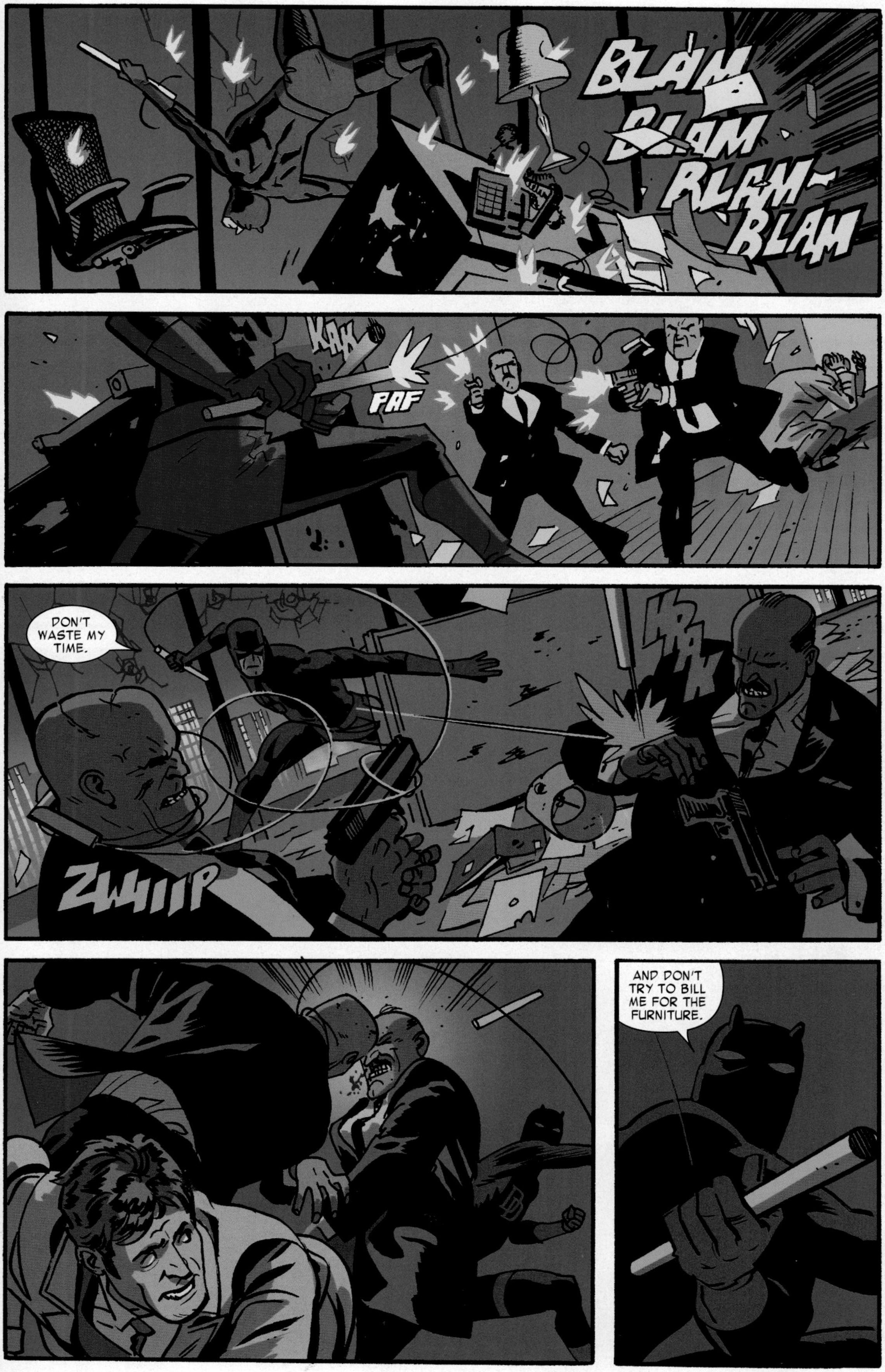
BLAM BLAM BLAM- BLAM
KAK
PAF
DON'T WASTE MY TIME.
ZWIIIP
AND DON'T TRY TO BILL ME FOR THE FURNITURE.

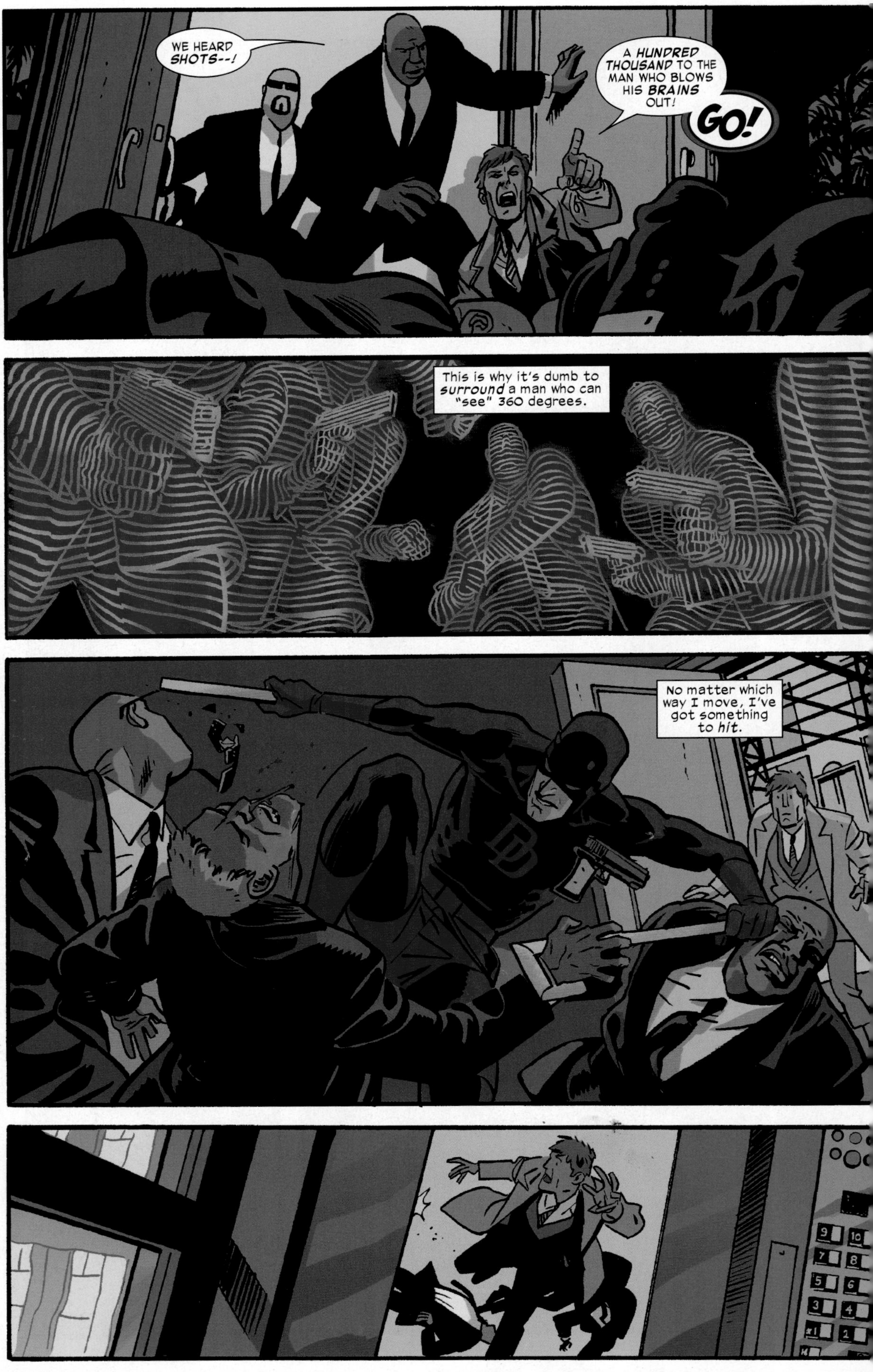
WE HEARD SHOTS--!
A HUNDRED THOUSAND TO THE MAN WHO BLOWS HIS BRAINS OUT!
GO!
This is why it's dumb to surround a man who can "see" 360 degrees.
No matter which way I move, I've got something to hit.

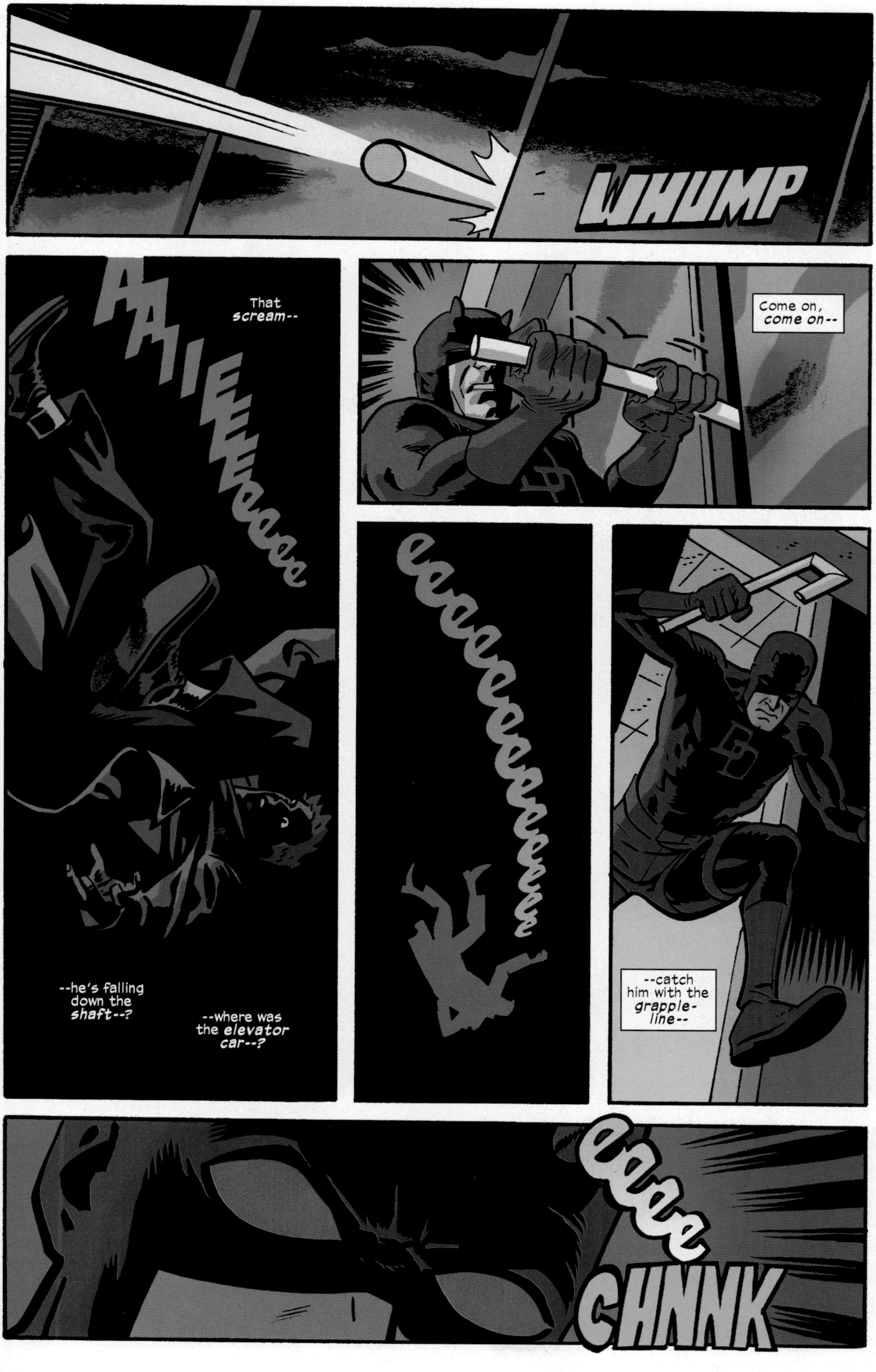
WHUMP
AAIIEEEeeee
That scream--
--he's falling down the shaft--?
--where was the elevator car--?
Come on, come on--
eeeeeeeeeeeeeeeeeeeeeeee
--catch him with the grapple-line--
eeee
CHNNK

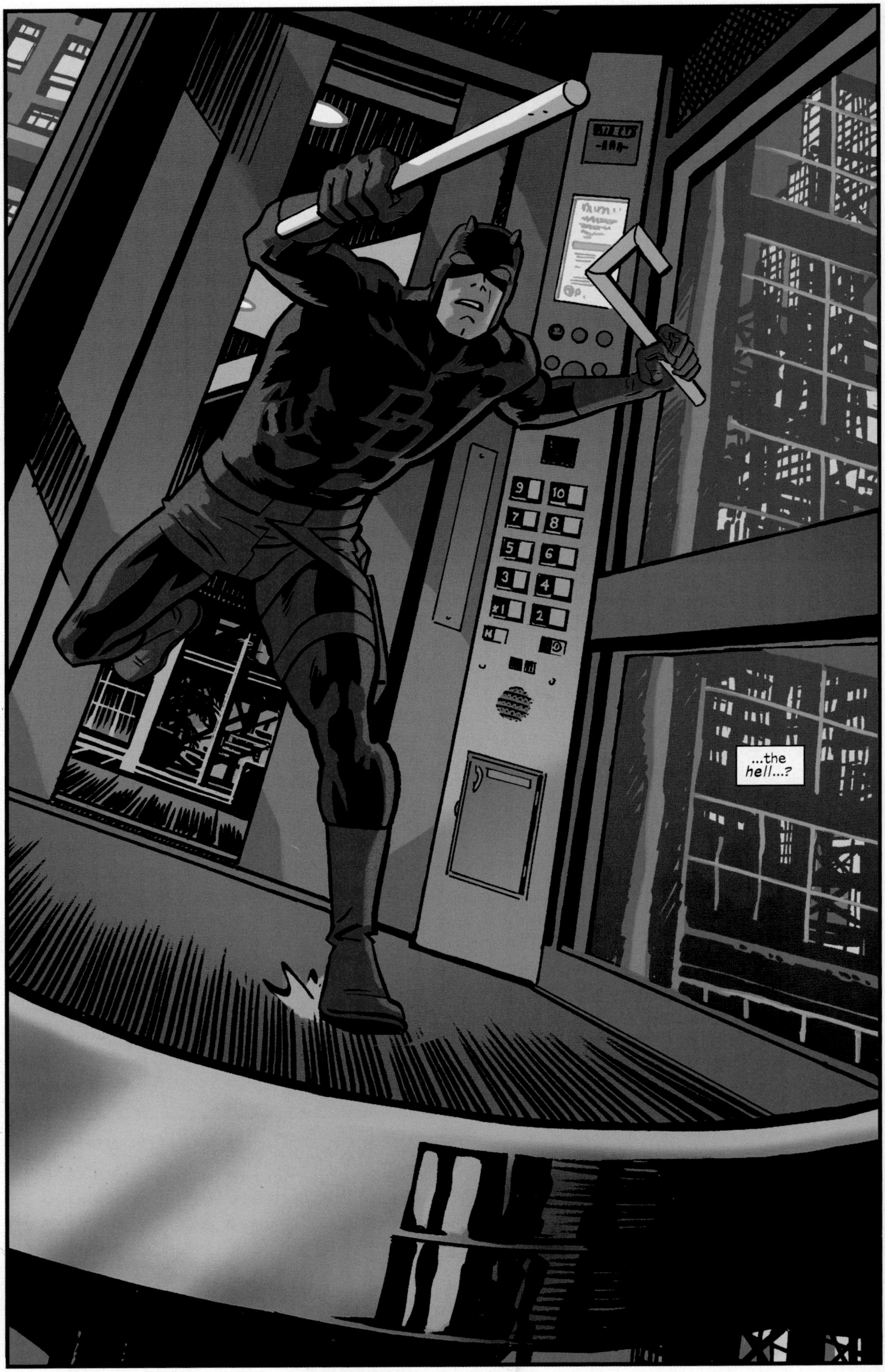
...the hell...?

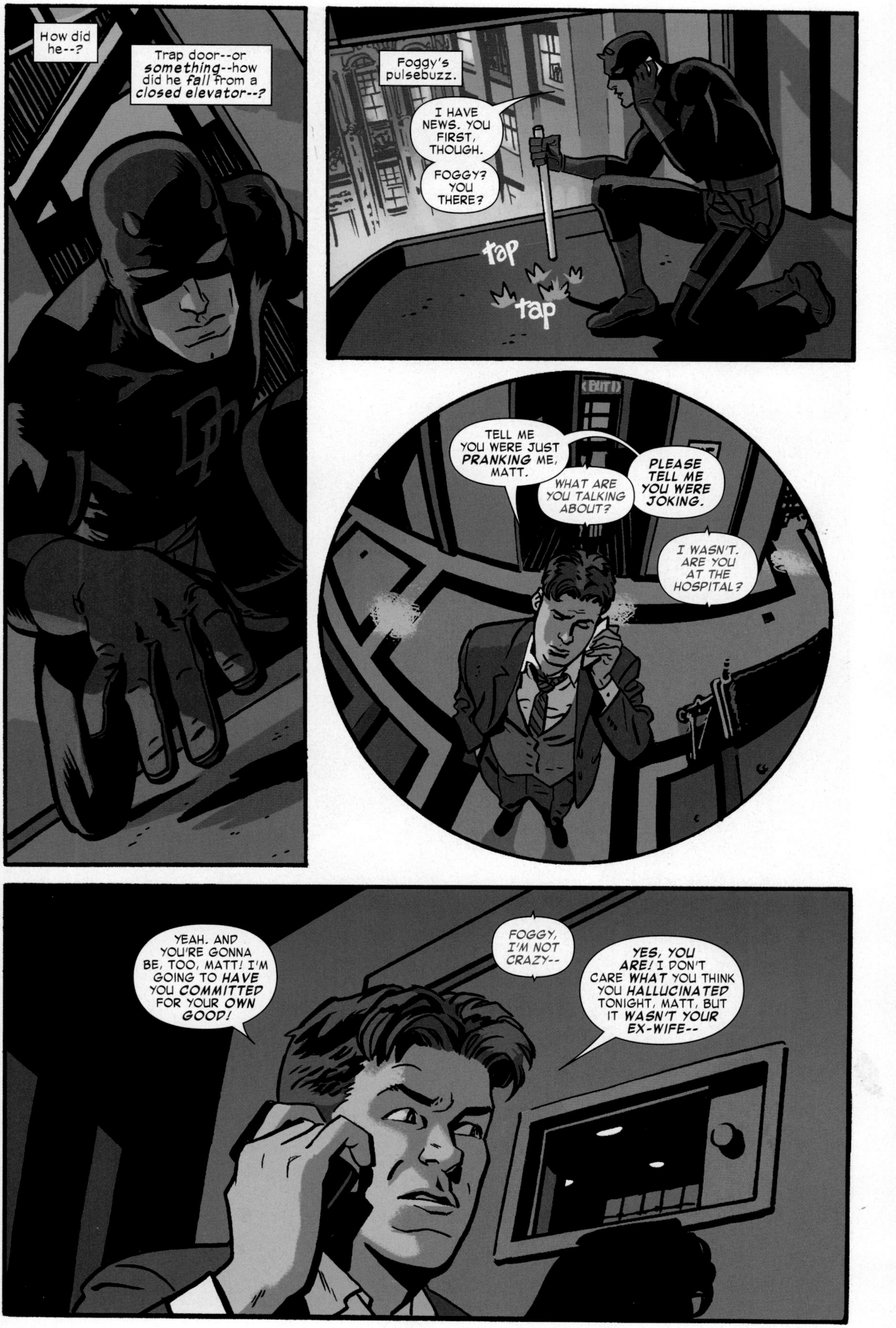
How did he--?
Trap door--or something--how did he fall from a closed elevator--?
Foggy's pulsebuzz.
I HAVE NEWS. YOU FIRST, THOUGH.
FOGGY? YOU THERE?
tap
tap
TELL ME YOU WERE JUST PRANKING ME, MATT.
WHAT ARE YOU TALKING ABOUT?
PLEASE TELL ME YOU WERE JOKING.
I WASN'T. ARE YOU AT THE HOSPITAL?
YEAH. AND YOU'RE GONNA BE, TOO, MATT! I'M GOING TO HAVE YOU COMMITTED FOR YOUR OWN GOOD!
FOGGY, I'M NOT CRAZY--
YES, YOU ARE! I DON'T CARE WHAT YOU THINK YOU HALLUCINATED TONIGHT, MATT, BUT IT WASN'T YOUR EX-WIFE--

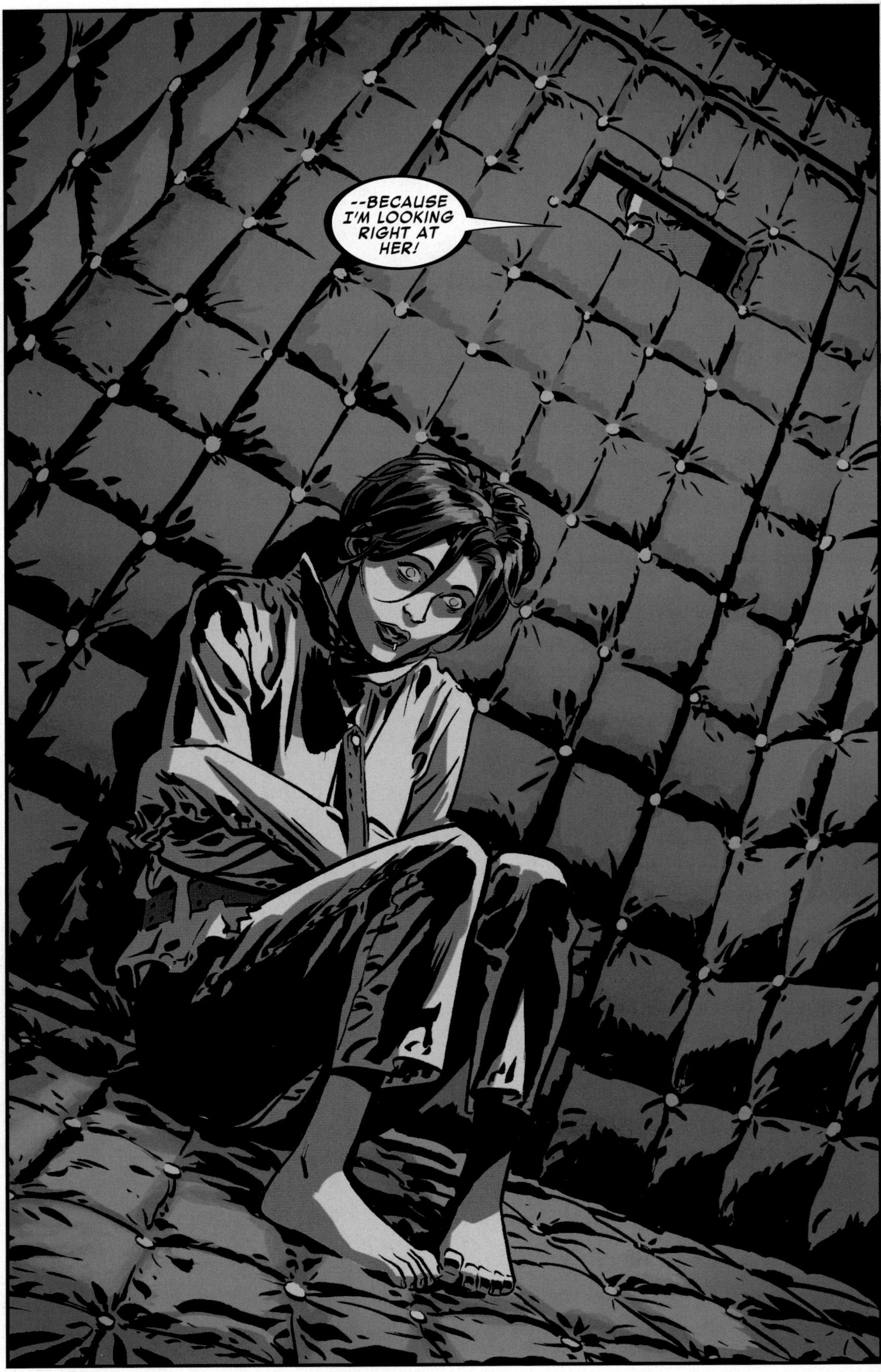
--BECAUSE I'M LOOKING RIGHT AT HER!

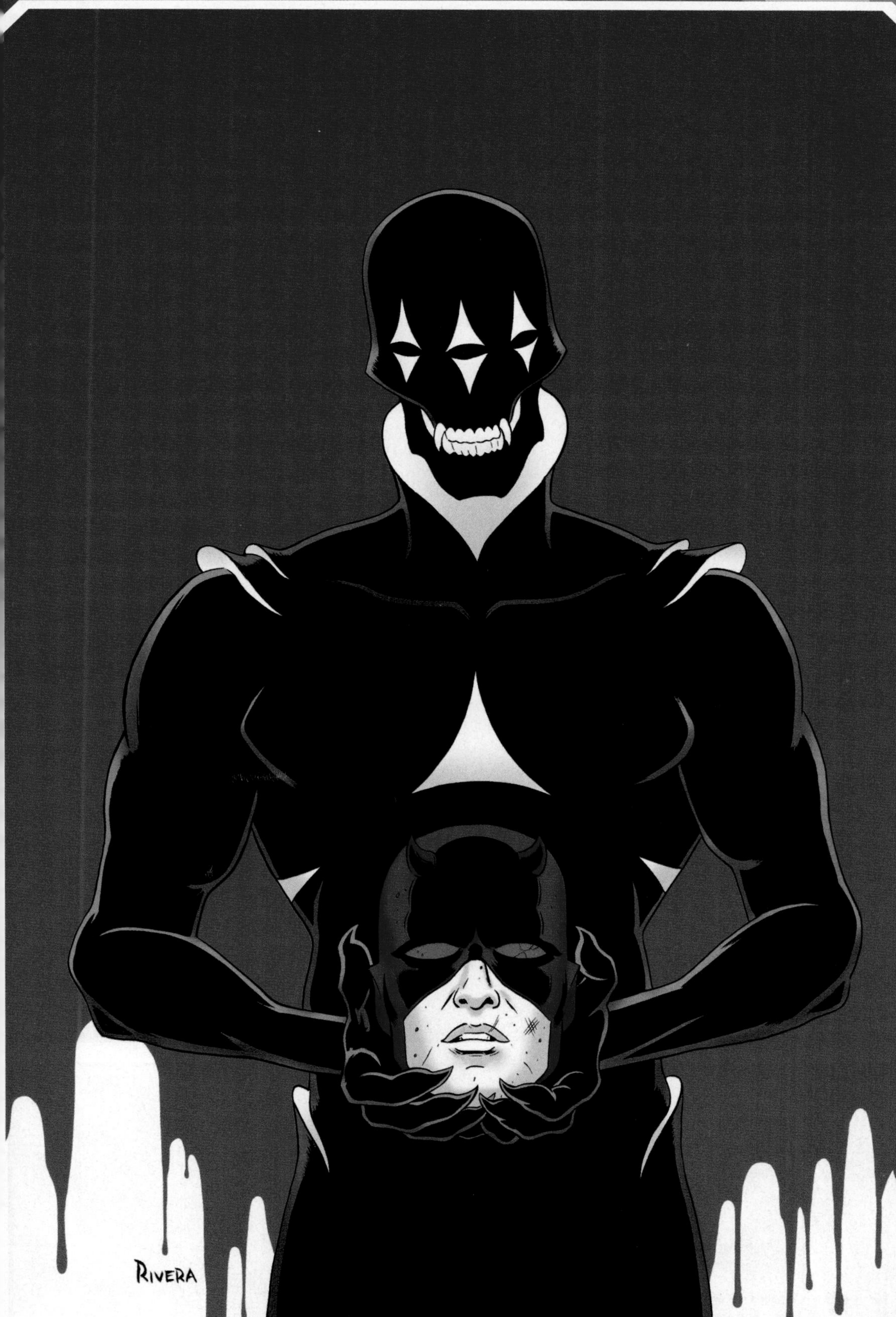
RIVERA

NINETEEN

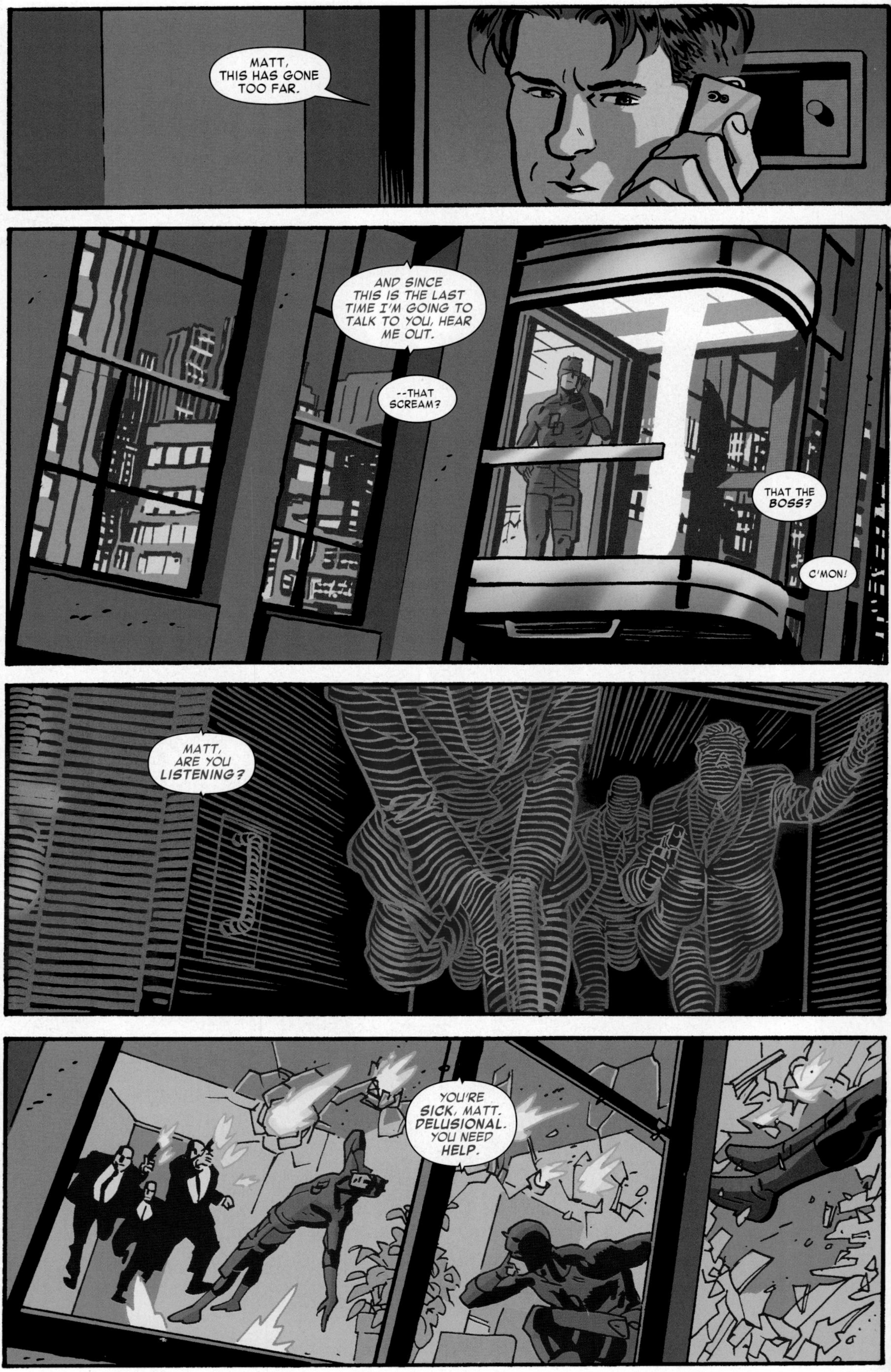
MATT, THIS HAS GONE TOO FAR.
AND SINCE THIS IS THE LAST TIME I'M GOING TO TALK TO YOU, HEAR ME OUT.
--THAT SCREAM?
THAT THE BOSS?
C'MON!
MATT, ARE YOU LISTENING?
YOU'RE SICK, MATT. DELUSIONAL. YOU NEED HELP.

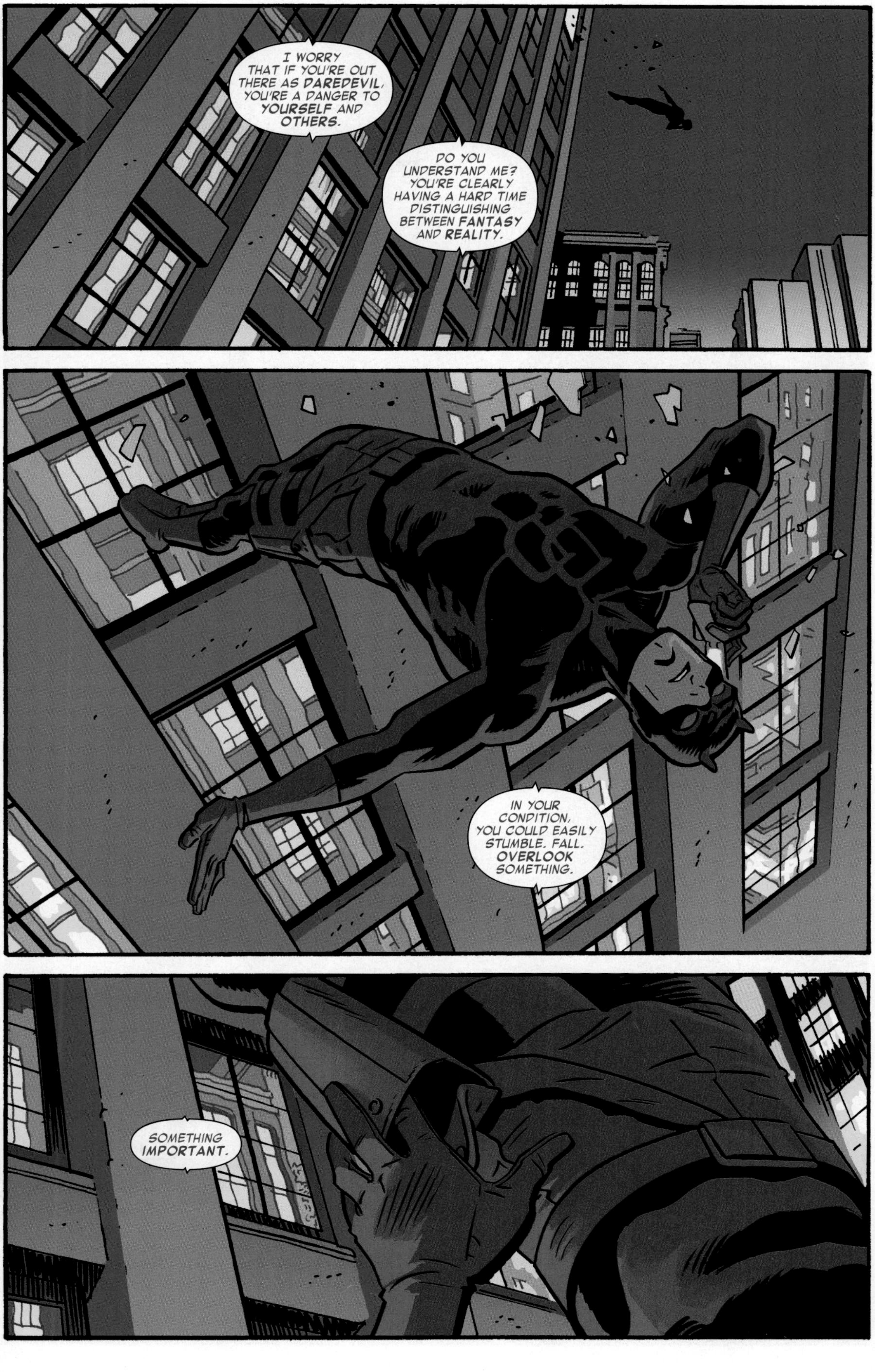
I WORRY THAT IF YOU'RE OUT THERE AS DAREDEVIL, YOU'RE A DANGER TO YOURSELF AND OTHERS.
DO YOU UNDERSTAND ME? YOU'RE CLEARLY HAVING A HARD TIME DISTINGUISHING BETWEEN FANTASY AND REALITY.
IN YOUR CONDITION, YOU COULD EASILY STUMBLE. FALL. OVERLOOK SOMETHING.
SOMETHING IMPORTANT.

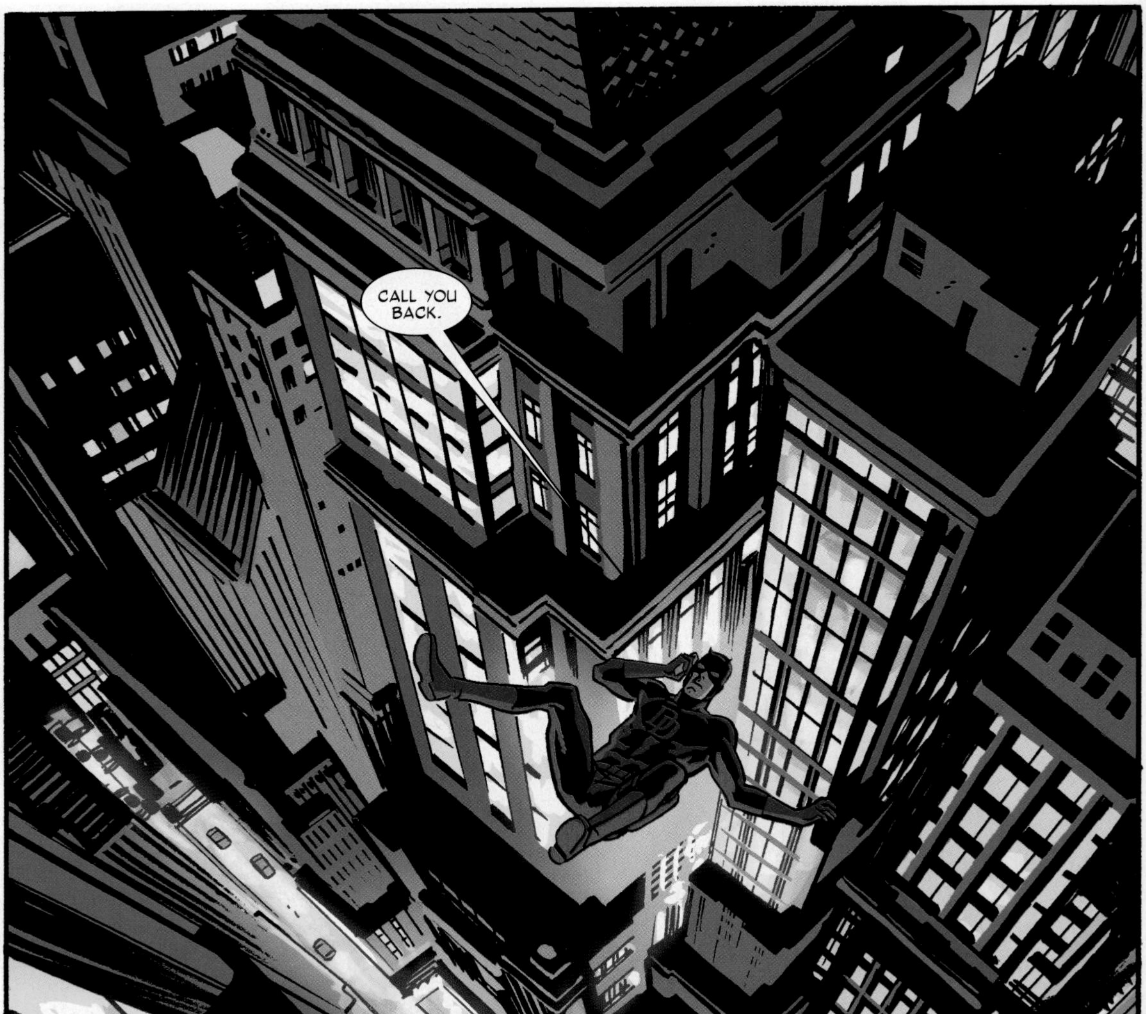
CALL YOU BACK.

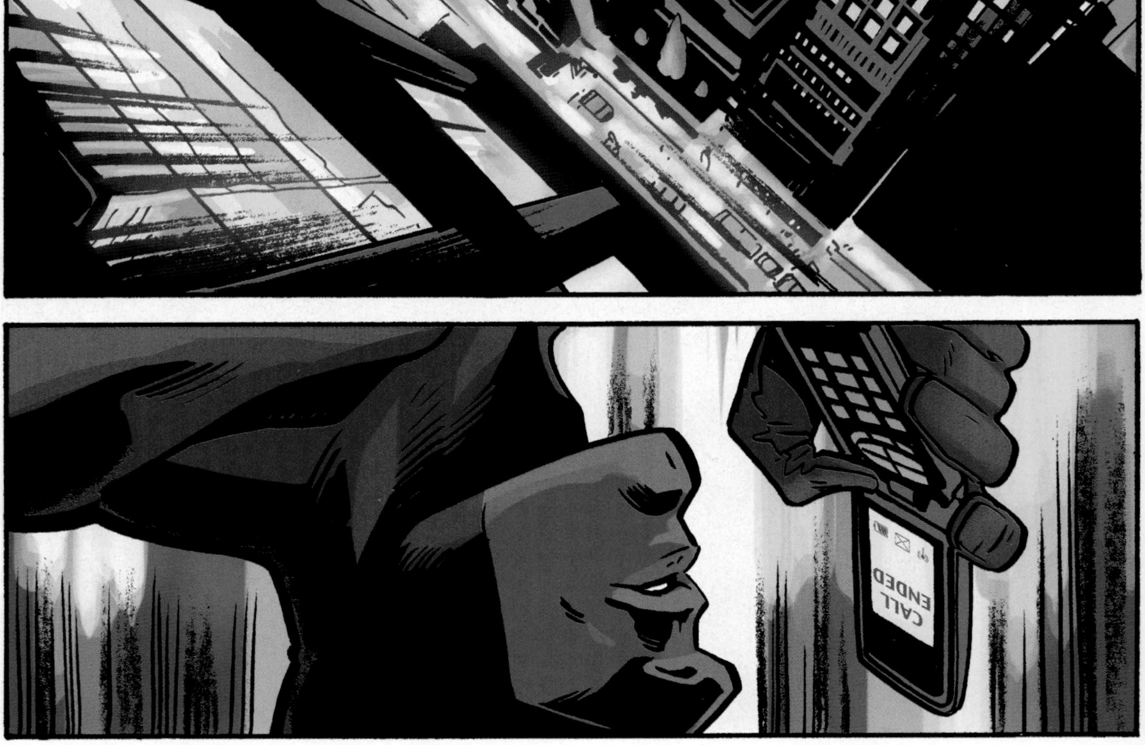
CALL ENDED

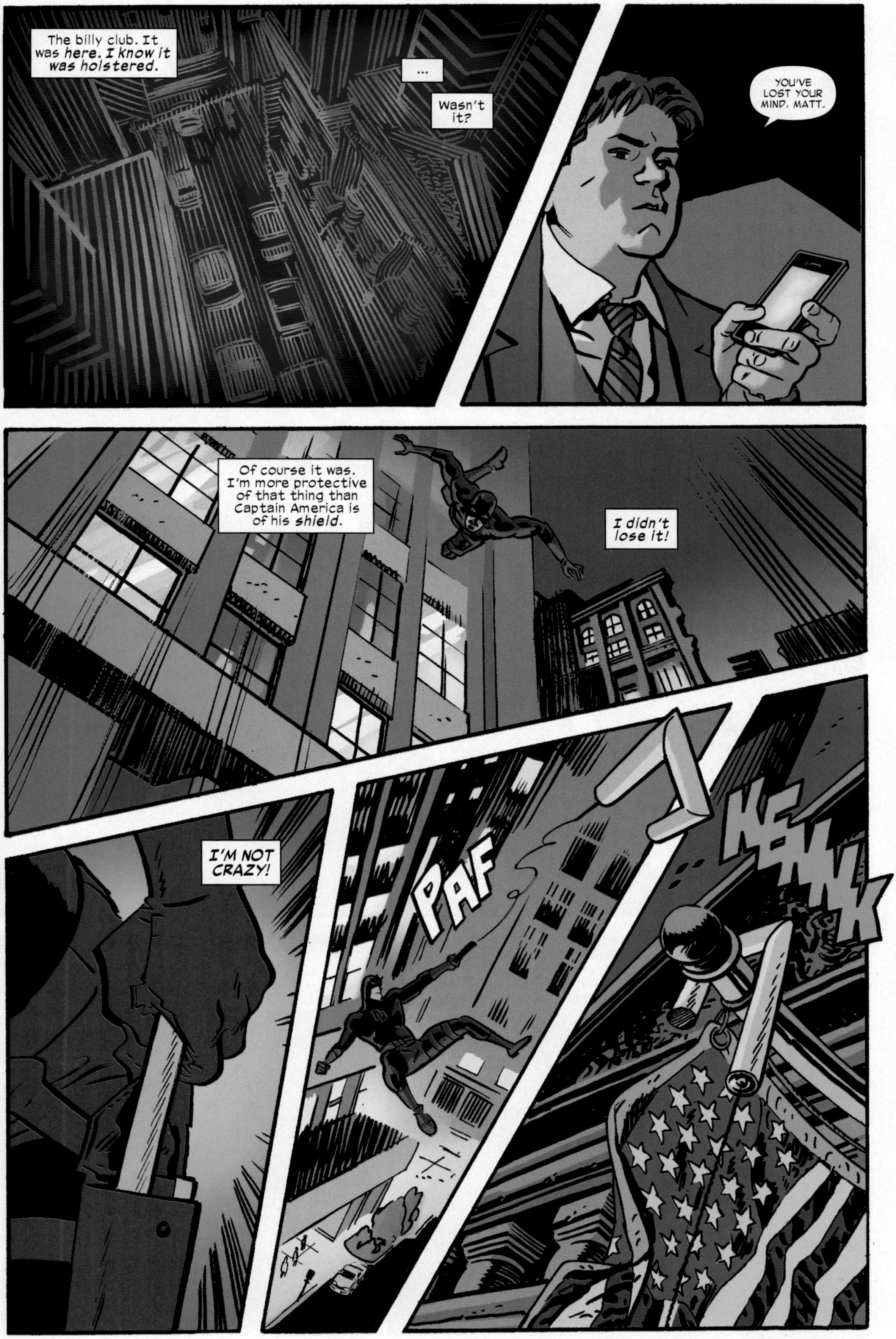
The billy club. It was *here*. *I know it was holstered*.
...
Wasn't it?
YOU'VE LOST YOUR MIND, MATT.
Of course it was. I'm more protective of that thing than Captain America is of his *shield*.
I didn't lose it!
I'M NOT CRAZY!
PAF
KLANNK

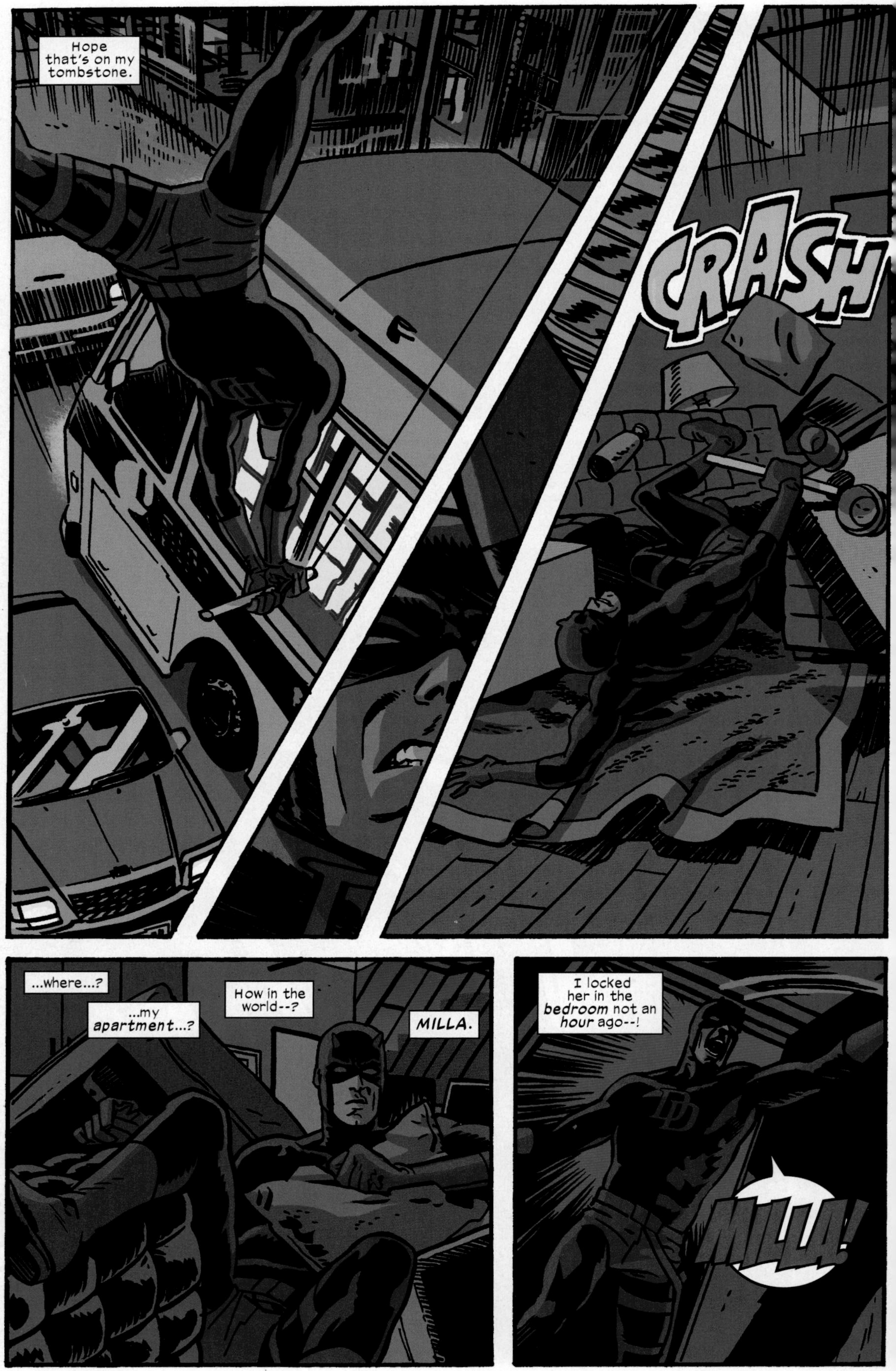
Hope that's on my tombstone.
CRASH
...where...?
...my apartment...?
How in the world--?
MILLA.
I locked her in the bedroom not an hour ago--!
MILLA!

Not only is she *gone*, but it's as if she were never *here*.

The bed's the way I make it--Milla never could learn the hospital corner--and the sheets smell of detergent, not of *her*.

Maybe Foggy's onto something. I think I'm fine, but history would argue that I'm not always the best judge of my own mental state.

I need to see a doctor.

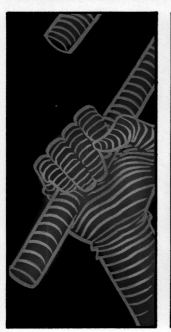

I should take a cab.

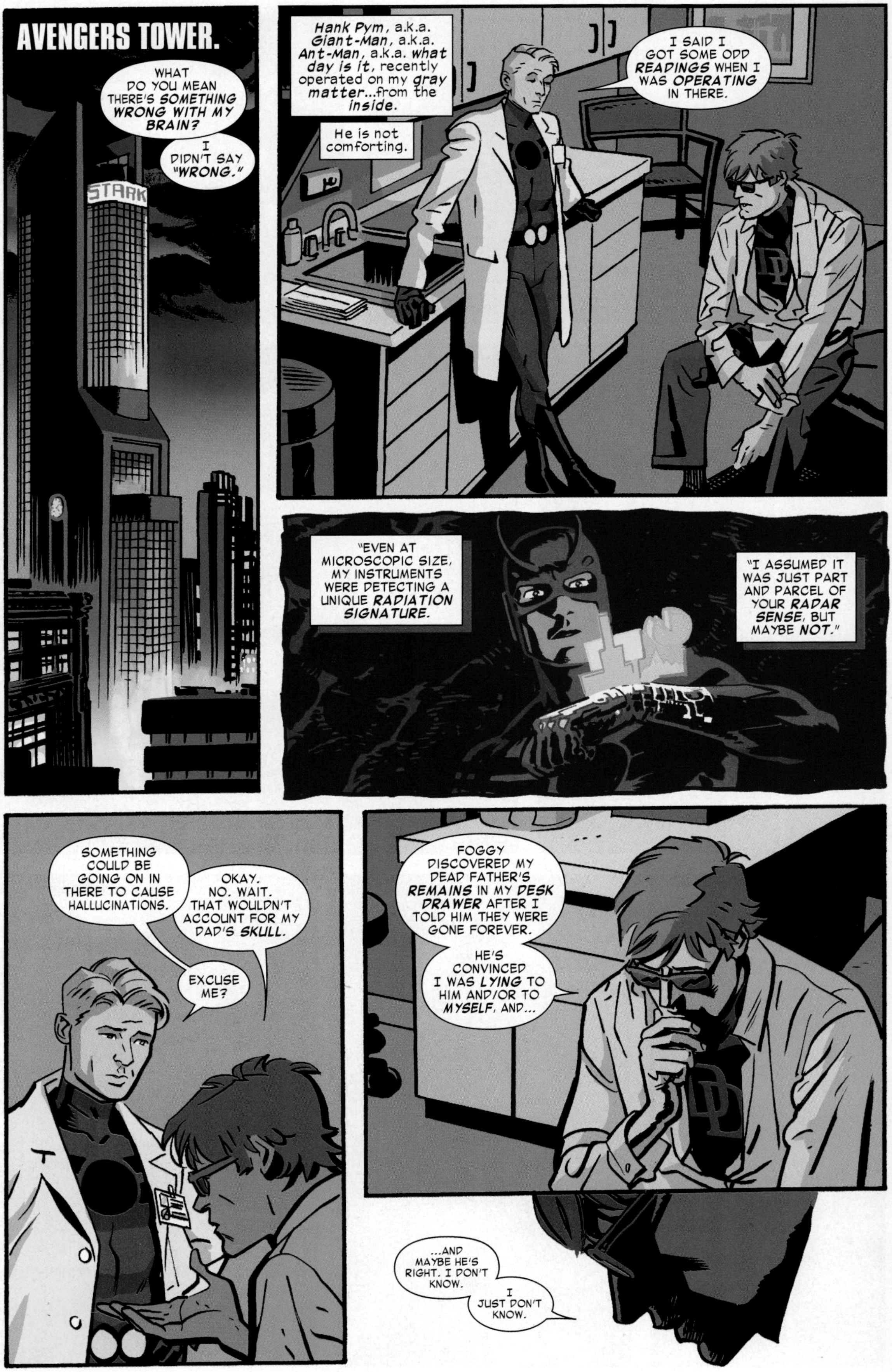
AVENGERS TOWER.
WHAT DO YOU MEAN THERE'S SOMETHING WRONG WITH MY BRAIN?
I DIDN'T SAY "WRONG."
STARK
Hank Pym, a.k.a. Giant-Man, a.k.a. Ant-Man, a.k.a. what day is it, recently operated on my gray matter...from the inside.
He is not comforting.
I SAID I GOT SOME ODD READINGS WHEN I WAS OPERATING IN THERE.
"EVEN AT MICROSCOPIC SIZE, MY INSTRUMENTS WERE DETECTING A UNIQUE RADIATION SIGNATURE.
"I ASSUMED IT WAS JUST PART AND PARCEL OF YOUR RADAR SENSE, BUT MAYBE NOT."
SOMETHING COULD BE GOING ON IN THERE TO CAUSE HALLUCINATIONS.
OKAY. NO. WAIT. THAT WOULDN'T ACCOUNT FOR MY DAD'S SKULL.
EXCUSE ME?
FOGGY DISCOVERED MY DEAD FATHER'S REMAINS IN MY DESK DRAWER AFTER I TOLD HIM THEY WERE GONE FOREVER.
HE'S CONVINCED I WAS LYING TO HIM AND/OR TO MYSELF, AND...
...AND MAYBE HE'S RIGHT. I DON'T KNOW.
I JUST DON'T KNOW.

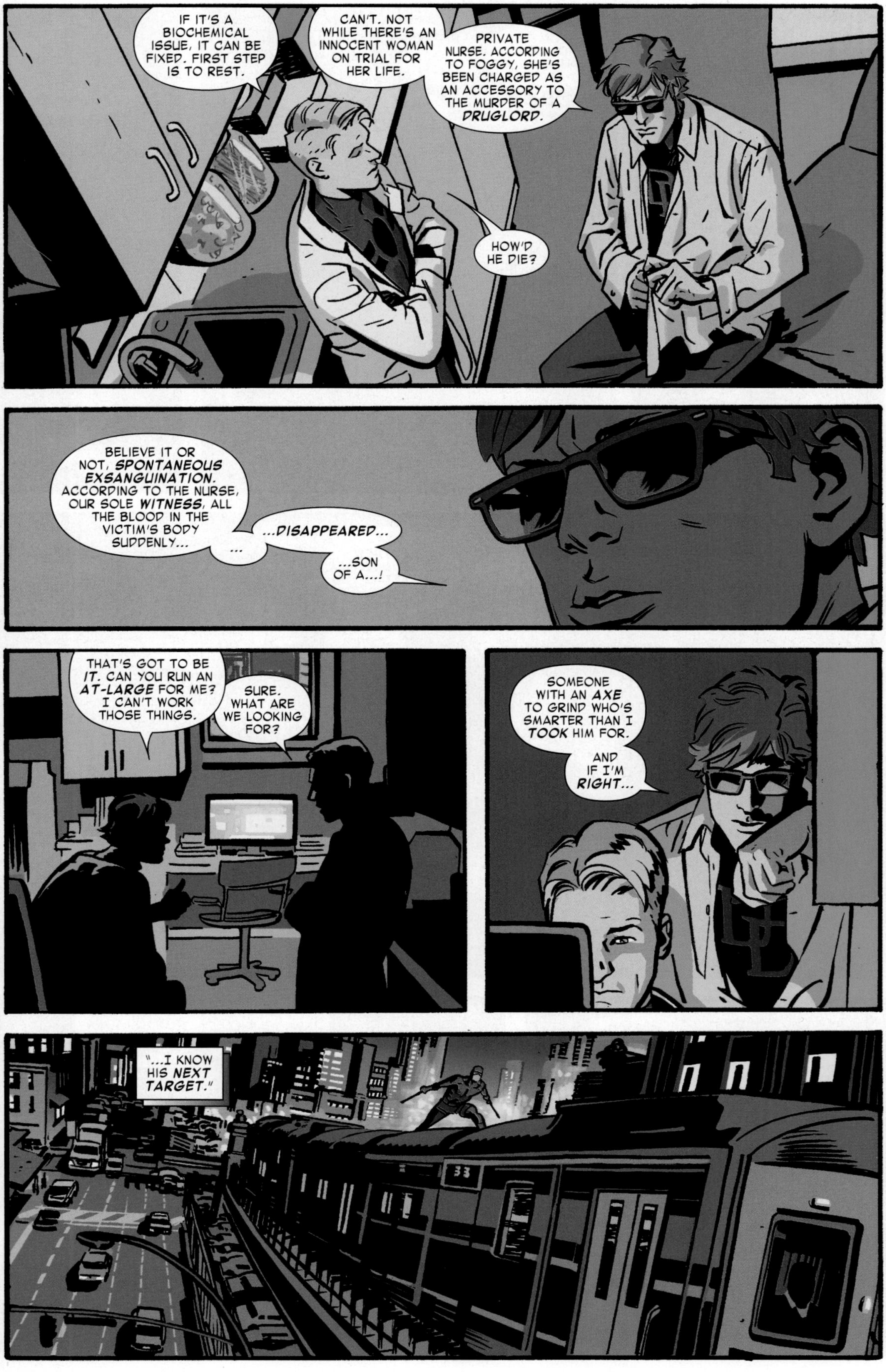
IF IT'S A BIOCHEMICAL ISSUE, IT CAN BE FIXED. FIRST STEP IS TO REST.
CAN'T. NOT WHILE THERE'S AN INNOCENT WOMAN ON TRIAL FOR HER LIFE.
PRIVATE NURSE. ACCORDING TO FOGGY, SHE'S BEEN CHARGED AS AN ACCESSORY TO THE MURDER OF A DRUGLORD.
HOW'D HE DIE?
BELIEVE IT OR NOT, SPONTANEOUS EXSANGUINATION. ACCORDING TO THE NURSE, OUR SOLE WITNESS, ALL THE BLOOD IN THE VICTIM'S BODY SUDDENLY...
...
...DISAPPEARED...
...SON OF A...!
THAT'S GOT TO BE IT. CAN YOU RUN AN AT-LARGE FOR ME? I CAN'T WORK THOSE THINGS.
SURE. WHAT ARE WE LOOKING FOR?
SOMEONE WITH AN AXE TO GRIND WHO'S SMARTER THAN I TOOK HIM FOR.
AND IF I'M RIGHT...
"...I KNOW HIS NEXT TARGET."

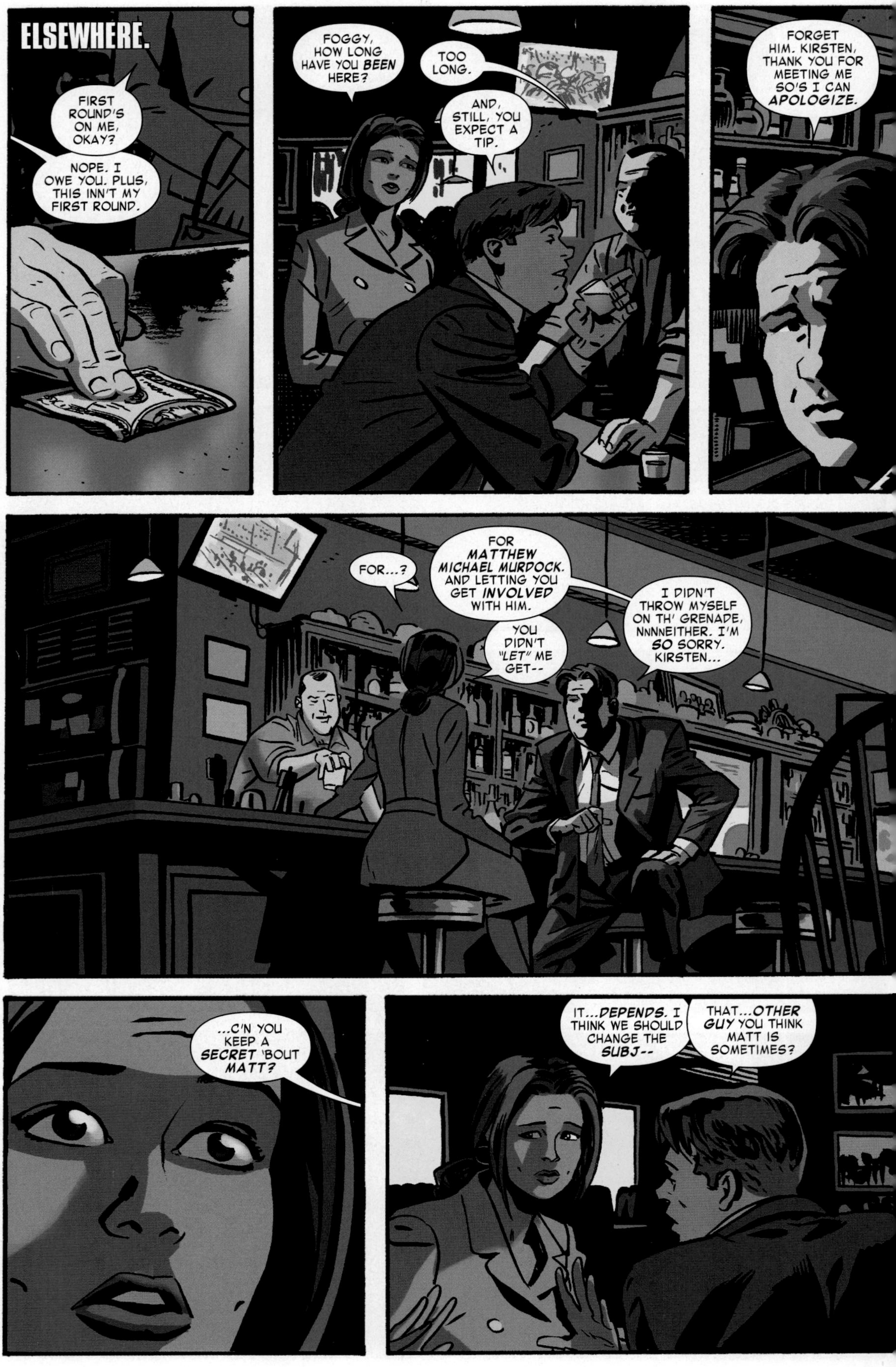
ELSEWHERE.
FIRST ROUND'S ON ME, OKAY?
NOPE. I OWE YOU. PLUS, THIS INN'T MY FIRST ROUND.
FOGGY, HOW LONG HAVE YOU BEEN HERE?
TOO LONG.
AND, STILL, YOU EXPECT A TIP.
FORGET HIM. KIRSTEN, THANK YOU FOR MEETING ME SO'S I CAN APOLOGIZE.
FOR...?
FOR MATTHEW MICHAEL MURDOCK. AND LETTING YOU GET INVOLVED WITH HIM.
YOU DIDN'T "LET" ME GET--
I DIDN'T THROW MYSELF ON TH' GRENADE, NNNNEITHER. I'M SO SORRY. KIRSTEN...
...C'N YOU KEEP A SECRET 'BOUT MATT?
IT...DEPENDS. I THINK WE SHOULD CHANGE THE SUBJ--
THAT...OTHER GUY YOU THINK MATT IS SOMETIMES?

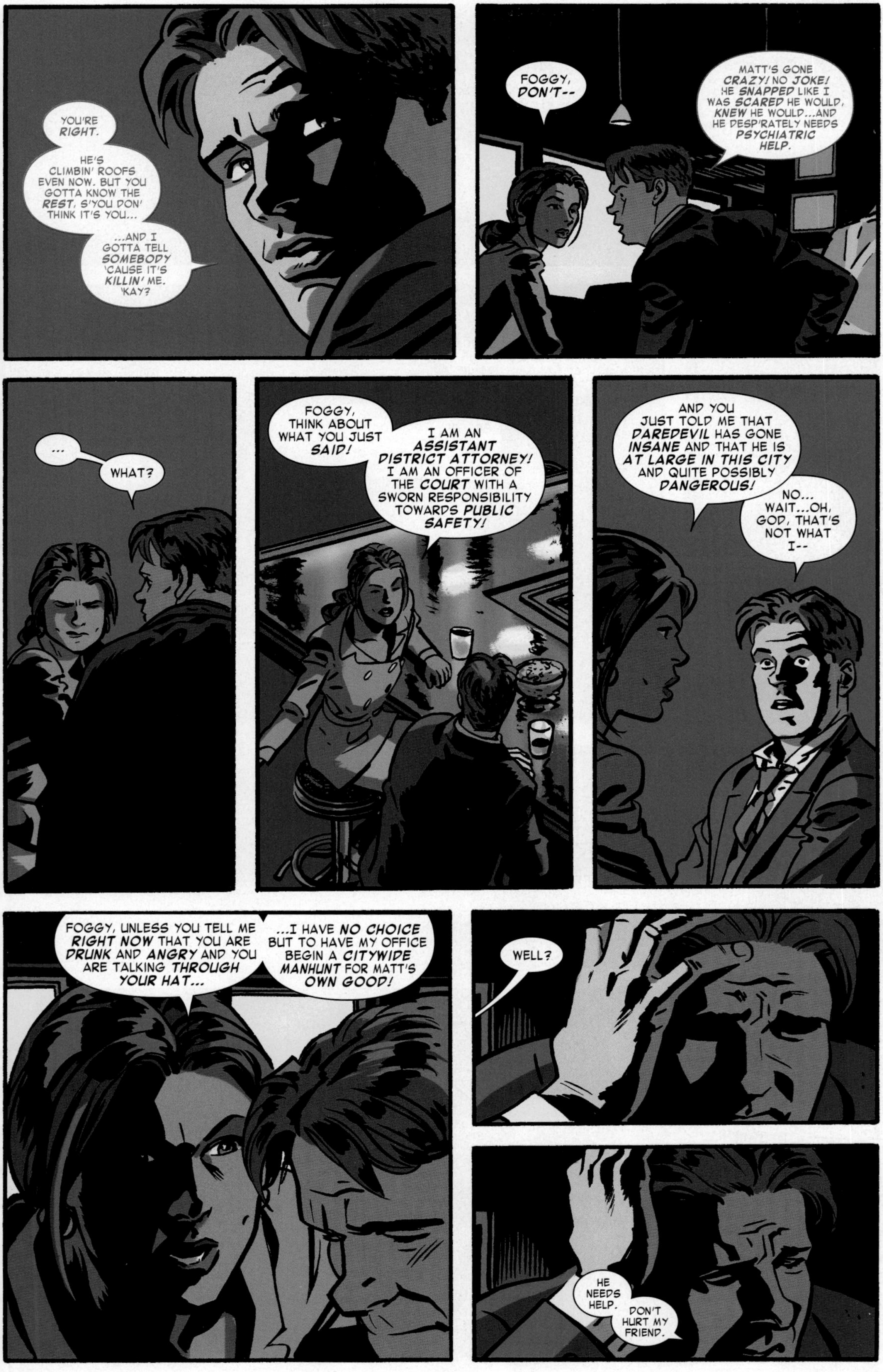
YOU'RE RIGHT.
HE'S CLIMBIN' ROOFS EVEN NOW. BUT YOU GOTTA KNOW THE REST, S'YOU DON' THINK IT'S YOU...
...AND I GOTTA TELL SOMEBODY 'CAUSE IT'S KILLIN' ME. 'KAY?
FOGGY, DON'T--
MATT'S GONE CRAZY! NO JOKE! HE SNAPPED LIKE I WAS SCARED HE WOULD, KNEW HE WOULD...AND HE DESP'RATELY NEEDS PSYCHIATRIC HELP.
...
WHAT?
FOGGY, THINK ABOUT WHAT YOU JUST SAID!
I AM AN ASSISTANT DISTRICT ATTORNEY! I AM AN OFFICER OF THE COURT WITH A SWORN RESPONSIBILITY TOWARDS PUBLIC SAFETY!
AND YOU JUST TOLD ME THAT DAREDEVIL HAS GONE INSANE AND THAT HE IS AT LARGE IN THIS CITY AND QUITE POSSIBLY DANGEROUS!
NO... WAIT...OH, GOD, THAT'S NOT WHAT I--
FOGGY, UNLESS YOU TELL ME RIGHT NOW THAT YOU ARE DRUNK AND ANGRY AND YOU ARE TALKING THROUGH YOUR HAT...
...I HAVE NO CHOICE BUT TO HAVE MY OFFICE BEGIN A CITYWIDE MANHUNT FOR MATT'S OWN GOOD!
WELL?
HE NEEDS HELP.
DON'T HURT MY FRIEND.

I know the *where*, but not the *when*.

So I'm at a garage in *Jersey* all night...

TORTINO SANITATION ENGINEERS

...despite the *stench*.

Now that Hierra *and* Salazar are dead, the tri-state's *other* "family members" will gather *fast* to decide how to fill the *vacuum*.

As the *senior don*, Anthony Tortino will have the others come to *his* place of business. Lucky *me*.

That's presuming that *Tortino's* still alive--

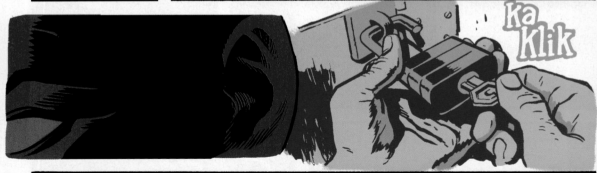

ka Klik

--for the next few *minutes*, at least.

THANK YOU ALL FOR COMING. I ASSURE YOU, YOU'RE SAFE HERE.

ARE YOU *KIDDING* ME?

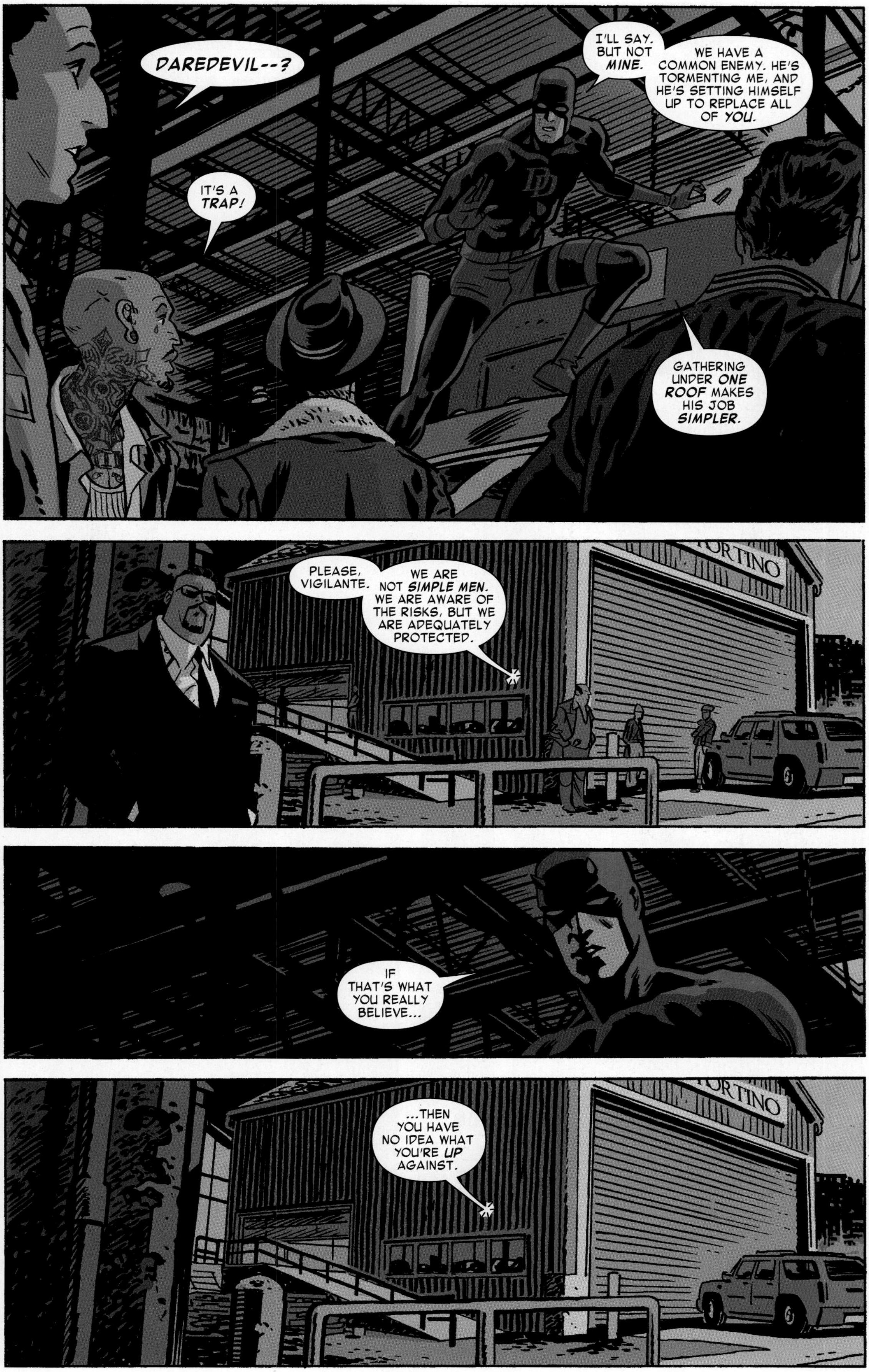
DAREDEVIL--?
IT'S A TRAP!
I'LL SAY. BUT NOT MINE.
WE HAVE A COMMON ENEMY. HE'S TORMENTING ME, AND HE'S SETTING HIMSELF UP TO REPLACE ALL OF YOU.
GATHERING UNDER ONE ROOF MAKES HIS JOB SIMPLER.
PLEASE, VIGILANTE.
WE ARE NOT SIMPLE MEN. WE ARE AWARE OF THE RISKS, BUT WE ARE ADEQUATELY PROTECTED.
IF THAT'S WHAT YOU REALLY BELIEVE...
...THEN YOU HAVE NO IDEA WHAT YOU'RE UP AGAINST.

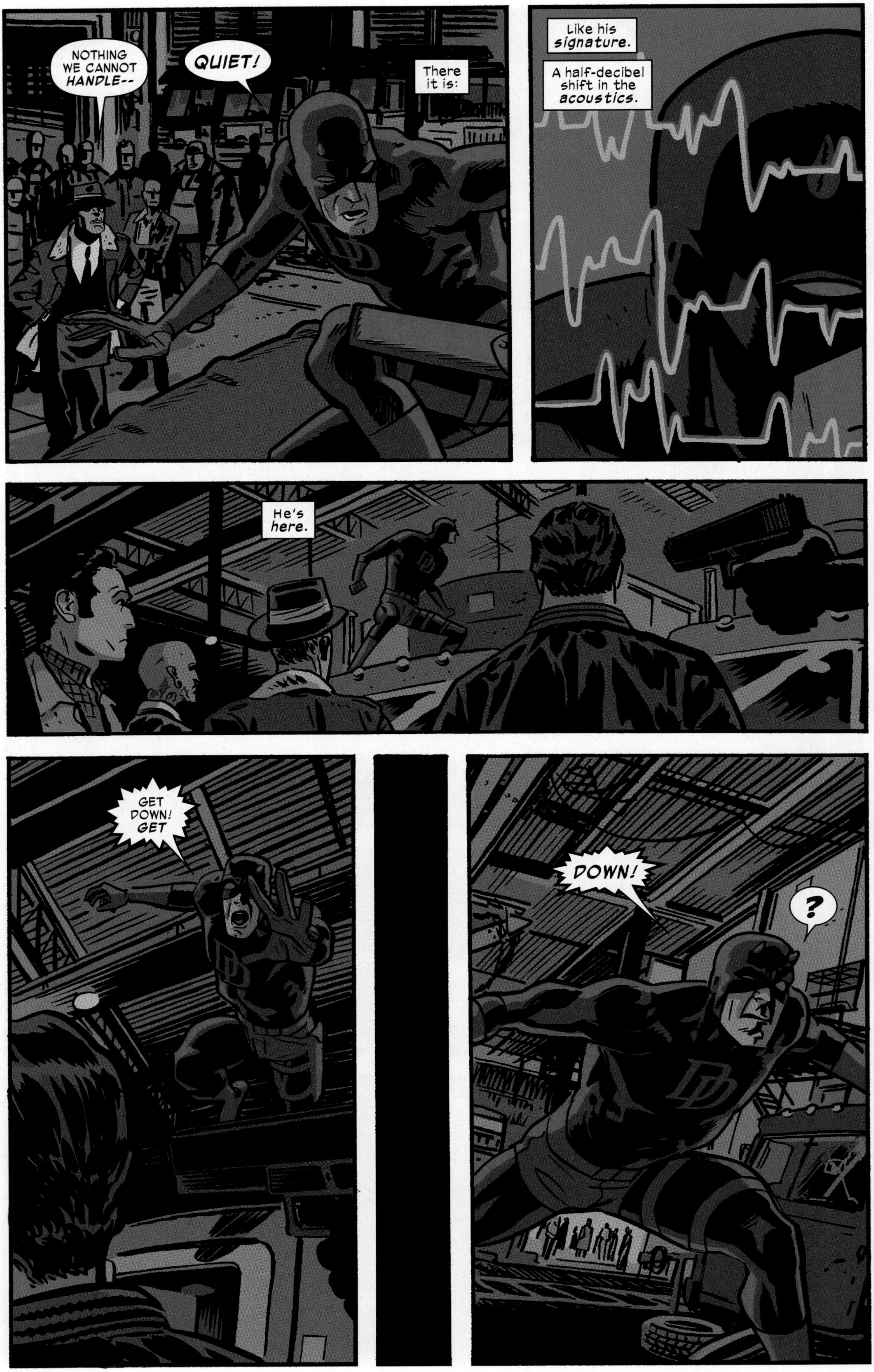

NOTHING WE CANNOT HANDLE--
QUIET!
There it is:
Like his signature.
A half-decibel shift in the acoustics.
He's here.
GET DOWN! GET
DOWN!
?

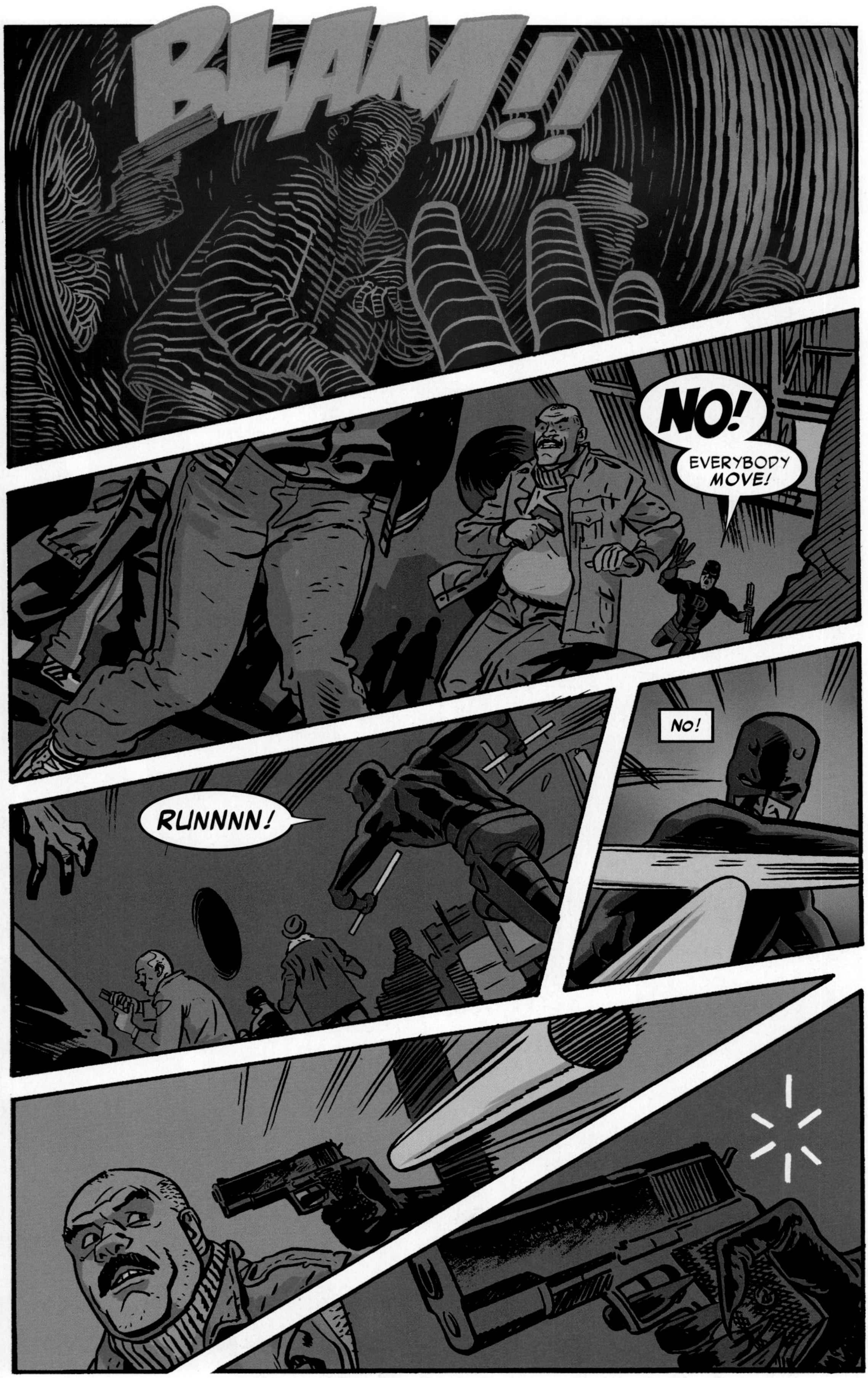
BLAM!!
NO!
EVERYBODY MOVE!
NO!
RUNNNN!

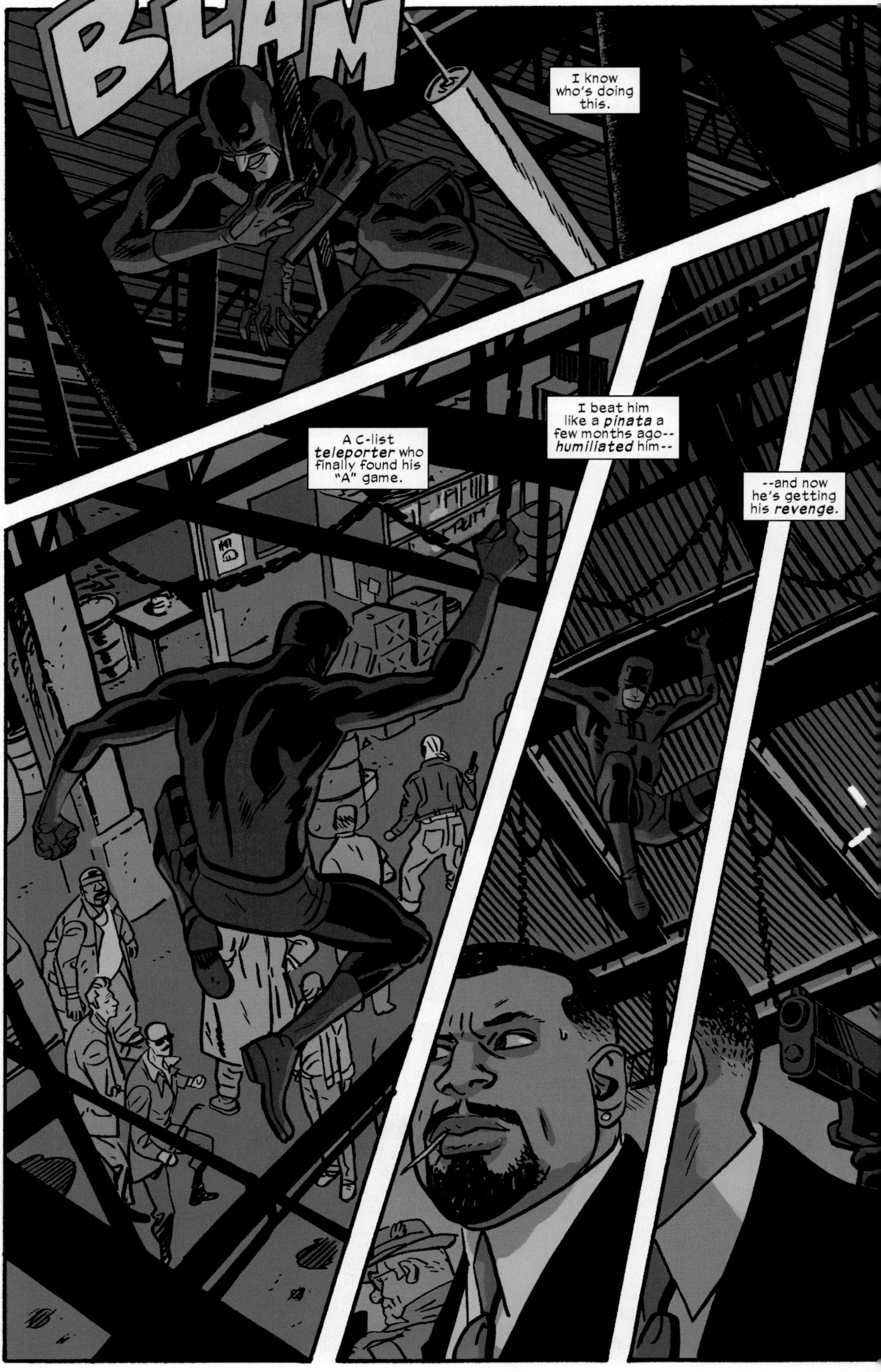
BLAM
I know who's doing this.
A C-list *teleporter* who finally found his "A" game.
I beat him like a *pinata* a few months ago-- *humiliated* him--
--and now he's getting his *revenge*.

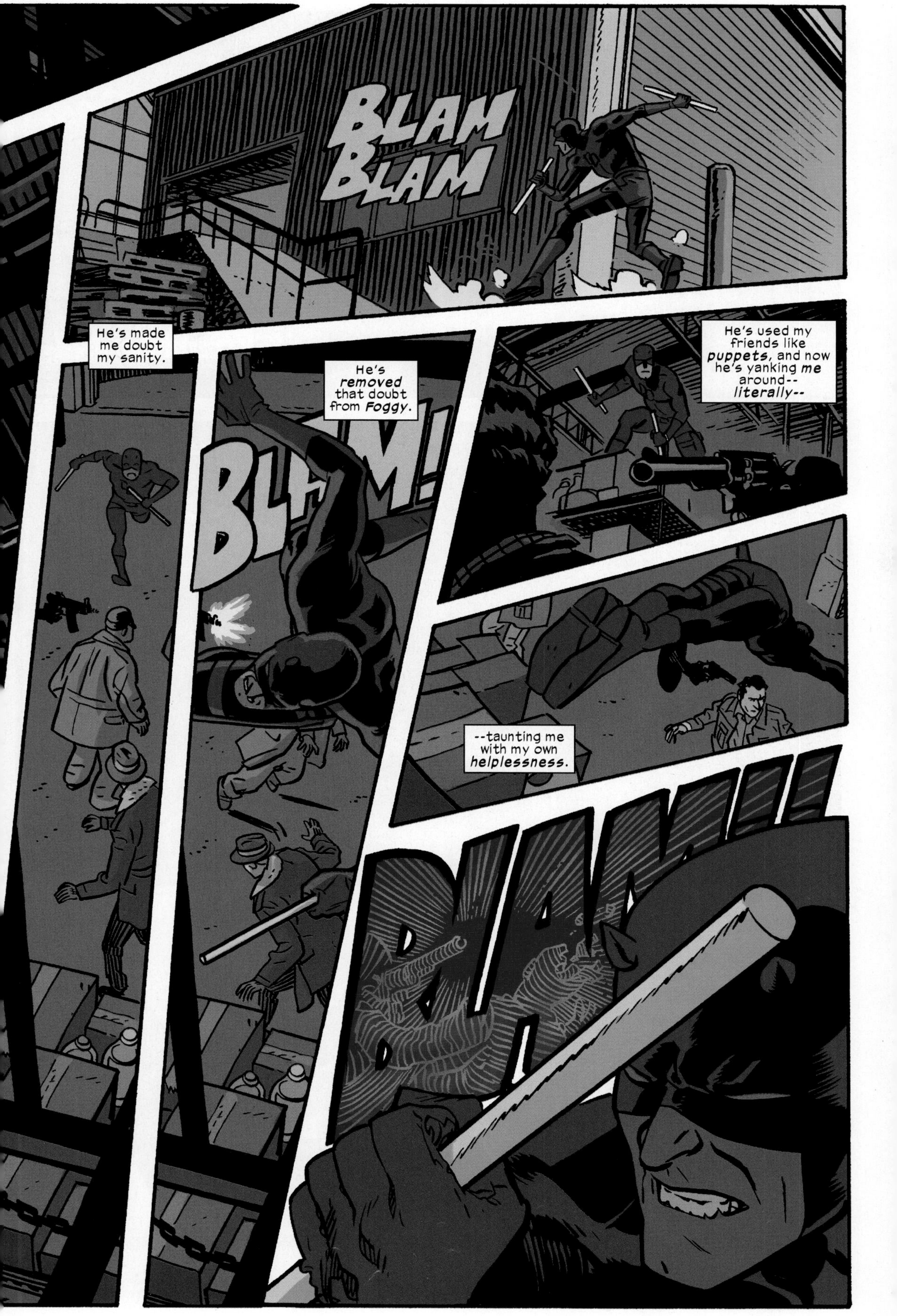

BLAM
BLAM
He's made me doubt my sanity.
He's *removed* that doubt from *Foggy*.
He's used my friends like *puppets*, and now he's yanking *me* around-- *literally*--
--taunting me with my own *helplessness*.

His name is
The Spot--

--and he is
done for.

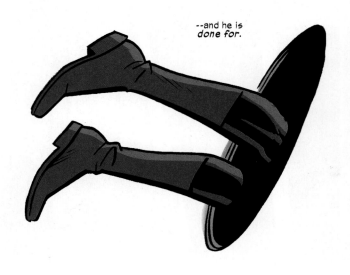

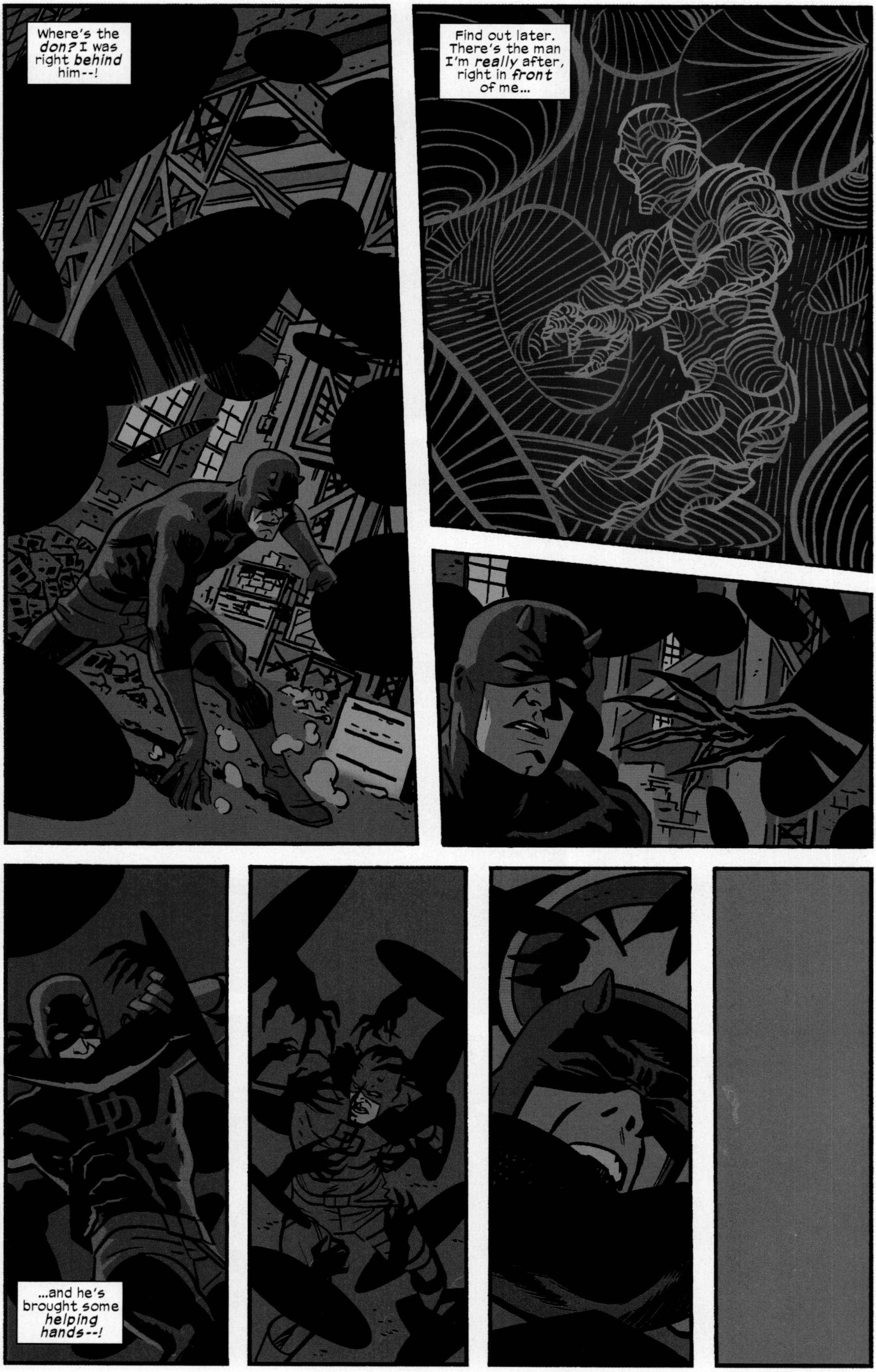
Where's the *don?* I was right *behind* him--!
Find out later. There's the man I'm *really* after, right in *front* of me...
...and he's brought some *helping hands*--!

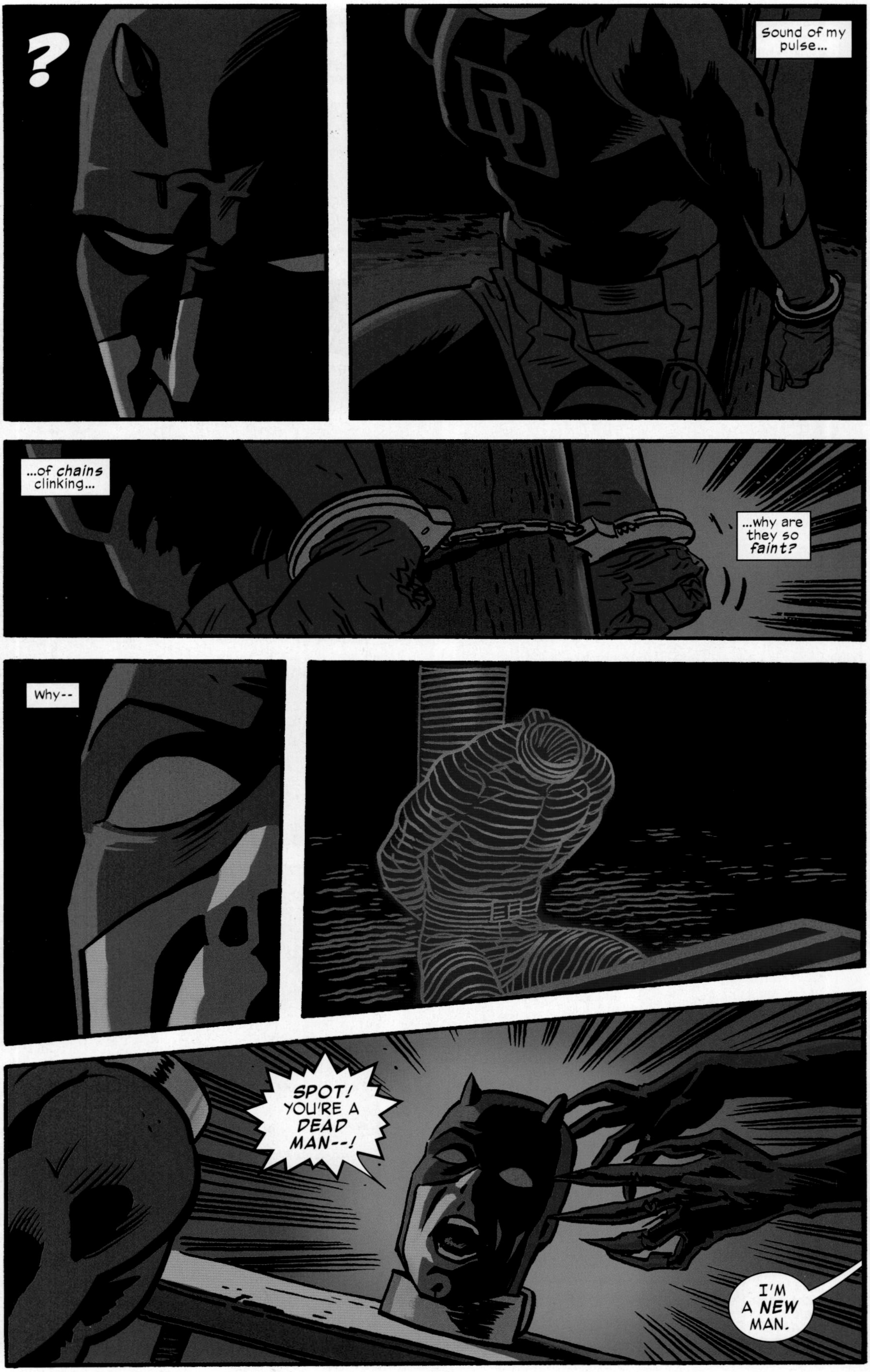
?
Sound of my pulse...
...of chains clinking...
...why are they so faint?
Why--
SPOT! YOU'RE A DEAD MAN--!
I'M A NEW MAN.

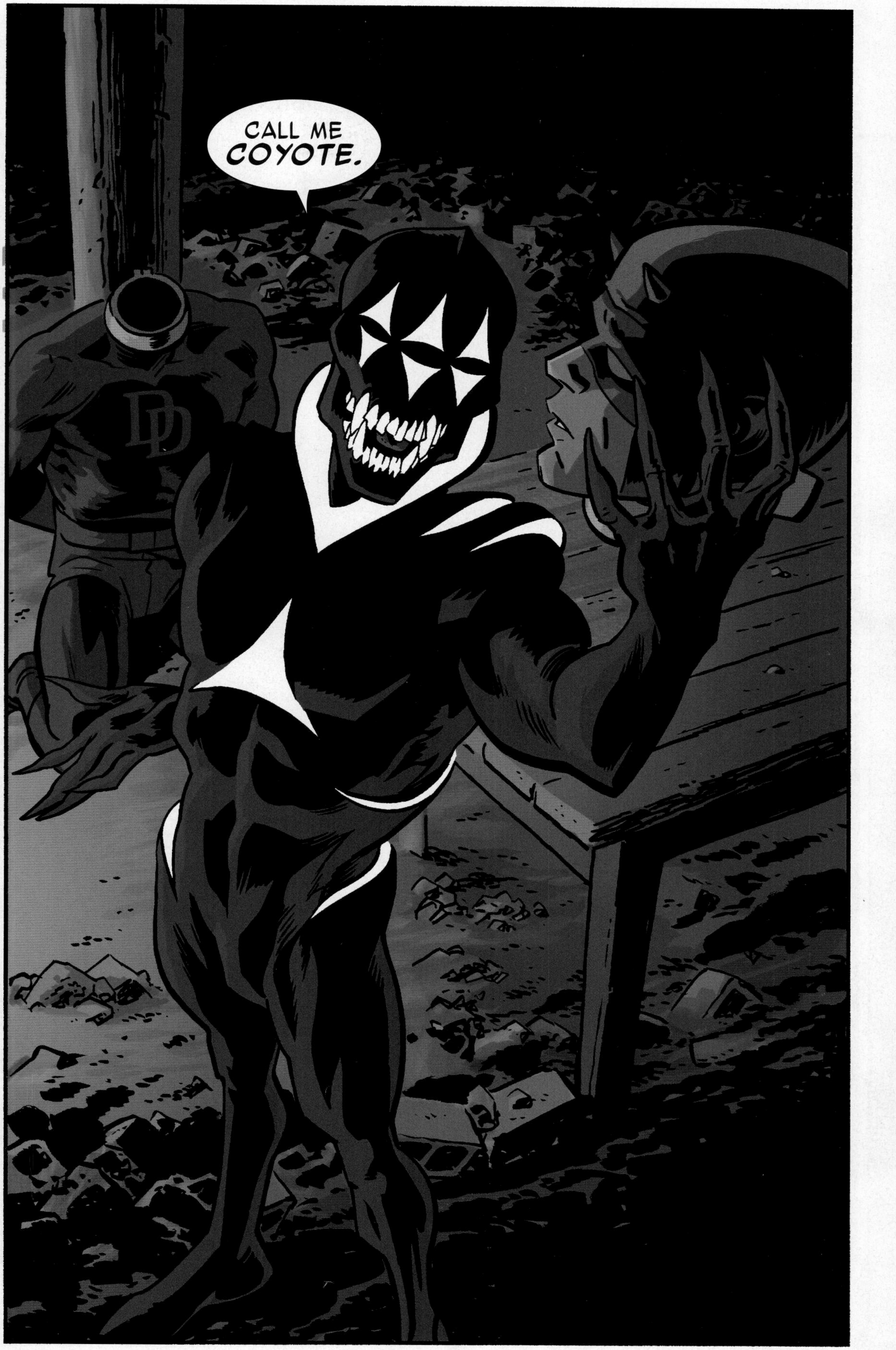
CALL ME COYOTE.

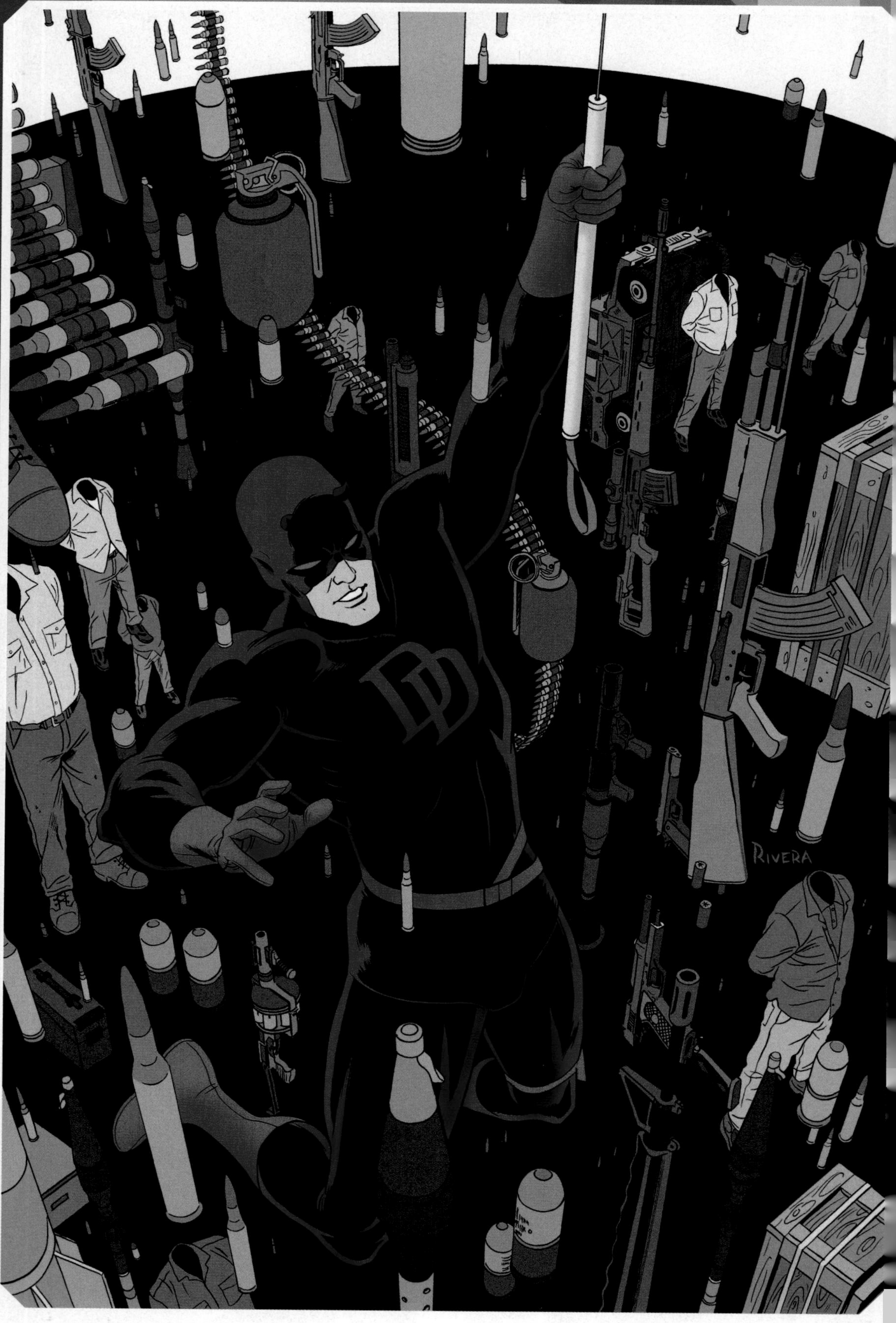
RIVERA

TWENTY

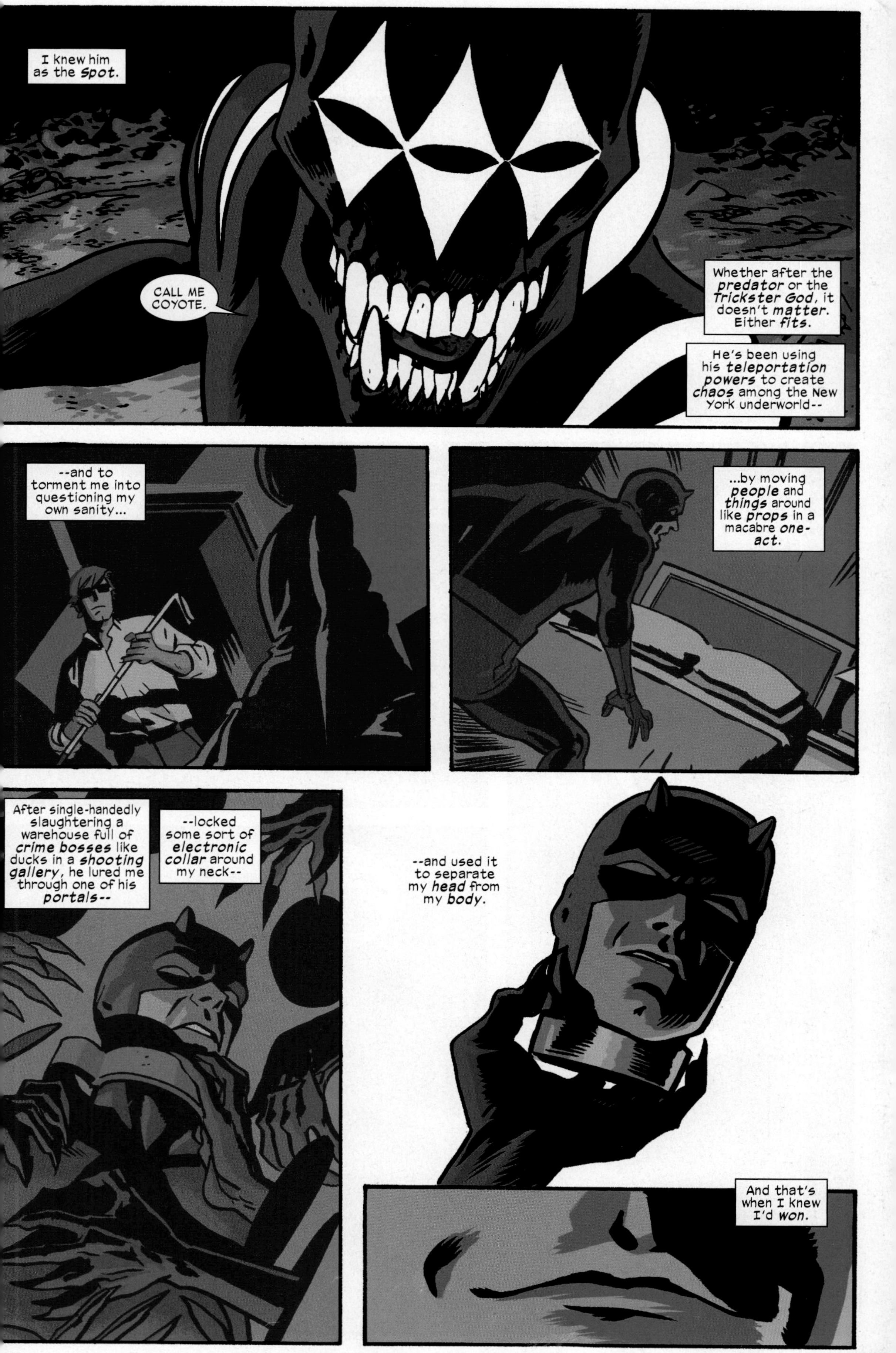

I knew him as the *Spot*.
CALL ME COYOTE.
Whether after the *predator* or the *Trickster God*, it doesn't *matter*. Either *fits*.
He's been using his *teleportation powers* to create *chaos* among the New York underworld--
--and to torment me into questioning my own sanity...
...by moving *people* and *things* around like *props* in a macabre *one-act*.
After single-handedly slaughtering a warehouse full of *crime bosses* like ducks in a *shooting gallery*, he lured me through one of his *portals*--
--locked some sort of *electronic collar* around my neck--
--and used it to separate my *head* from my *body*.
And that's when I knew I'd *won*.

Another change: he *speaks* now. Good.

I absolutely have to keep him *talking.*

A hostile line of questioning should do it...

SO...*YOU'VE* COME UP IN THE WORLD. I GUESS I OWE SPIDER-MAN *TWENTY BUCKS.*

DECIDED TO TAKE OVER THE TRI-STATE *DRUG TRADE*, I GATHER?

NOT MY STYLE.

HOW SO? IT'S NOT A *ROAD RUNNER CARTOON?*

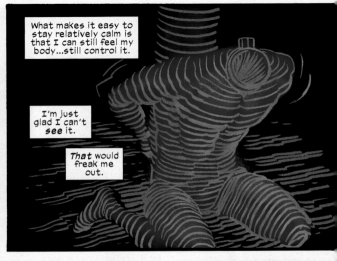

What makes it easy to stay relatively calm is that I can still feel my body...still control it.

I'm just glad I can't *see* it.

That would freak me out.

TOO MUCH *FUSS.* I *HAVE* BEGUN *ONE* SOLO ENTERPRISE, BUT WE'LL GET TO THAT. BY AND LARGE, I'M STILL A *CONTRACTOR* AT HEART. WORK FOR HIRE, AND ALL THAT.

BUT SINCE THERE'S NOTHING CLIENTS CAN *PAY* ME THAT I CAN'T SIMPLY *TAKE*...

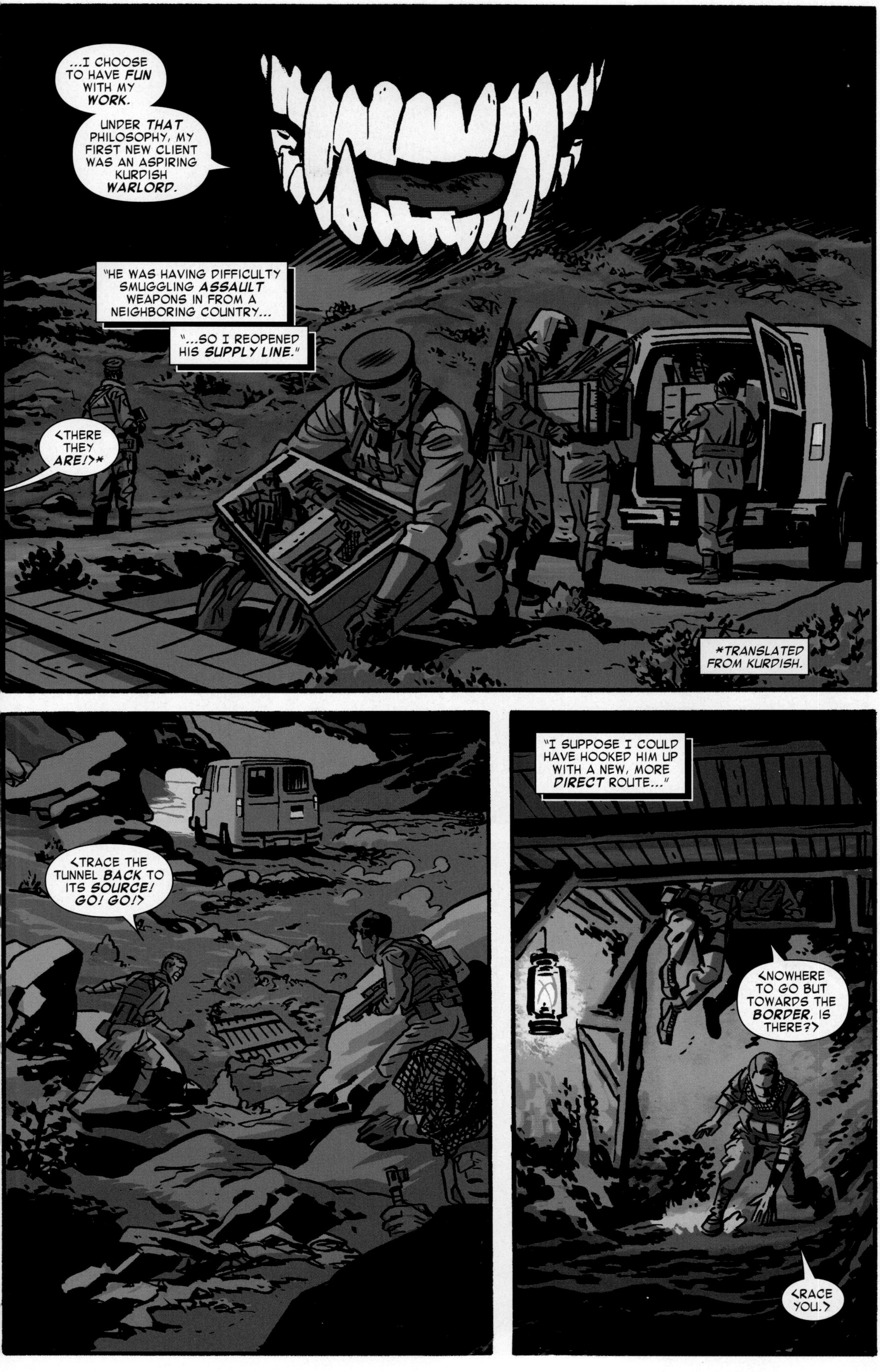
...I CHOOSE TO HAVE FUN WITH MY WORK.
UNDER THAT PHILOSOPHY, MY FIRST NEW CLIENT WAS AN ASPIRING KURDISH WARLORD.
"HE WAS HAVING DIFFICULTY SMUGGLING ASSAULT WEAPONS IN FROM A NEIGHBORING COUNTRY...
"...SO I REOPENED HIS SUPPLY LINE."
<THERE THEY ARE!>*
*TRANSLATED FROM KURDISH.
<TRACE THE TUNNEL BACK TO ITS SOURCE! GO! GO!>
"I SUPPOSE I COULD HAVE HOOKED HIM UP WITH A NEW, MORE DIRECT ROUTE..."
<NOWHERE TO GO BUT TOWARDS THE BORDER, IS THERE?>
<RACE YOU.>

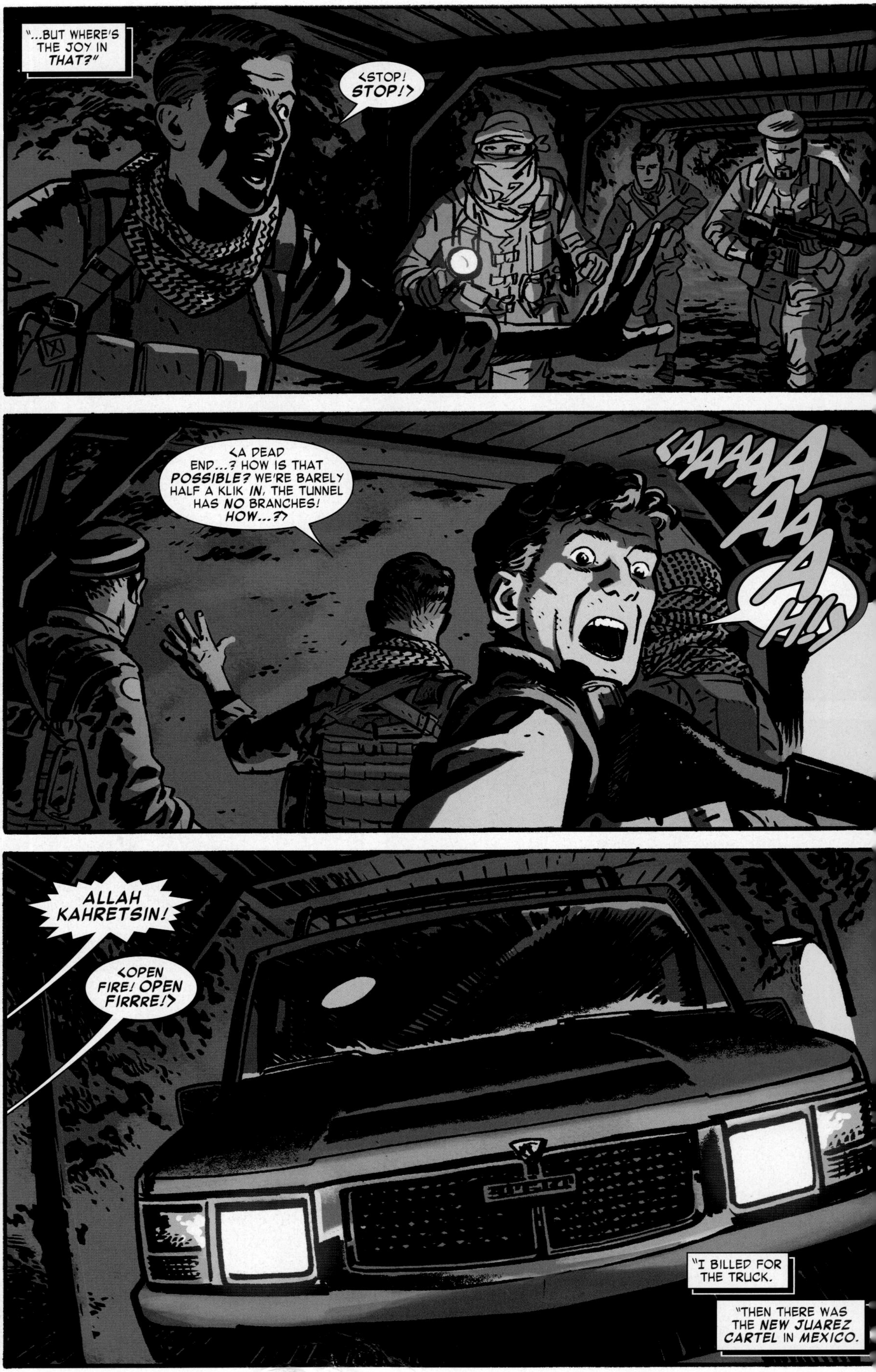

"...BUT WHERE'S THE JOY IN *THAT?*"
<STOP! *STOP!*>
<A DEAD END...? HOW IS THAT *POSSIBLE?* WE'RE BARELY HALF A KLIK *IN*, THE TUNNEL HAS *NO* BRANCHES! *HOW...?*>
AAAAAAAAAH!!
ALLAH KAHRETSIN!
<OPEN FIRE! OPEN FIRRRE!>
"I BILLED FOR THE TRUCK.
"THEN THERE WAS THE *NEW JUAREZ CARTEL* IN *MEXICO.*

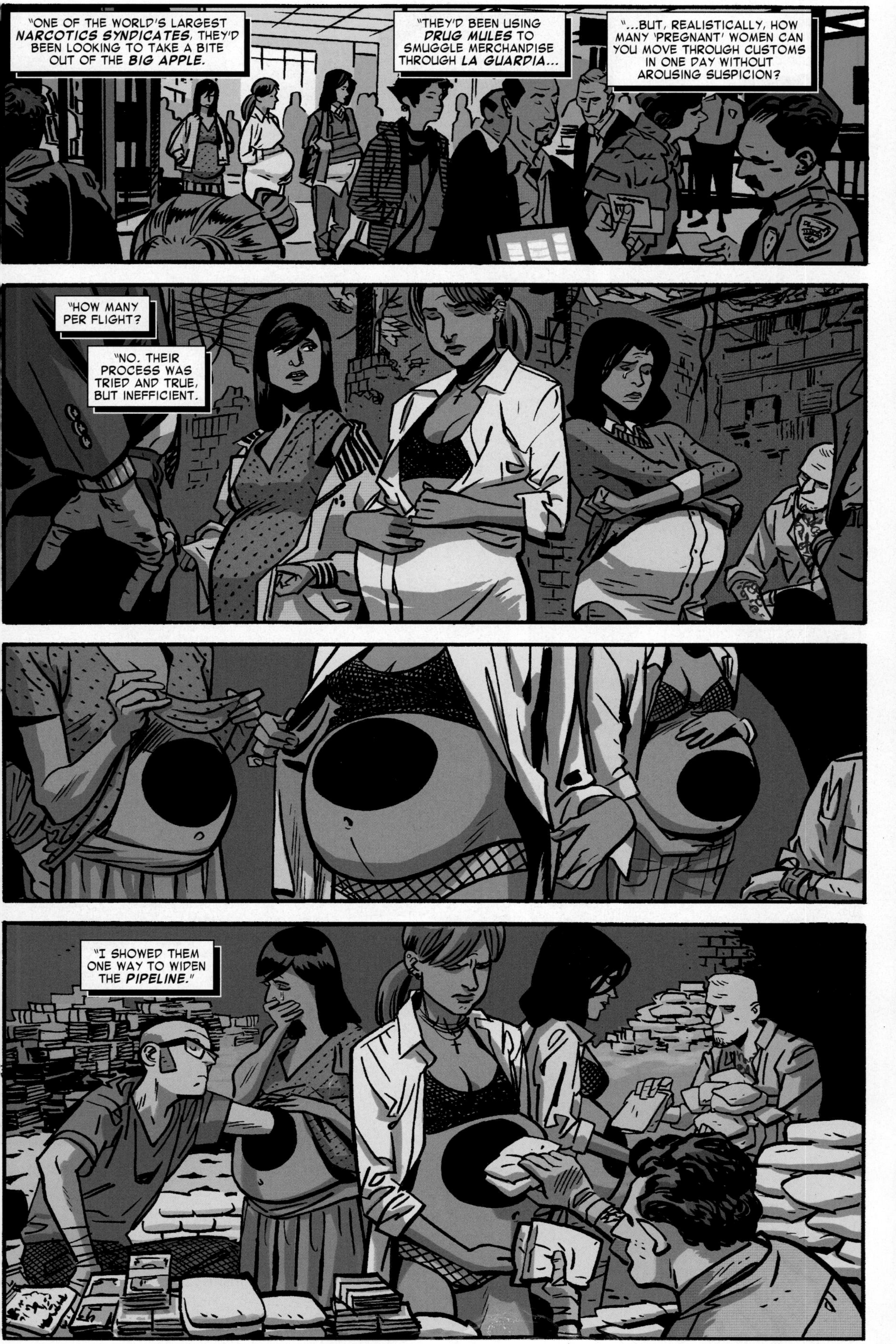
"ONE OF THE WORLD'S LARGEST NARCOTICS SYNDICATES, THEY'D BEEN LOOKING TO TAKE A BITE OUT OF THE BIG APPLE.
"THEY'D BEEN USING DRUG MULES TO SMUGGLE MERCHANDISE THROUGH LA GUARDIA...
"...BUT, REALISTICALLY, HOW MANY 'PREGNANT' WOMEN CAN YOU MOVE THROUGH CUSTOMS IN ONE DAY WITHOUT AROUSING SUSPICION?
"HOW MANY PER FLIGHT?
"NO. THEIR PROCESS WAS TRIED AND TRUE, BUT INEFFICIENT.
"I SHOWED THEM ONE WAY TO WIDEN THE PIPELINE."

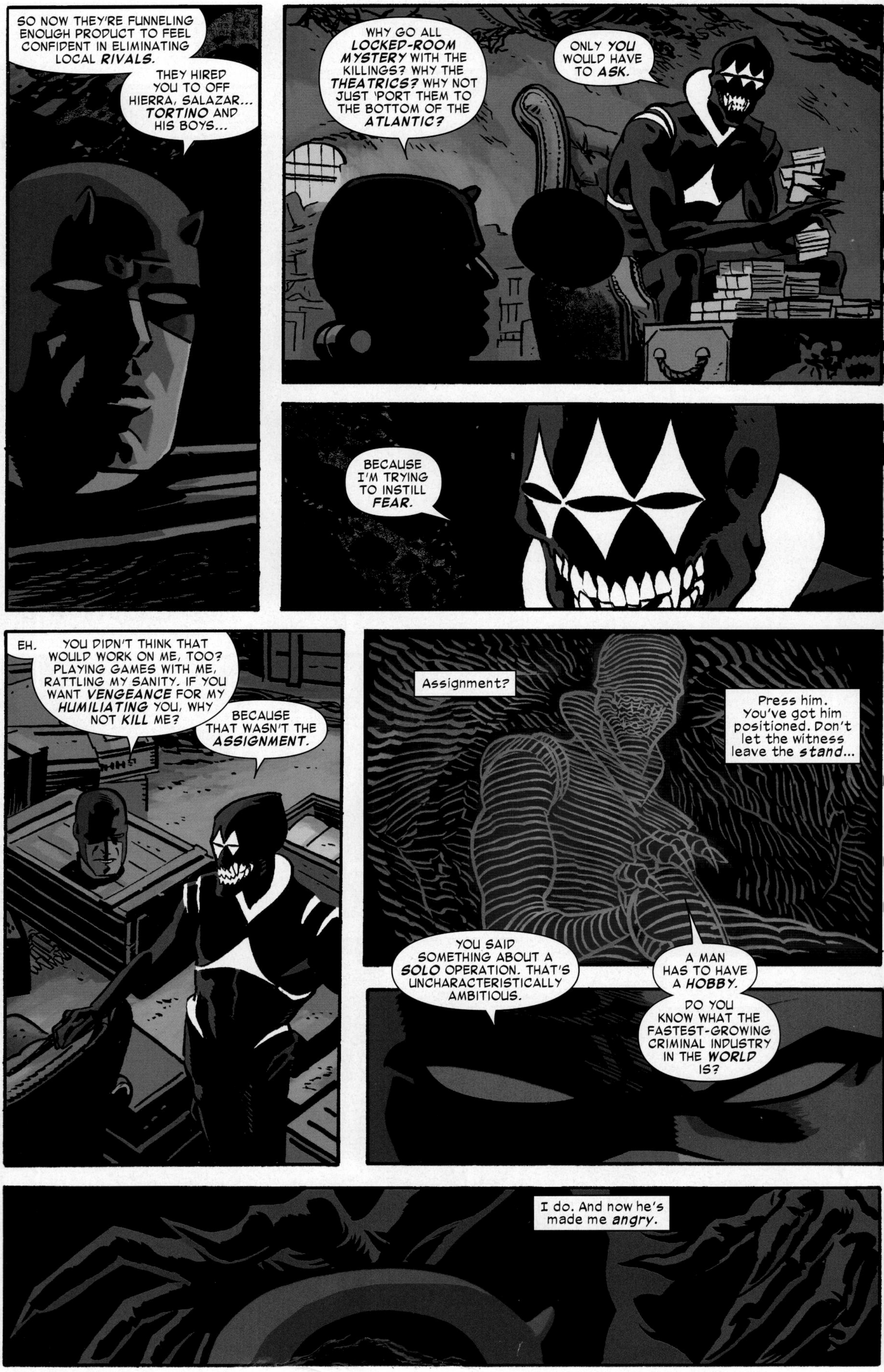
SO NOW THEY'RE FUNNELING ENOUGH PRODUCT TO FEEL CONFIDENT IN ELIMINATING LOCAL RIVALS.
THEY HIRED YOU TO OFF HIERRA, SALAZAR... TORTINO AND HIS BOYS...
WHY GO ALL LOCKED-ROOM MYSTERY WITH THE KILLINGS? WHY THE THEATRICS? WHY NOT JUST 'PORT THEM TO THE BOTTOM OF THE ATLANTIC?
ONLY YOU WOULD HAVE TO ASK.
BECAUSE I'M TRYING TO INSTILL FEAR.
EH.
YOU DIDN'T THINK THAT WOULD WORK ON ME, TOO? PLAYING GAMES WITH ME, RATTLING MY SANITY. IF YOU WANT VENGEANCE FOR MY HUMILIATING YOU, WHY NOT KILL ME?
BECAUSE THAT WASN'T THE ASSIGNMENT.
Assignment?
Press him. You've got him positioned. Don't let the witness leave the stand...
YOU SAID SOMETHING ABOUT A SOLO OPERATION. THAT'S UNCHARACTERISTICALLY AMBITIOUS.
A MAN HAS TO HAVE A HOBBY.
DO YOU KNOW WHAT THE FASTEST-GROWING CRIMINAL INDUSTRY IN THE WORLD IS?
I do. And now he's made me angry.

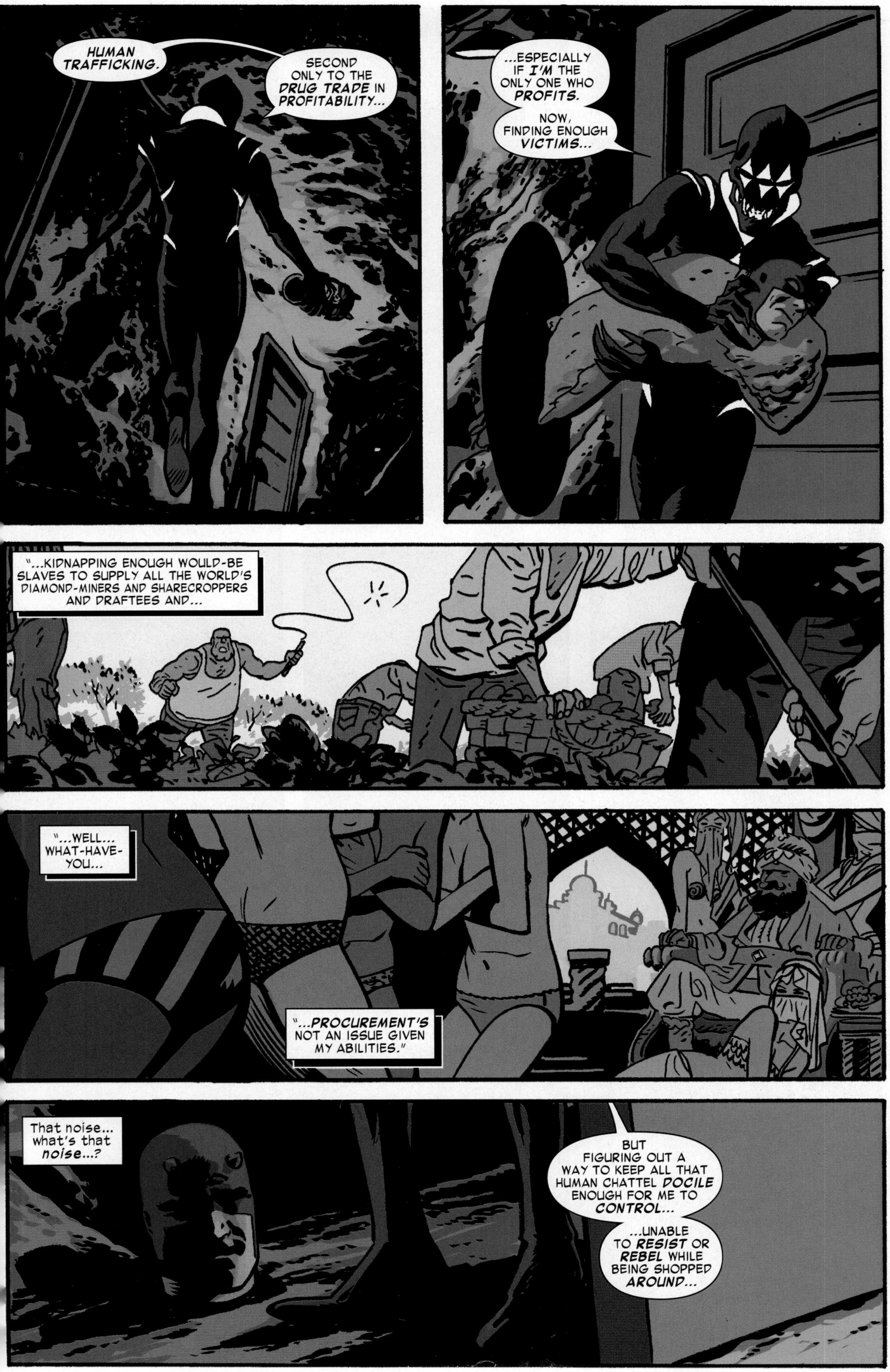

HUMAN TRAFFICKING.
SECOND ONLY TO THE DRUG TRADE IN PROFITABILITY...
...ESPECIALLY IF I'M THE ONLY ONE WHO PROFITS.
NOW, FINDING ENOUGH VICTIMS...
"...KIDNAPPING ENOUGH WOULD-BE SLAVES TO SUPPLY ALL THE WORLD'S DIAMOND-MINERS AND SHARECROPPERS AND DRAFTEES AND...
"...WELL... WHAT-HAVE-YOU...
"...PROCUREMENT'S NOT AN ISSUE GIVEN MY ABILITIES."
That noise... what's that noise...?
BUT FIGURING OUT A WAY TO KEEP ALL THAT HUMAN CHATTEL DOCILE ENOUGH FOR ME TO CONTROL...
...UNABLE TO RESIST OR REBEL WHILE BEING SHOPPED AROUND...

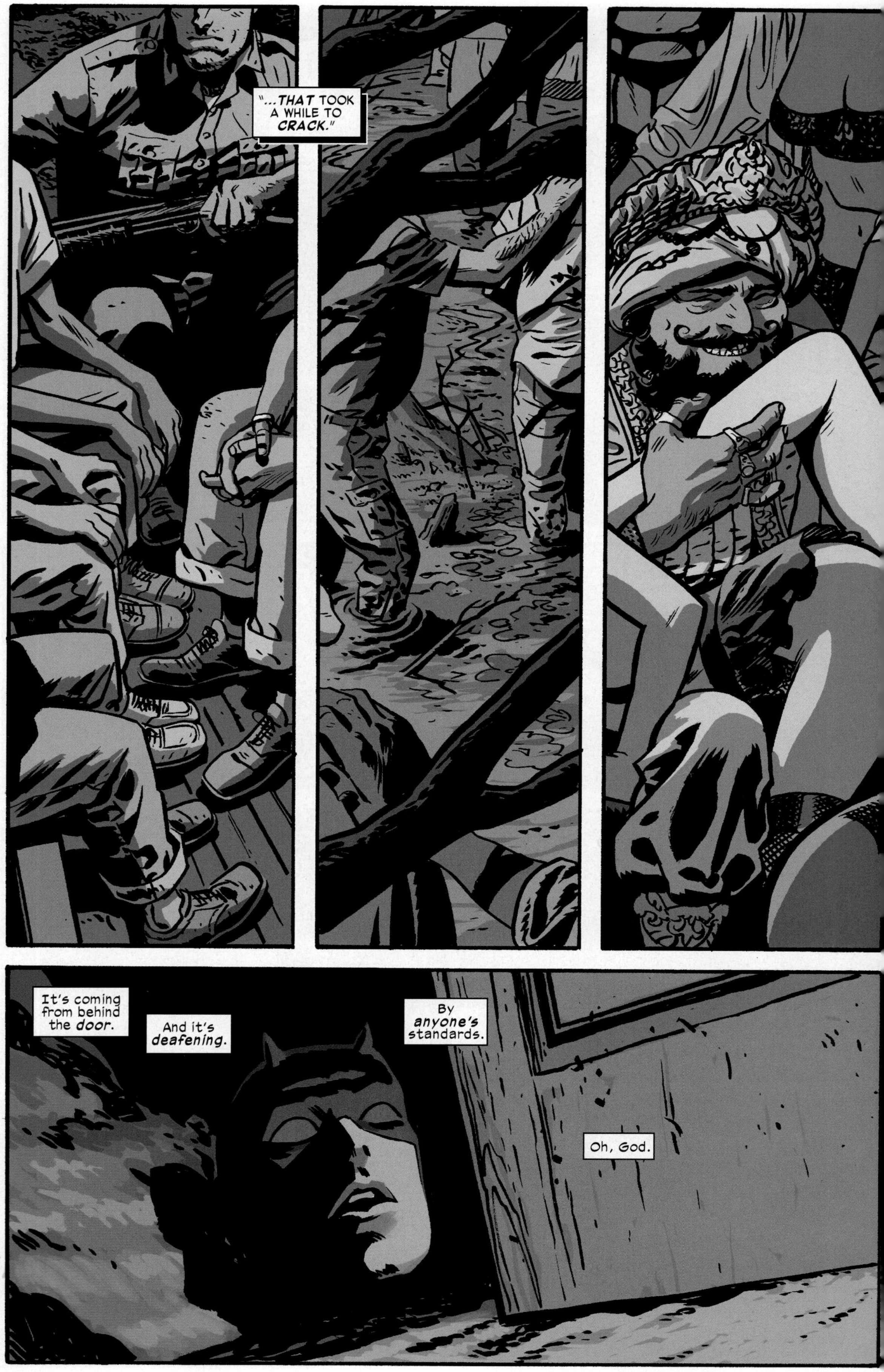
"...THAT TOOK A WHILE TO CRACK."
It's coming from behind the door.
And it's deafening.
By anyone's standards.
Oh, God.

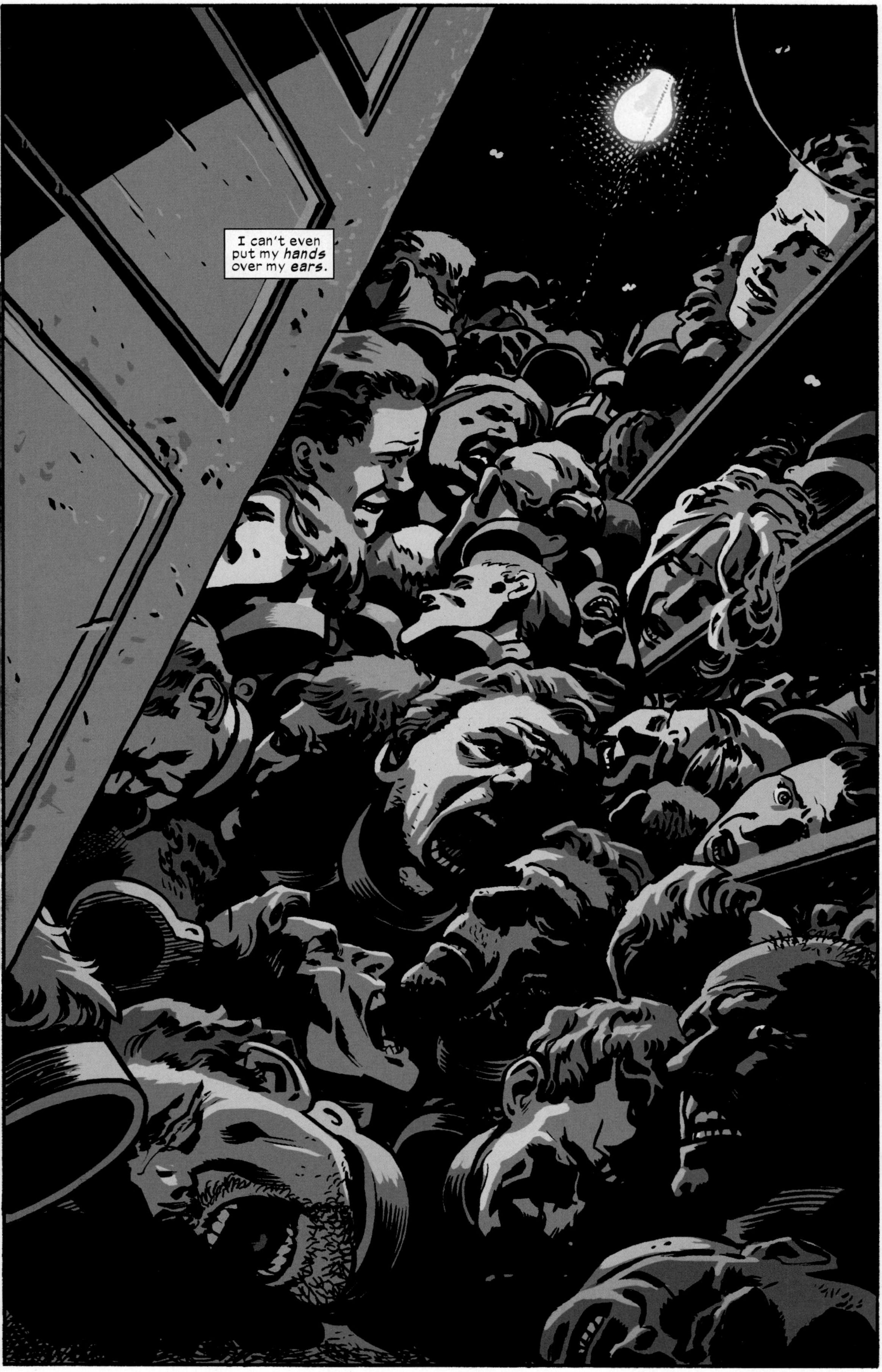
I can't even put my *hands* over my *ears*.

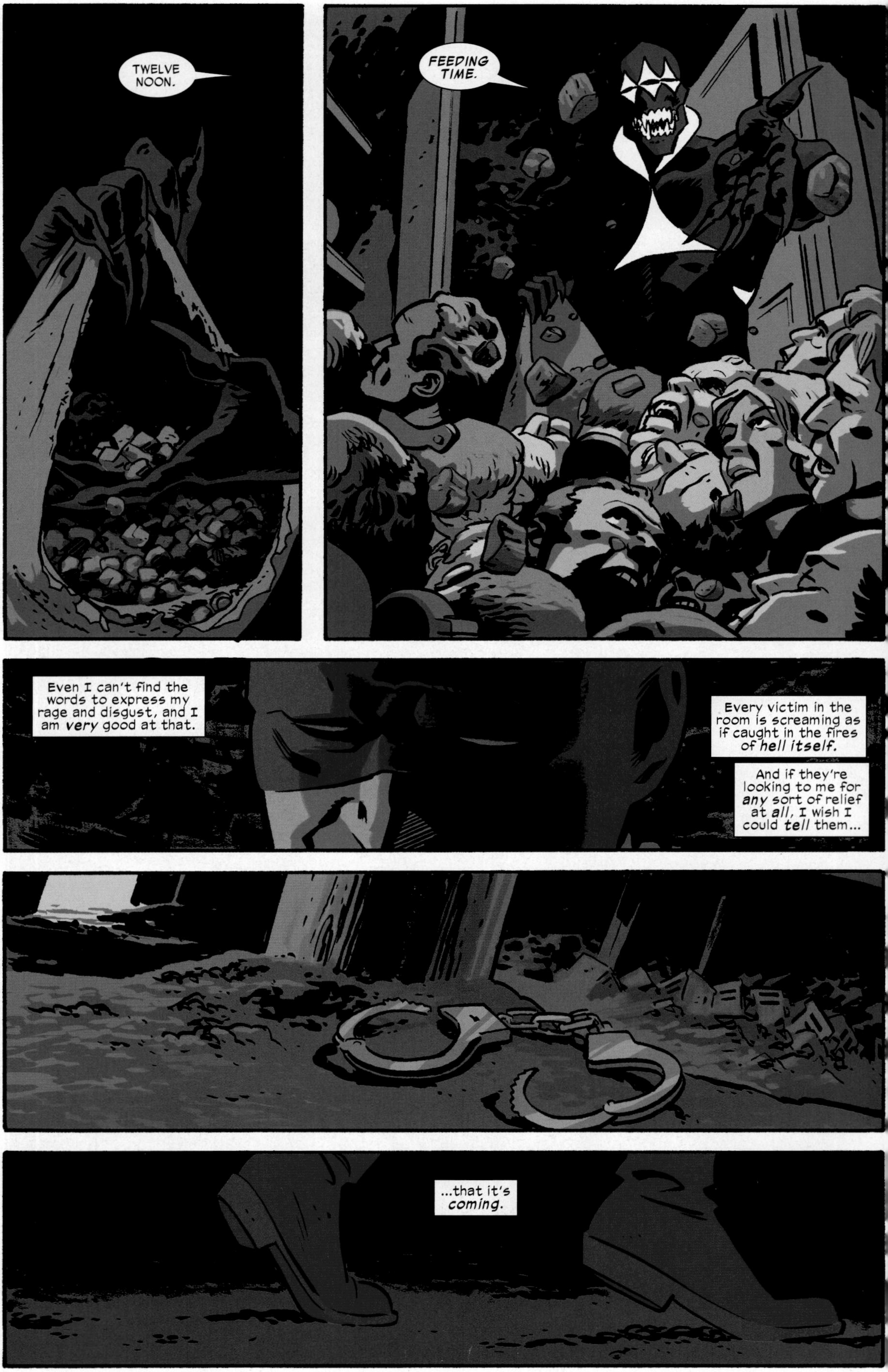
TWELVE NOON.
FEEDING TIME.
Even I can't find the words to express my rage and disgust, and I am *very* good at that.
Every victim in the room is screaming as if caught in the fires of *hell itself.*
And if they're looking to me for *any* sort of relief at *all*, I wish I could *tell* them...
...that it's *coming*.

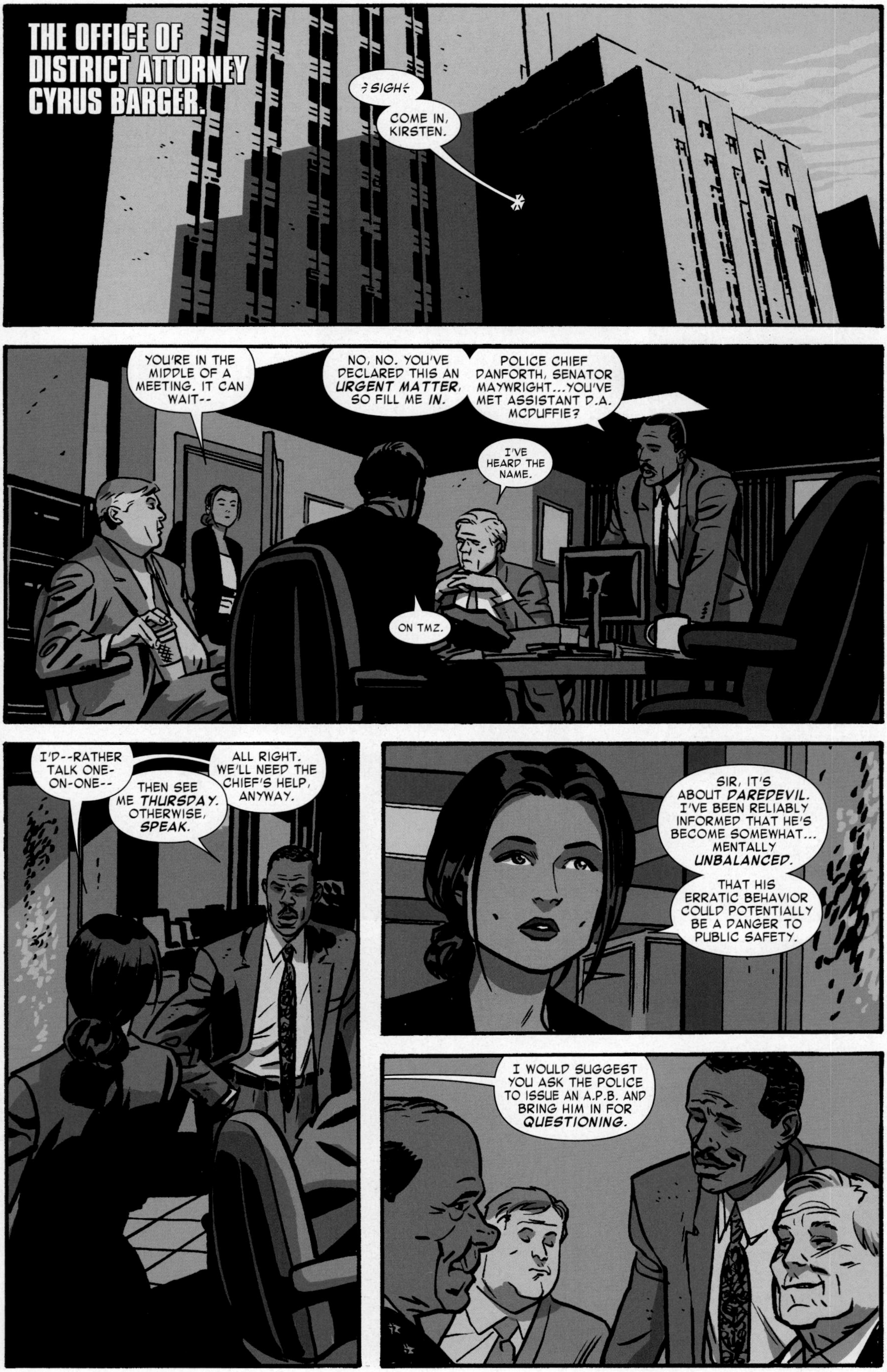
THE OFFICE OF DISTRICT ATTORNEY CYRUS BARGER.
SIGH
COME IN, KIRSTEN.
YOU'RE IN THE MIDDLE OF A MEETING. IT CAN WAIT--
NO, NO. YOU'VE DECLARED THIS AN URGENT MATTER, SO FILL ME IN.
POLICE CHIEF DANFORTH, SENATOR MAYWRIGHT...YOU'VE MET ASSISTANT D.A. MCDUFFIE?
I'VE HEARD THE NAME.
ON TMZ.
I'D--RATHER TALK ONE-ON-ONE--
THEN SEE ME THURSDAY. OTHERWISE, SPEAK.
ALL RIGHT. WE'LL NEED THE CHIEF'S HELP, ANYWAY.
SIR, IT'S ABOUT DAREDEVIL. I'VE BEEN RELIABLY INFORMED THAT HE'S BECOME SOMEWHAT... MENTALLY UNBALANCED.
THAT HIS ERRATIC BEHAVIOR COULD POTENTIALLY BE A DANGER TO PUBLIC SAFETY.
I WOULD SUGGEST YOU ASK THE POLICE TO ISSUE AN A.P.B. AND BRING HIM IN FOR QUESTIONING.

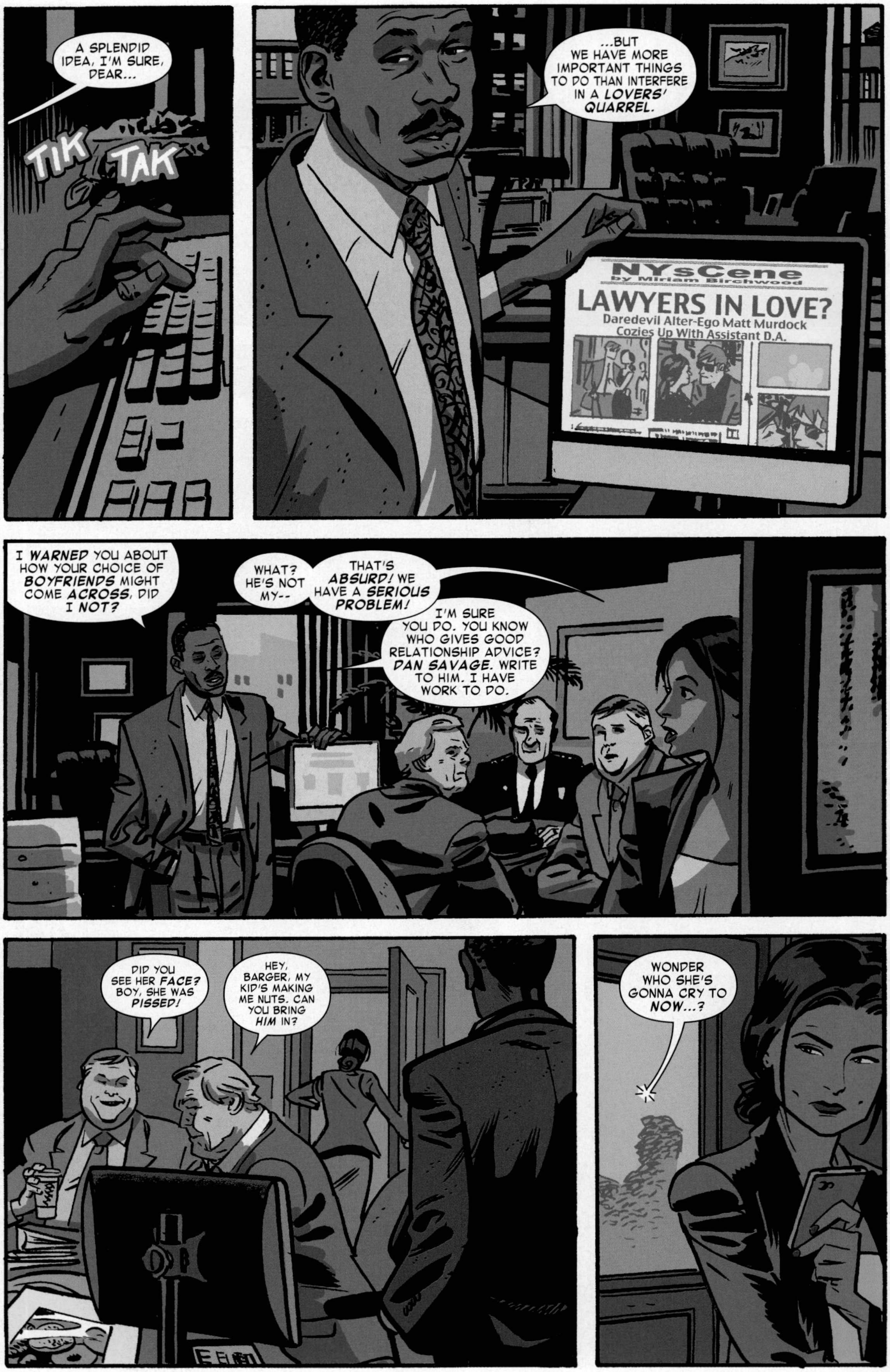
A SPLENDID IDEA, I'M SURE, DEAR...
TIK
TAK
...BUT WE HAVE MORE IMPORTANT THINGS TO DO THAN INTERFERE IN A LOVERS' QUARREL.
NYsCene
by Miriam Birchwood
LAWYERS IN LOVE?
Daredevil Alter-Ego Matt Murdock Cozies Up With Assistant D.A.
I WARNED YOU ABOUT HOW YOUR CHOICE OF BOYFRIENDS MIGHT COME ACROSS, DID I NOT?
WHAT? HE'S NOT MY--
THAT'S ABSURD! WE HAVE A SERIOUS PROBLEM!
I'M SURE YOU DO. YOU KNOW WHO GIVES GOOD RELATIONSHIP ADVICE? DAN SAVAGE. WRITE TO HIM. I HAVE WORK TO DO.
DID YOU SEE HER FACE? BOY, SHE WAS PISSED!
HEY, BARGER, MY KID'S MAKING ME NUTS. CAN YOU BRING HIM IN?
WONDER WHO SHE'S GONNA CRY TO NOW...?

Coyote's trap is gruesomely clever, no question.

But it has *one flaw.* Unlike *him*...

...it's powered *artificially.*

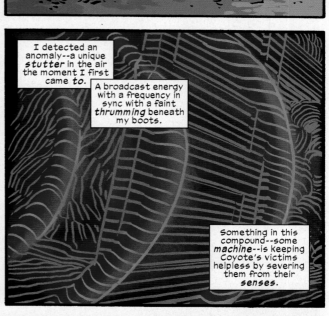

I detected an anomaly--a unique *stutter* in the air the moment I first came *to.*

A broadcast energy with a frequency in sync with a faint *thrumming* beneath my boots.

Something in this compound--some *machine*--is keeping Coyote's victims helpless by severing them from their *senses.*

SNAK

After all, what are their bodies going to do without *sight?*

CHAK

Just *grope around?*

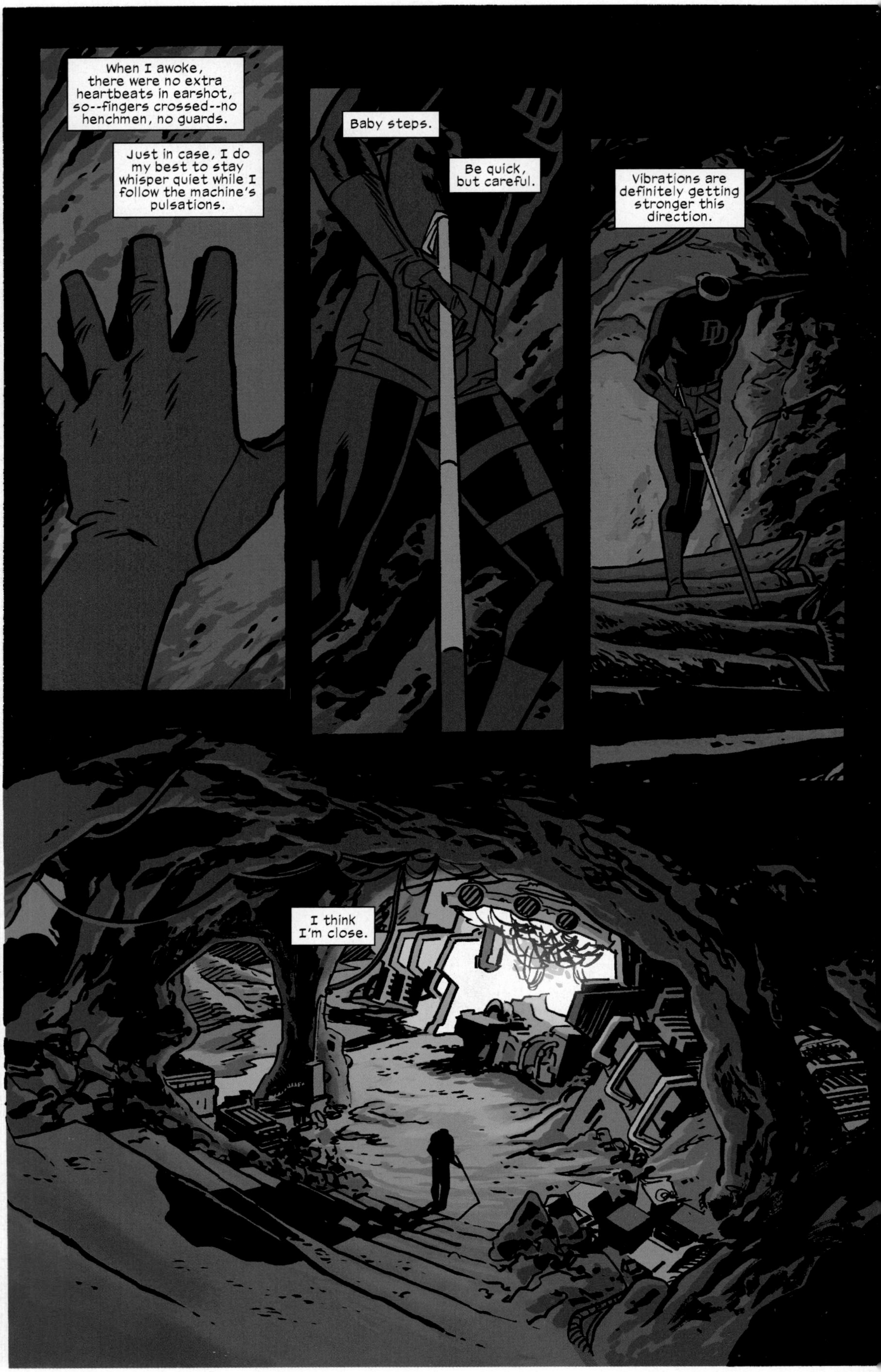
When I awoke, there were no extra heartbeats in earshot, so--fingers crossed--no henchmen, no guards.
Just in case, I do my best to stay whisper quiet while I follow the machine's pulsations.
Baby steps.
Be quick, but careful.
Vibrations are definitely getting stronger this direction.
I think I'm close.

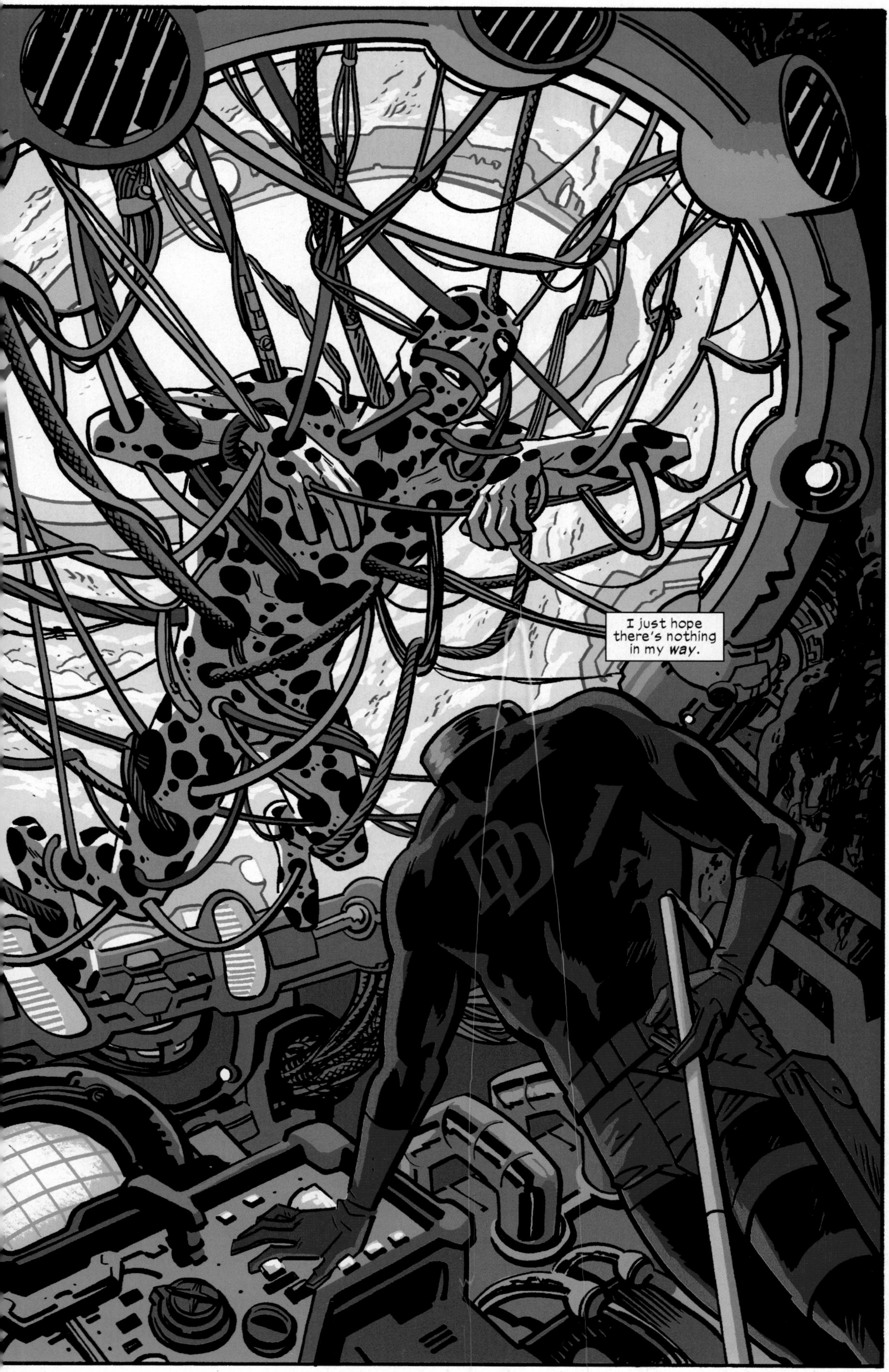
I just hope there's nothing in my way.

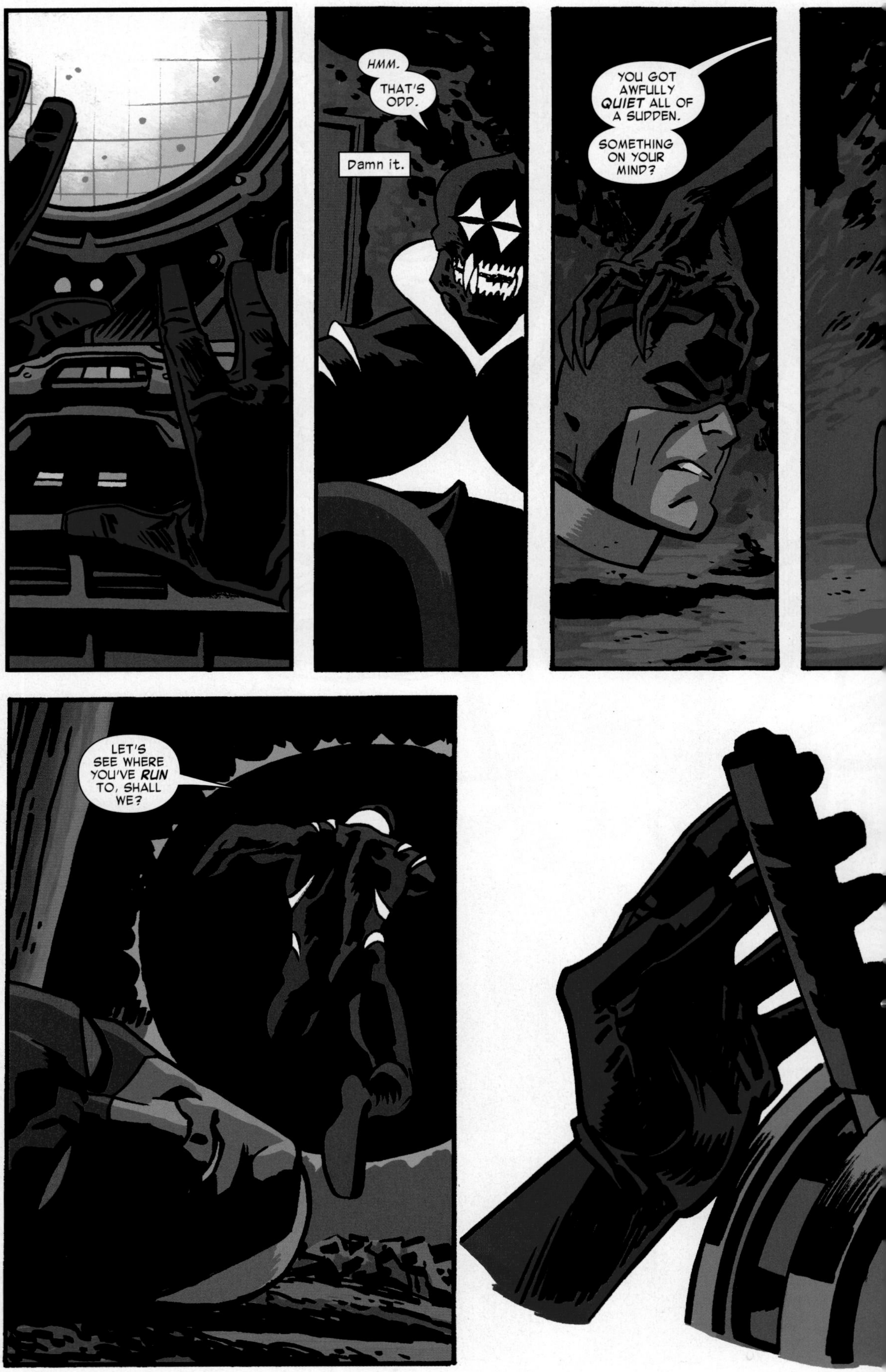
HMM.
THAT'S ODD.
Damn it.
YOU GOT AWFULLY QUIET ALL OF A SUDDEN.
SOMETHING ON YOUR MIND?
LET'S SEE WHERE YOU'VE RUN TO, SHALL WE?

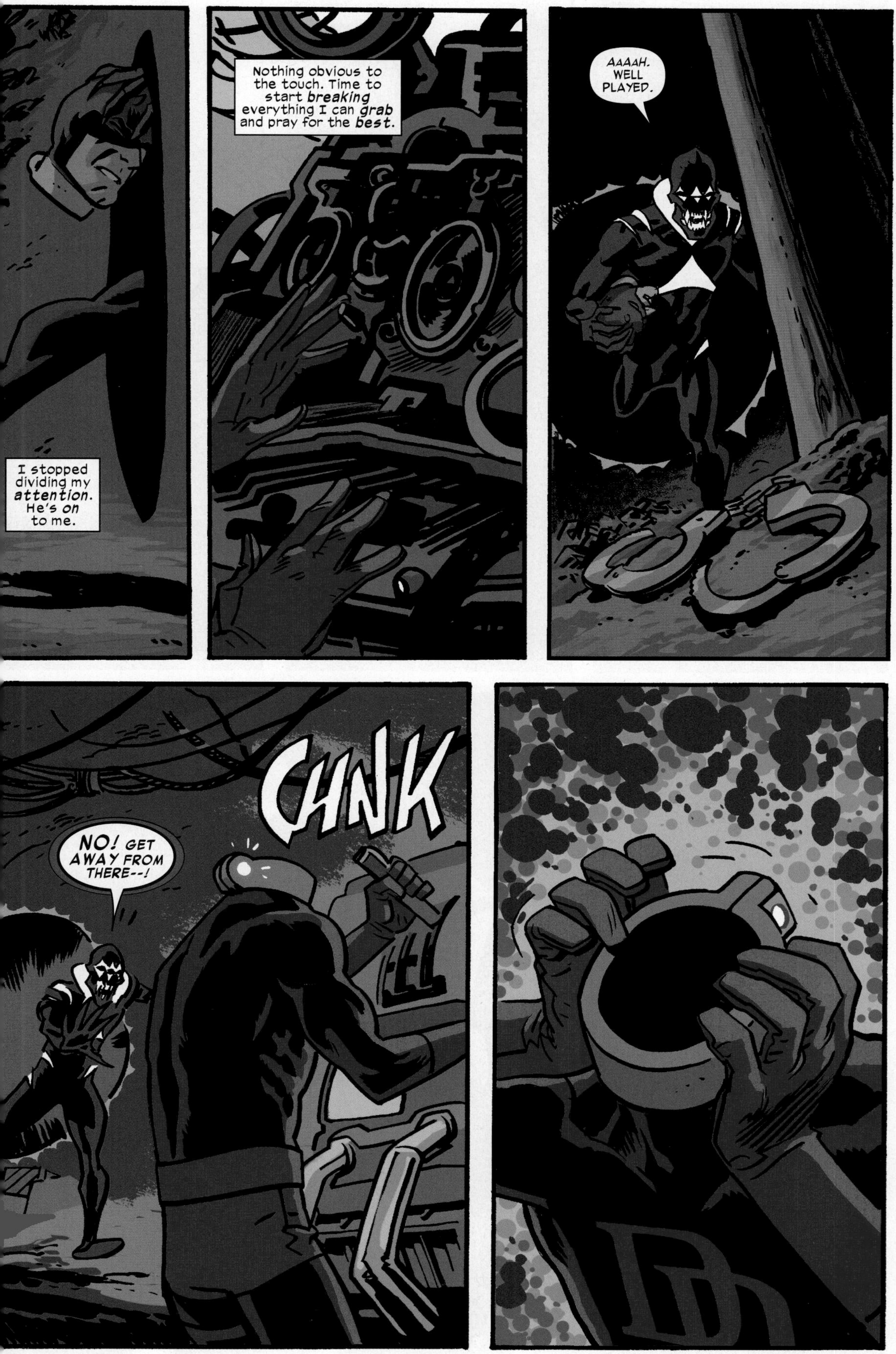

Nothing obvious to the touch. Time to start *breaking* everything I can *grab* and pray for the *best*.
I stopped dividing my *attention*. He's *on* to me.
AAAAH. WELL PLAYED.
CHNK
NO! GET AWAY FROM THERE--!

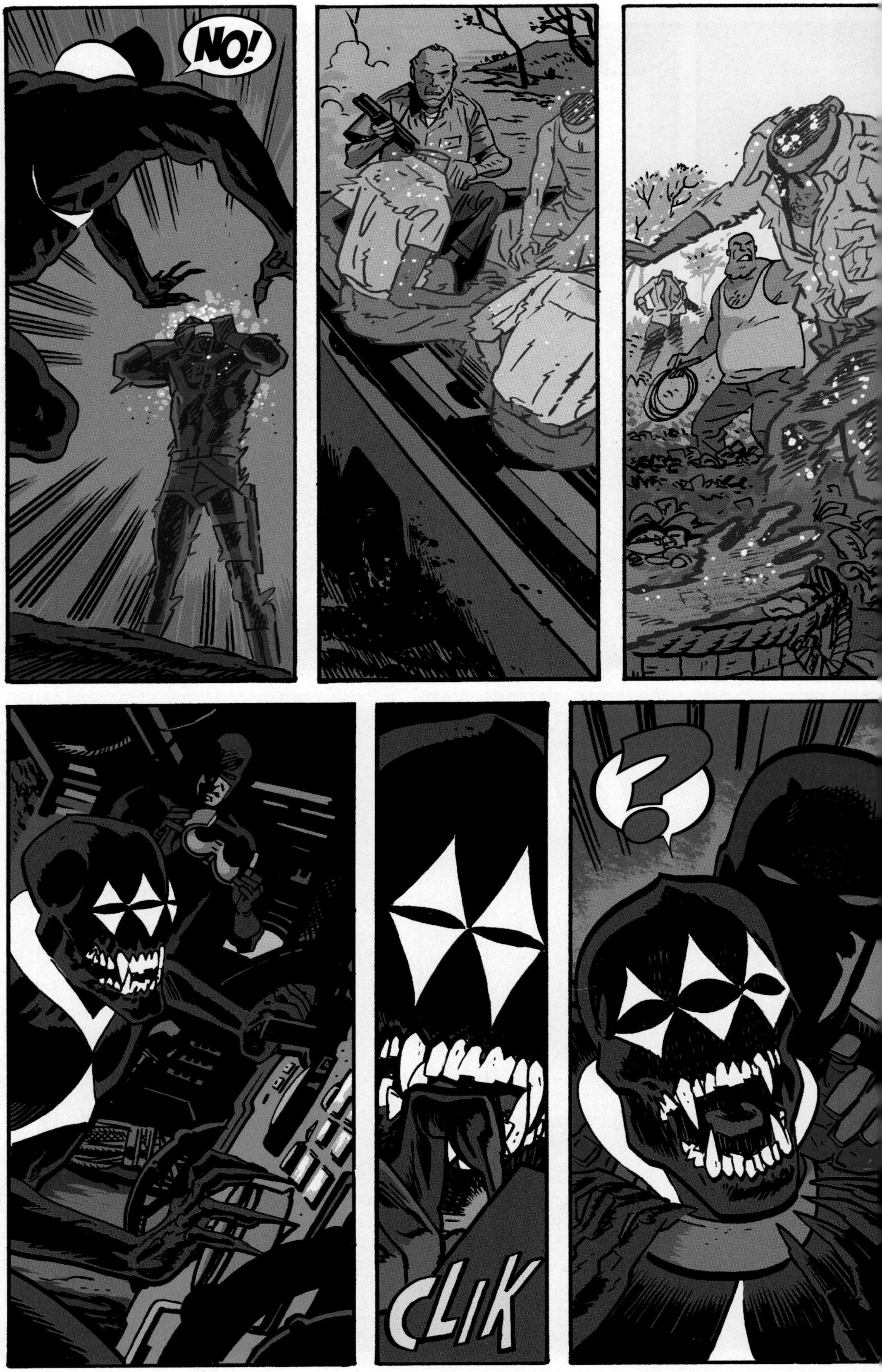
NO!
?
CLIK

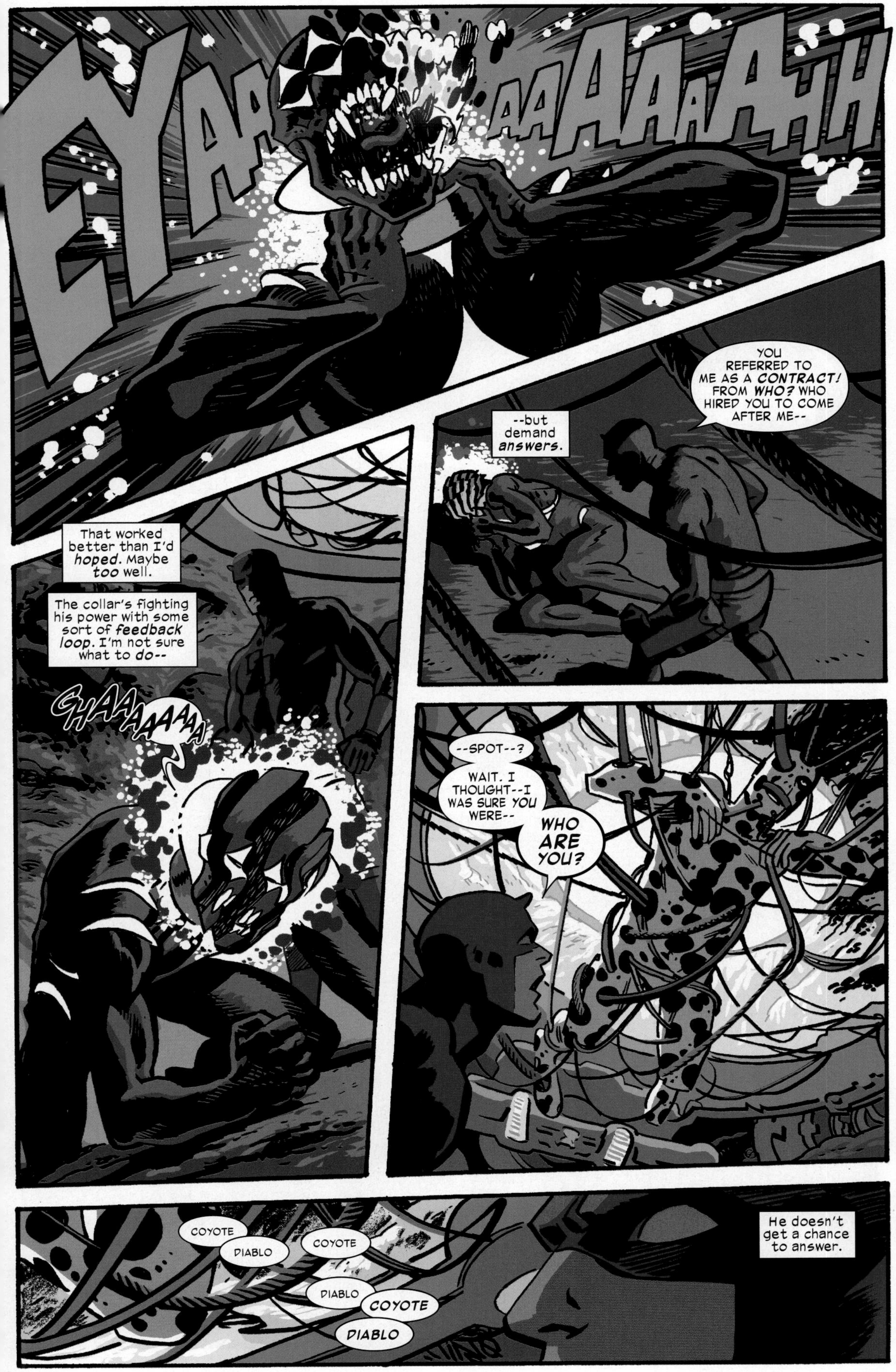
EYAAAAAAAAAAAH
That worked better than I'd hoped. Maybe too well.
The collar's fighting his power with some sort of feedback loop. I'm not sure what to do--
GHAAAAAAAA
--but demand answers.
YOU REFERRED TO ME AS A CONTRACT! FROM WHO? WHO HIRED YOU TO COME AFTER ME--
--SPOT--?
WAIT. I THOUGHT--I WAS SURE YOU WERE--
WHO ARE YOU?
COYOTE
DIABLO
COYOTE
DIABLO
COYOTE
DIABLO
He doesn't get a chance to answer.

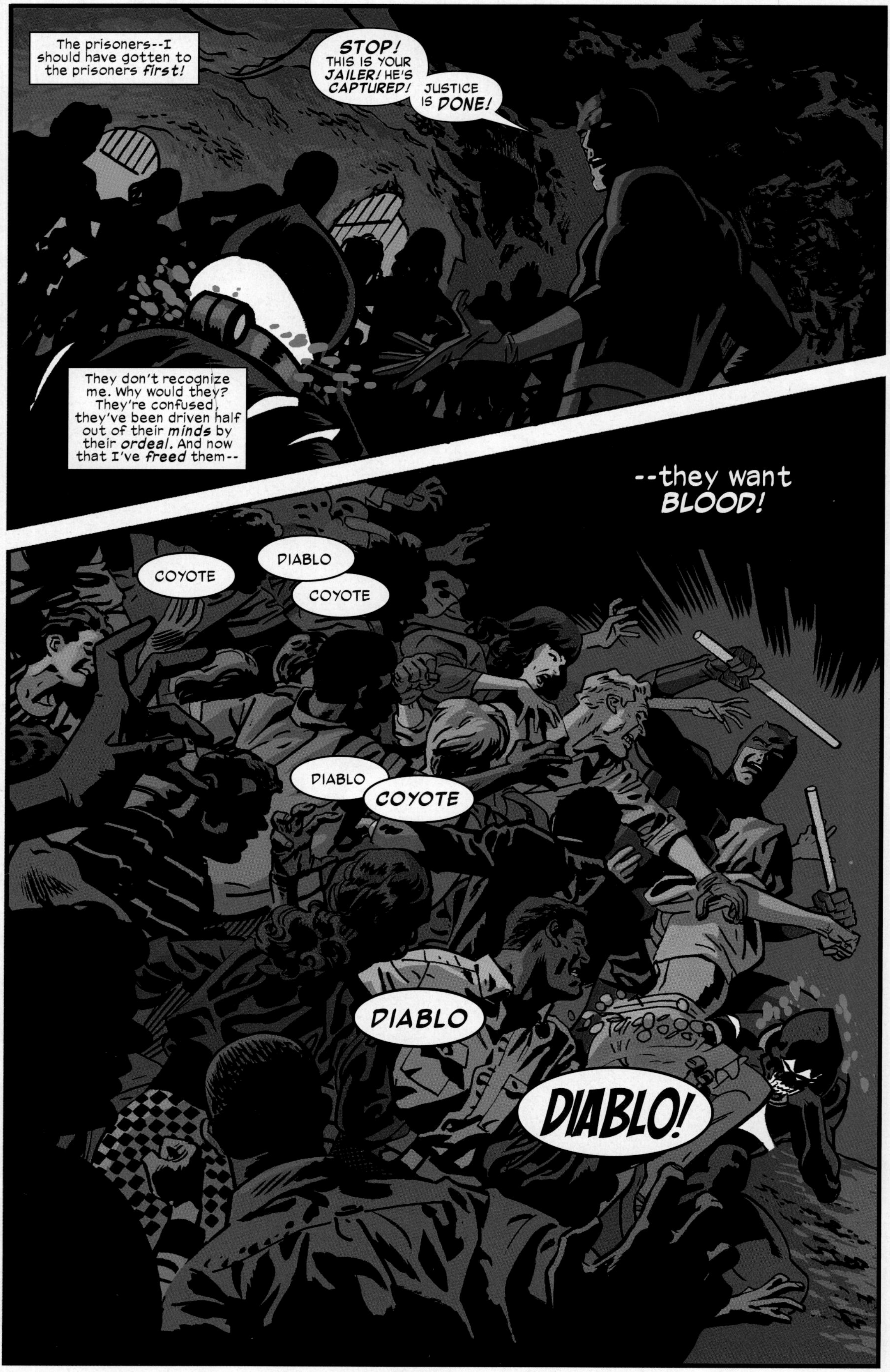
The prisoners--I should have gotten to the prisoners first!
STOP! THIS IS YOUR JAILER! HE'S CAPTURED!
JUSTICE IS DONE!
They don't recognize me. Why would they? They're confused, they've been driven half out of their minds by their ordeal. And now that I've freed them--
--they want BLOOD!
COYOTE
DIABLO
COYOTE
DIABLO
COYOTE
DIABLO
DIABLO!

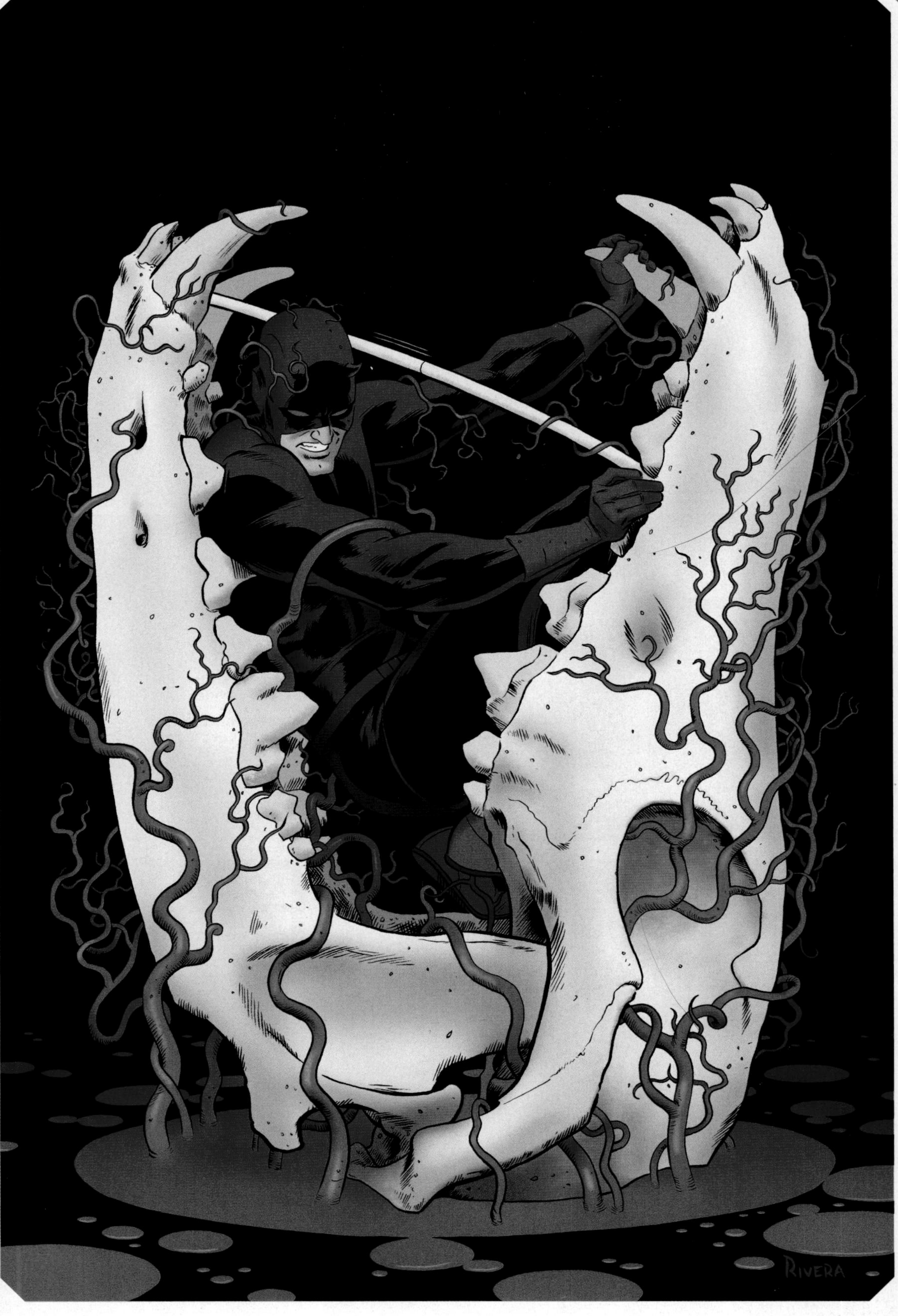
RIVERA

TWENTY-ONE

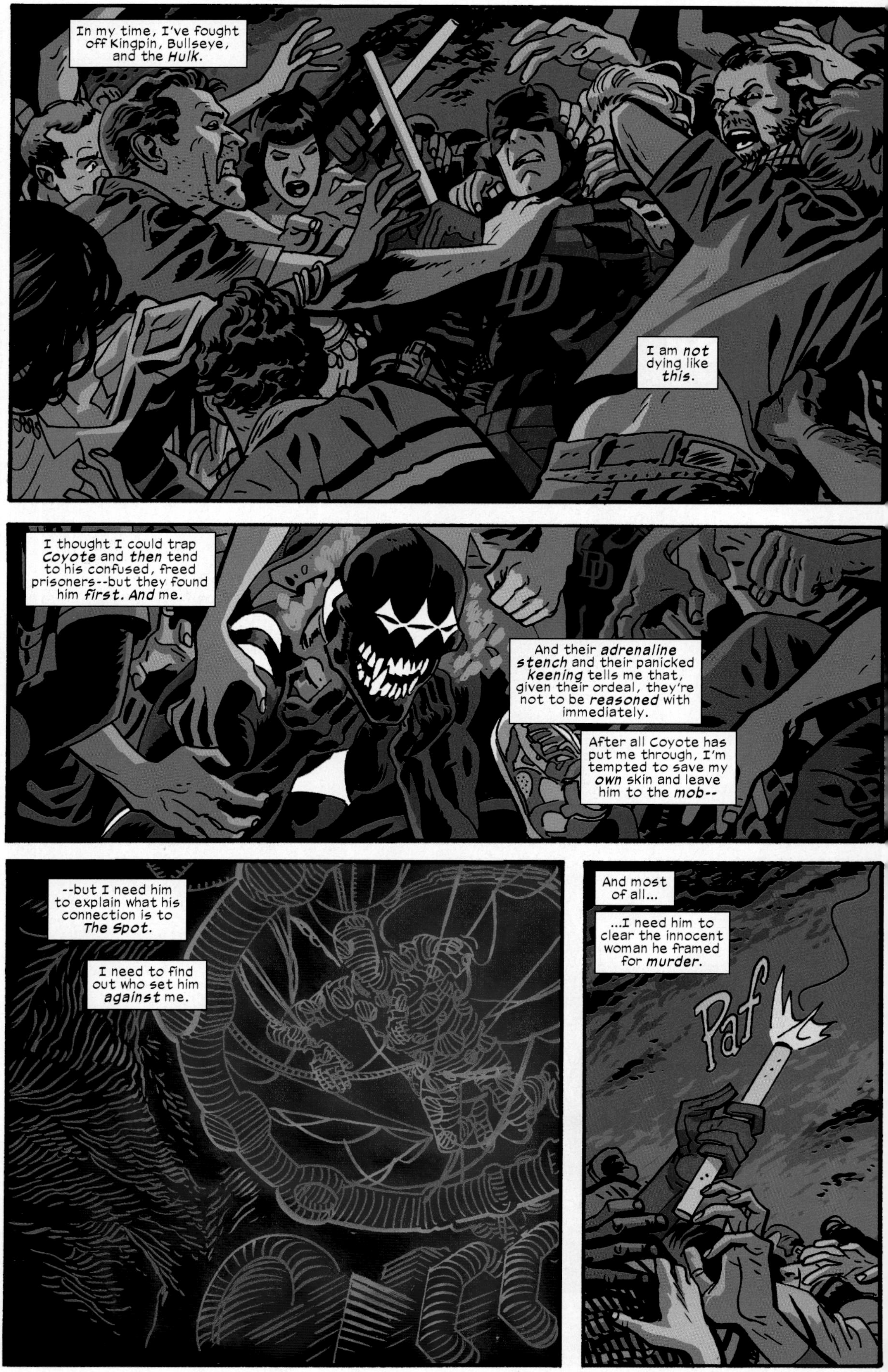
In my time, I've fought off Kingpin, Bullseye, and the *Hulk*.
I am *not* dying like *this*.
I thought I could trap *Coyote* and *then* tend to his confused, freed prisoners--but they found him *first. And* me.
And their *adrenaline stench* and their panicked *keening* tells me that, given their ordeal, they're not to be *reasoned* with immediately.
After all Coyote has put me through, I'm tempted to save my *own* skin and leave him to the *mob*--
--but I need him to explain what his connection is to *The Spot*.
I need to find out who set him *against* me.
And most of all...
...I need him to clear the innocent woman he framed for *murder*.
Paf

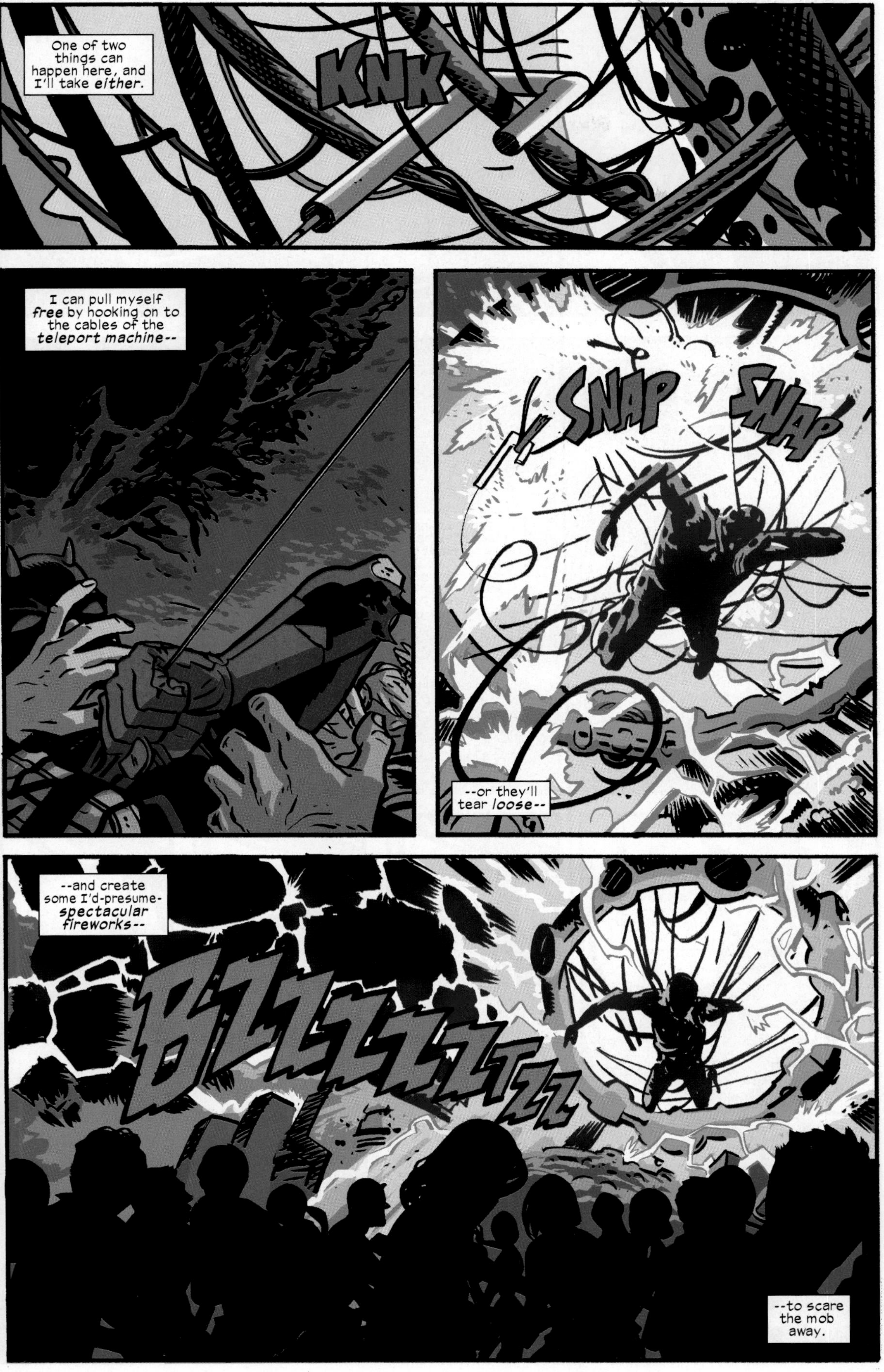
One of two things can happen here, and I'll take *either*.
KNK
I can pull myself *free* by hooking on to the cables of the *teleport machine*--
SNAP
SNAP
--or they'll tear *loose*--
--and create some I'd-presume-*spectacular fireworks*--
BZZZZZZTZZ
--to scare the mob away.

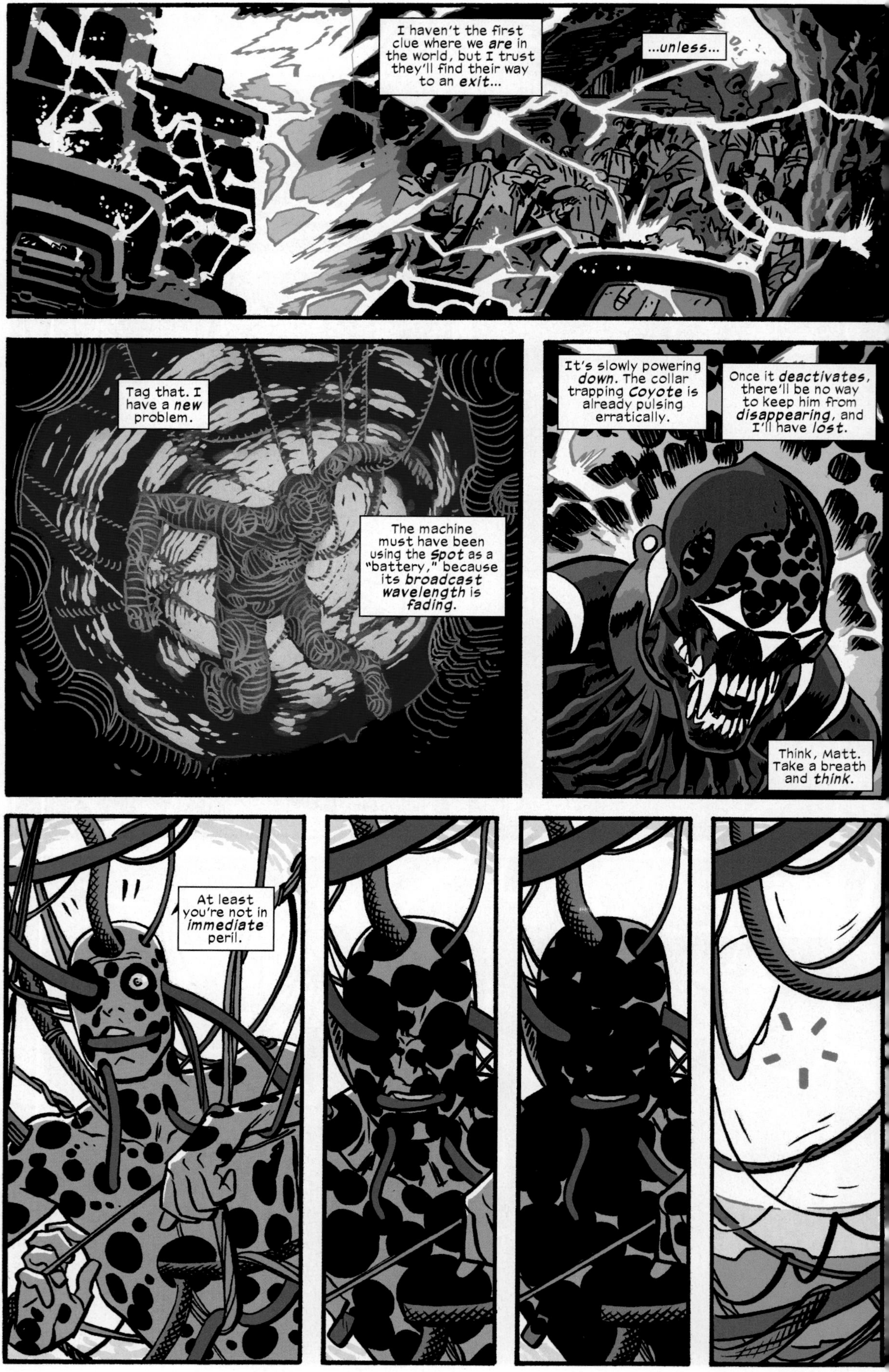

I haven't the first clue where we are in the world, but I trust they'll find their way to an exit...
...unless...
Tag that. I have a new problem.
The machine must have been using the Spot as a "battery," because its broadcast wavelength is fading.
It's slowly powering down. The collar trapping Coyote is already pulsing erratically.
Once it deactivates, there'll be no way to keep him from disappearing, and I'll have lost.
Think, Matt. Take a breath and think.
At least you're not in immediate peril.

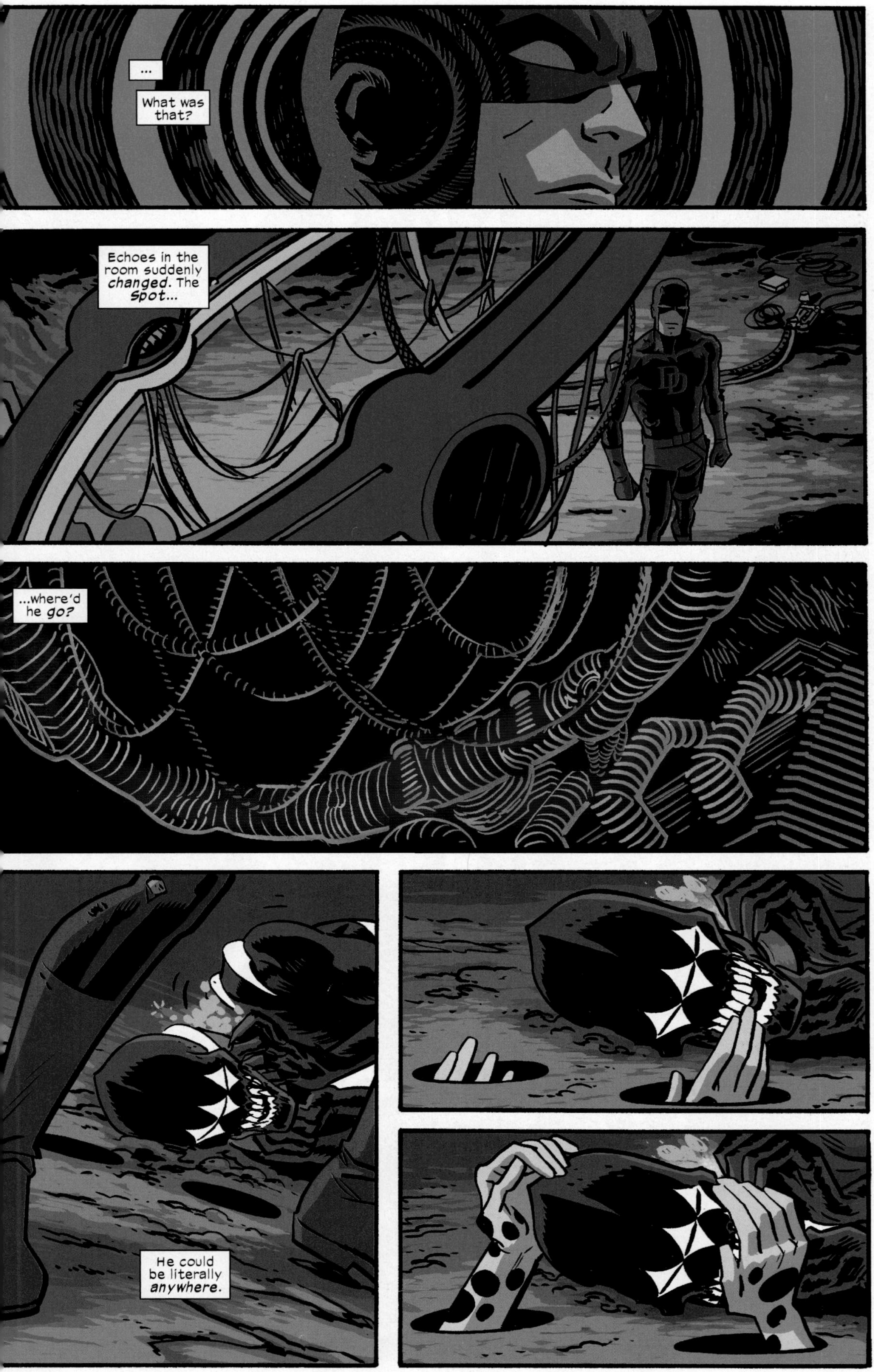
...
What was that?
Echoes in the room suddenly *changed*. The *Spot*...
...where'd he *go?*
He could be literally *anywhere*.

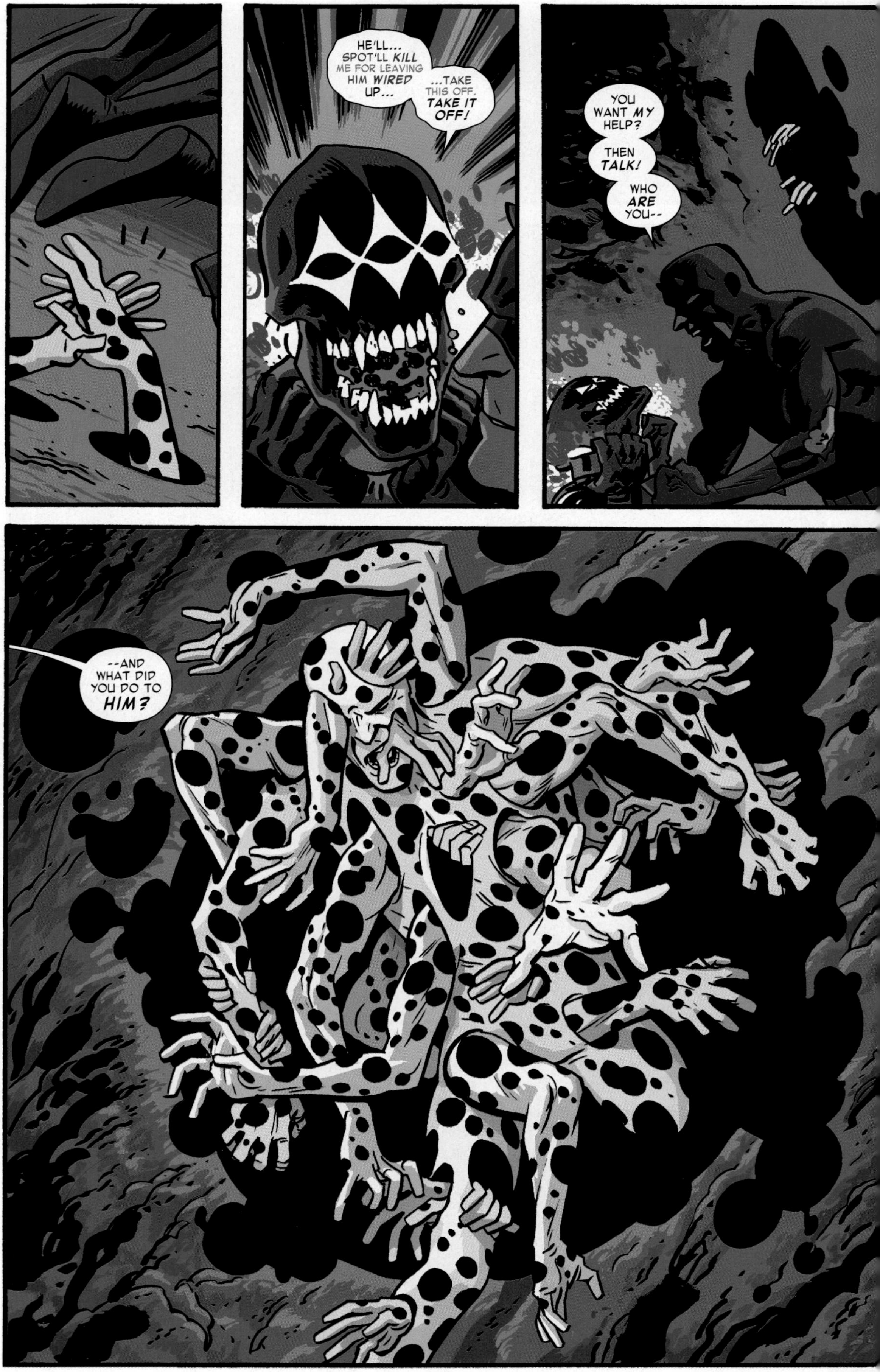
HE'LL... SPOT'LL KILL ME FOR LEAVING HIM WIRED UP...
...TAKE THIS OFF. TAKE IT OFF!
YOU WANT MY HELP?
THEN TALK!
WHO ARE YOU--
--AND WHAT DID YOU DO TO HIM?

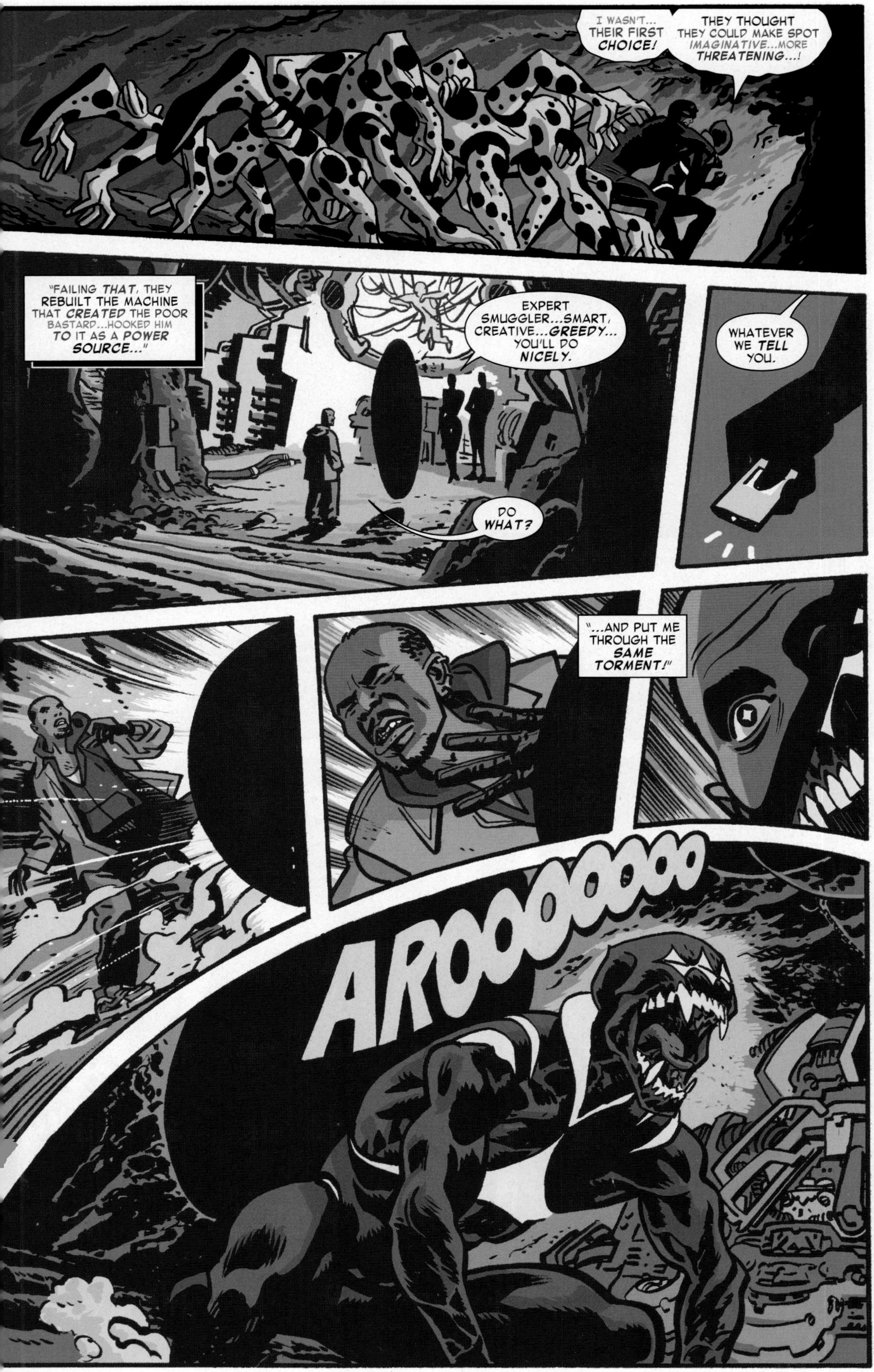
I WASN'T... THEIR FIRST CHOICE!
THEY THOUGHT THEY COULD MAKE SPOT IMAGINATIVE...MORE THREATENING...!
"FAILING THAT, THEY REBUILT THE MACHINE THAT CREATED THE POOR BASTARD...HOOKED HIM TO IT AS A POWER SOURCE..."
EXPERT SMUGGLER...SMART, CREATIVE...GREEDY... YOU'LL DO NICELY.
DO WHAT?
WHATEVER WE TELL YOU.
"...AND PUT ME THROUGH THE SAME TORMENT!"
AROOOOOOOO

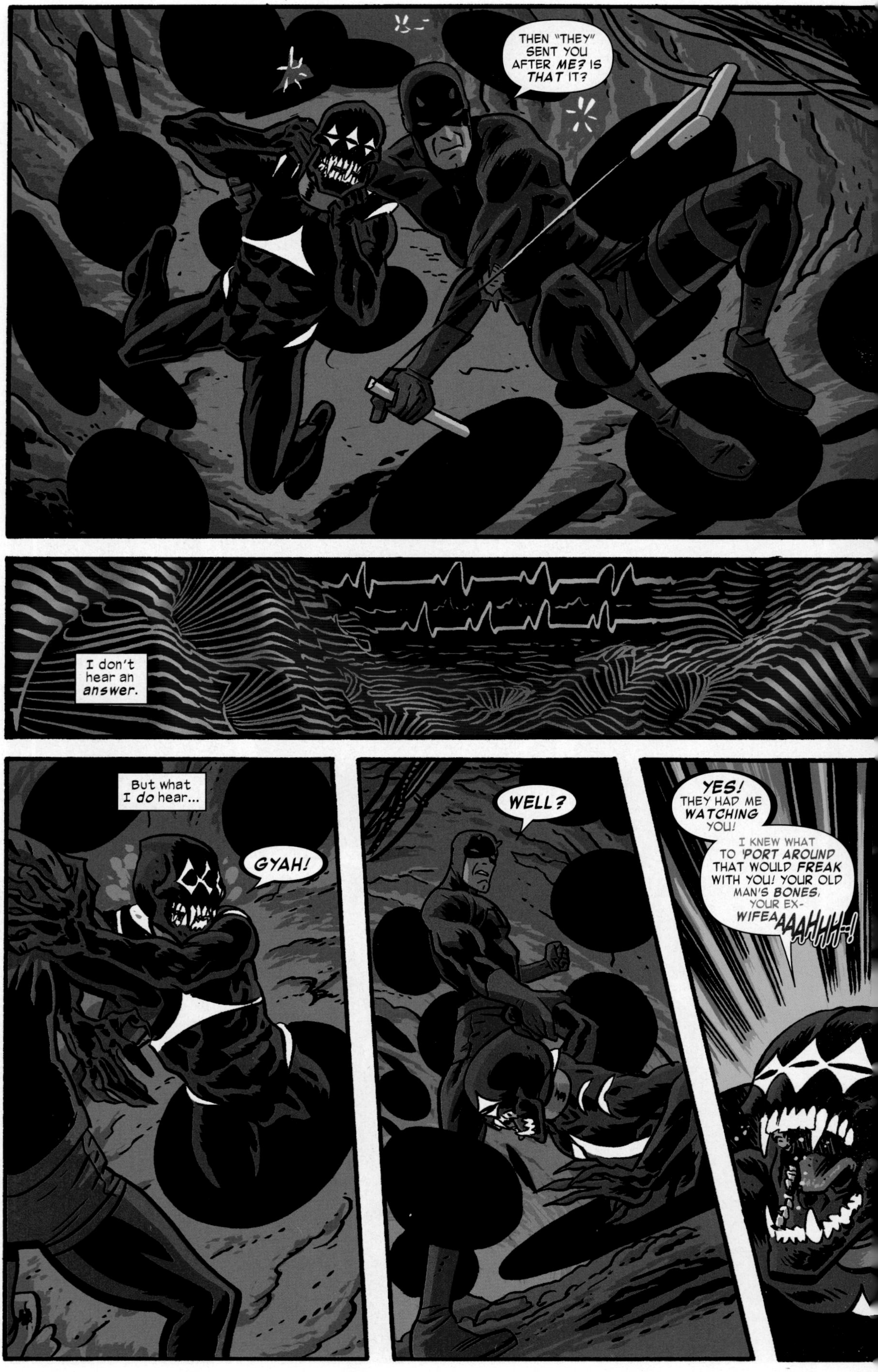
THEN "THEY" SENT YOU AFTER ME? IS THAT IT?
I don't hear an answer.
But what I do hear...
GYAH!
WELL?
YES! THEY HAD ME WATCHING YOU!
I KNEW WHAT TO 'PORT AROUND THAT WOULD FREAK WITH YOU! YOUR OLD MAN'S BONES, YOUR EX-WIFEAAAHHH-!

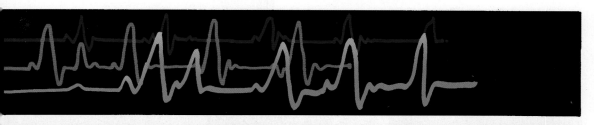

AND "THEY" HAD YOU TARGETING THE *NEW YORK DRUGLORDS* WITH YOUR *TELEPORTALS*, DIDN'T THEY? HIERRA? *SALAZAR?*

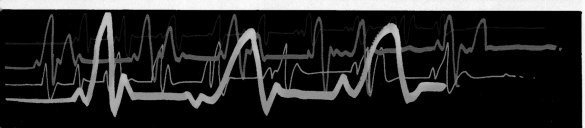

YOU OPENED UP THE *FLOOR* OF SALAZAR'S *ELEVATOR!* YOU DRAINED HIERRA'S *BLOOD* FROM *AFAR* AND LEFT HIS *NURSE* TO TAKE THE *FALL!*

DO YOU *ADMIT* THOSE THINGS?

Y--

THWAM

≋HNNGH≋

--YES! YES! YOU ALREADY KNOW ALL THAT!

TRUE.

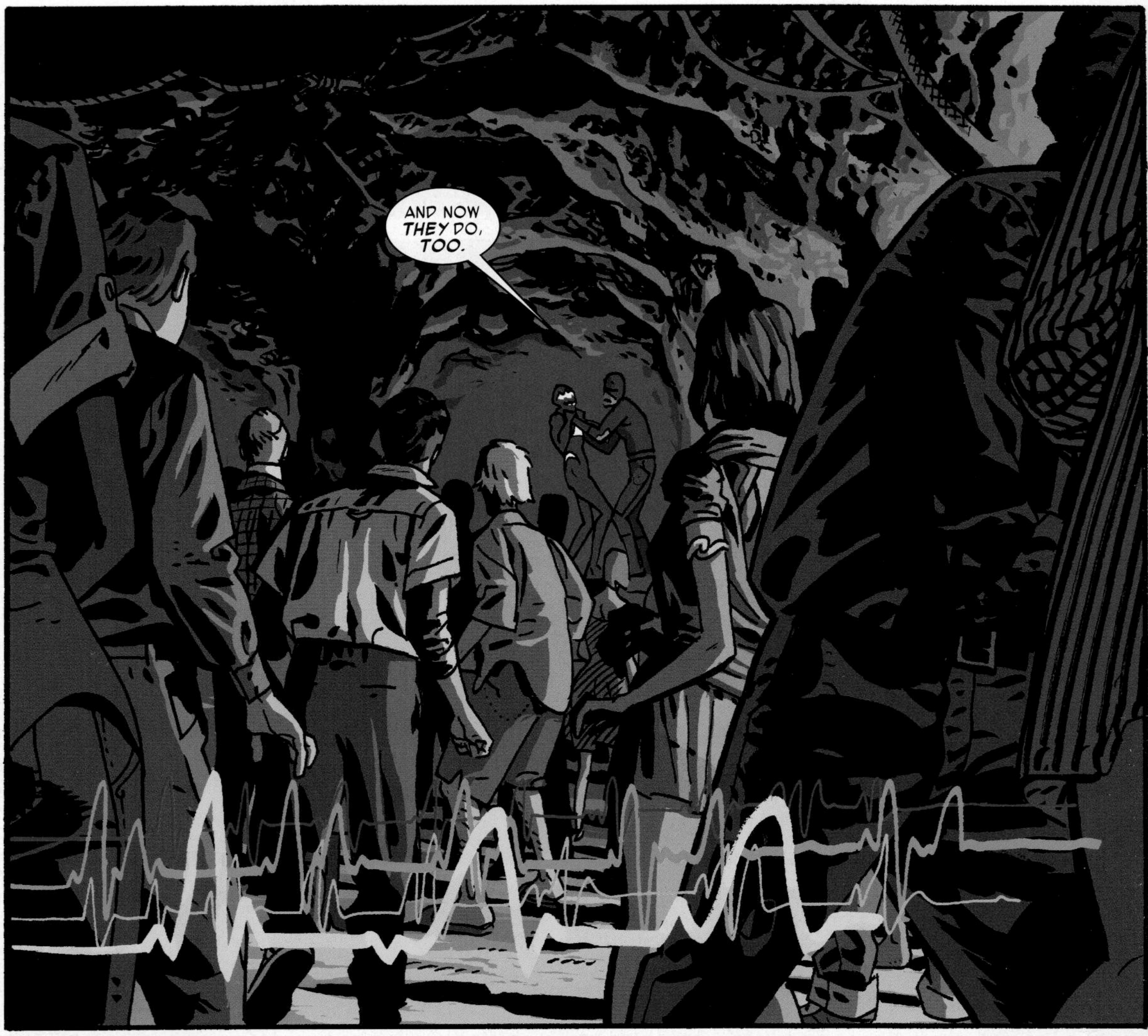
AND NOW THEY DO, TOO.

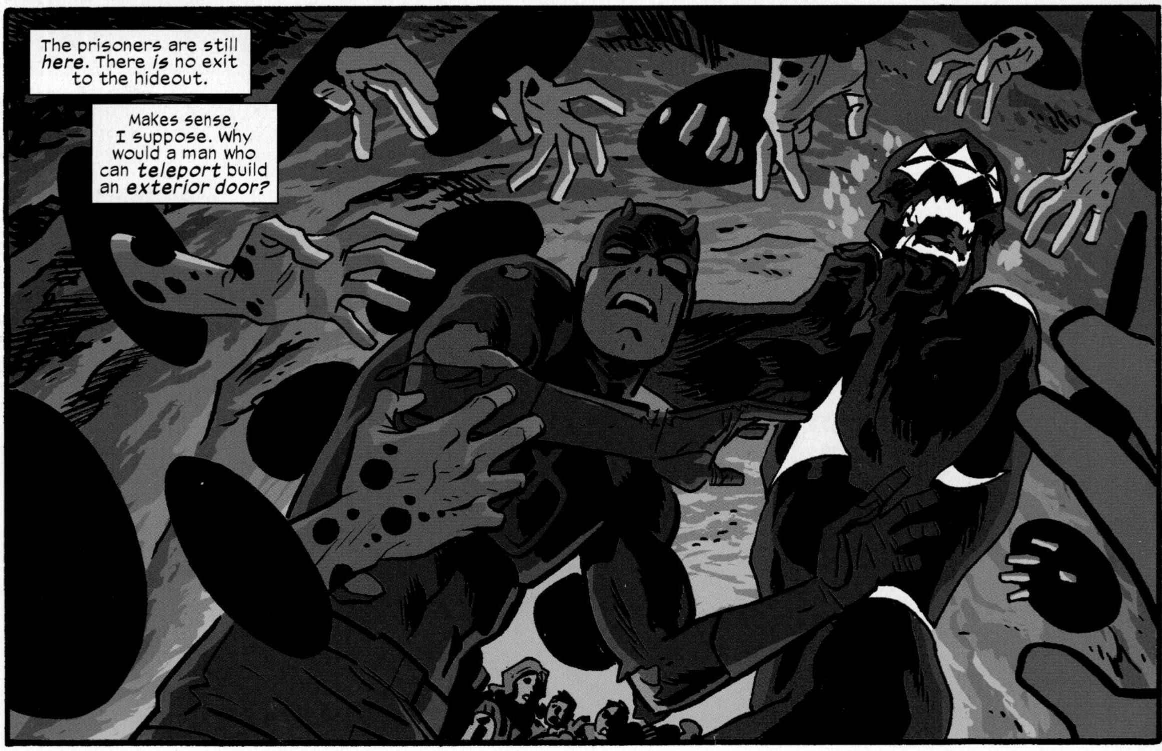
The prisoners are still here. There is no exit to the hideout.
Makes sense, I suppose. Why would a man who can teleport build an exterior door?

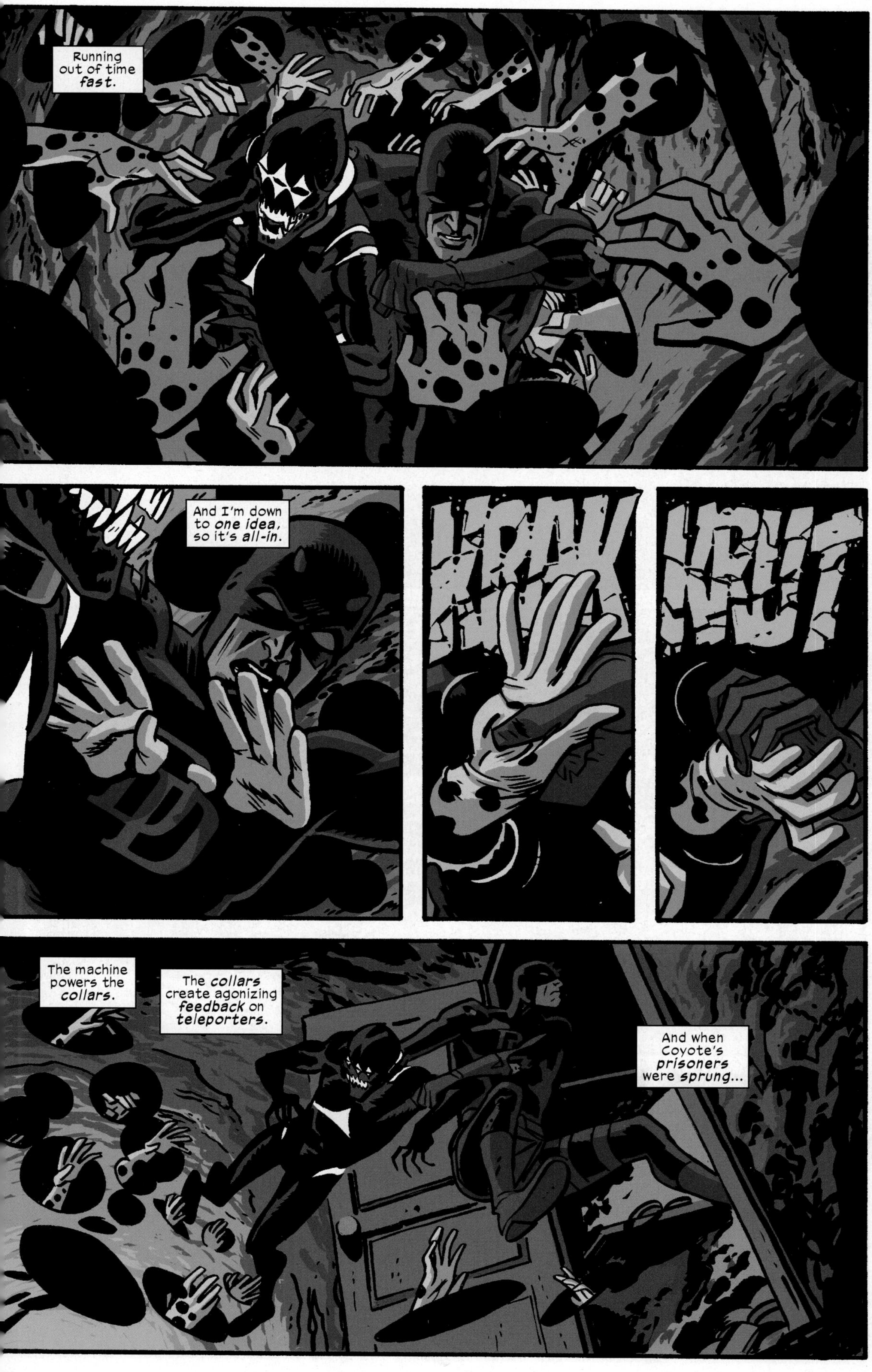
Running out of time *fast*.
And I'm down to *one idea*, so it's *all-in*.
The machine powers the *collars*.
The *collars* create agonizing *feedback* on *teleporters*.
And when Coyote's *prisoners* were *sprung*...

...they left behind *dozens* of collars!

For a long second, nothing much *happens.*

God keeps me in *suspense.*

But then it gets *ugly.*

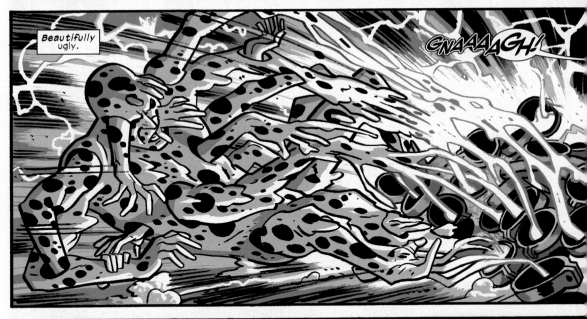

Beautifully ugly.

GNAAAAGH!

And then--

AAAACHHAAAAA!

YOU'RE CAUGHT IN A *BACKLASH!* HOLD *STILL!*

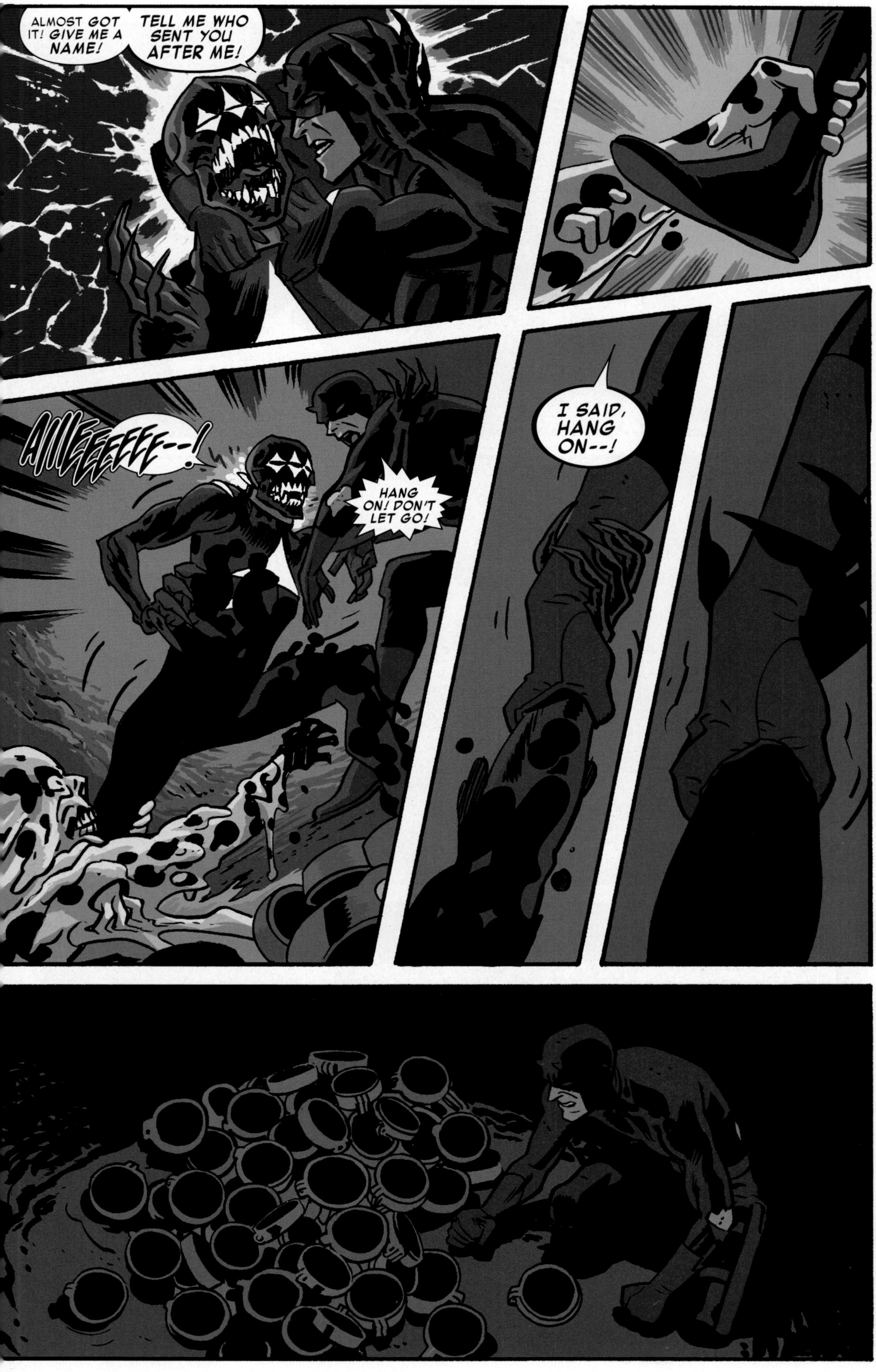
ALMOST GOT IT! GIVE ME A NAME!
TELL ME WHO SENT YOU AFTER ME!
AIIIEEEEEEE--!
HANG ON! DON'T LET GO!
I SAID, HANG ON--!

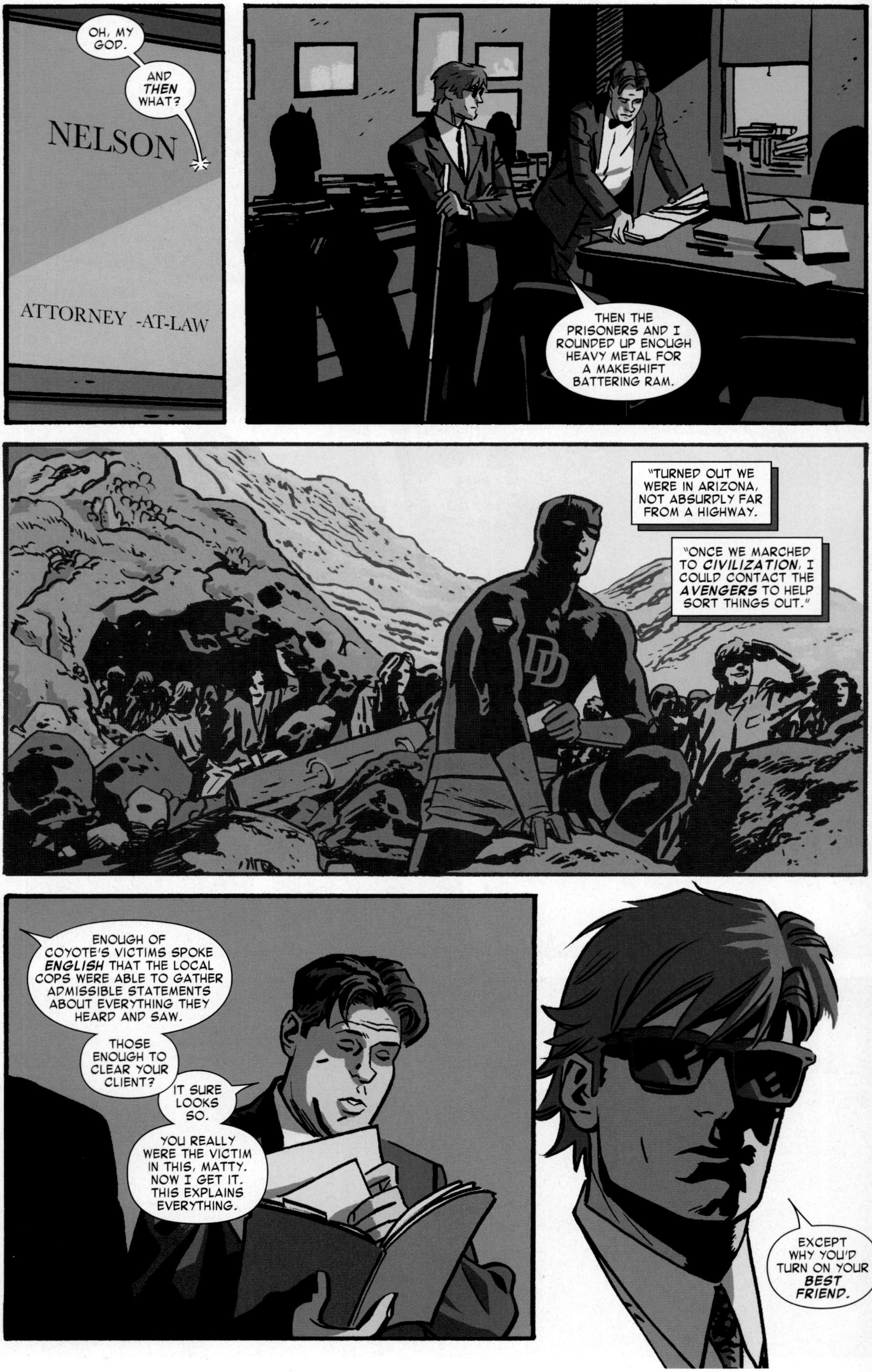
OH, MY GOD.
AND THEN WHAT?
NELSON
ATTORNEY -AT-LAW
THEN THE PRISONERS AND I ROUNDED UP ENOUGH HEAVY METAL FOR A MAKESHIFT BATTERING RAM.
"TURNED OUT WE WERE IN ARIZONA, NOT ABSURDLY FAR FROM A HIGHWAY.
"ONCE WE MARCHED TO CIVILIZATION, I COULD CONTACT THE AVENGERS TO HELP SORT THINGS OUT."
ENOUGH OF COYOTE'S VICTIMS SPOKE ENGLISH THAT THE LOCAL COPS WERE ABLE TO GATHER ADMISSIBLE STATEMENTS ABOUT EVERYTHING THEY HEARD AND SAW.
THOSE ENOUGH TO CLEAR YOUR CLIENT?
IT SURE LOOKS SO.
YOU REALLY WERE THE VICTIM IN THIS, MATTY. NOW I GET IT. THIS EXPLAINS EVERYTHING.
EXCEPT WHY YOU'D TURN ON YOUR BEST FRIEND.

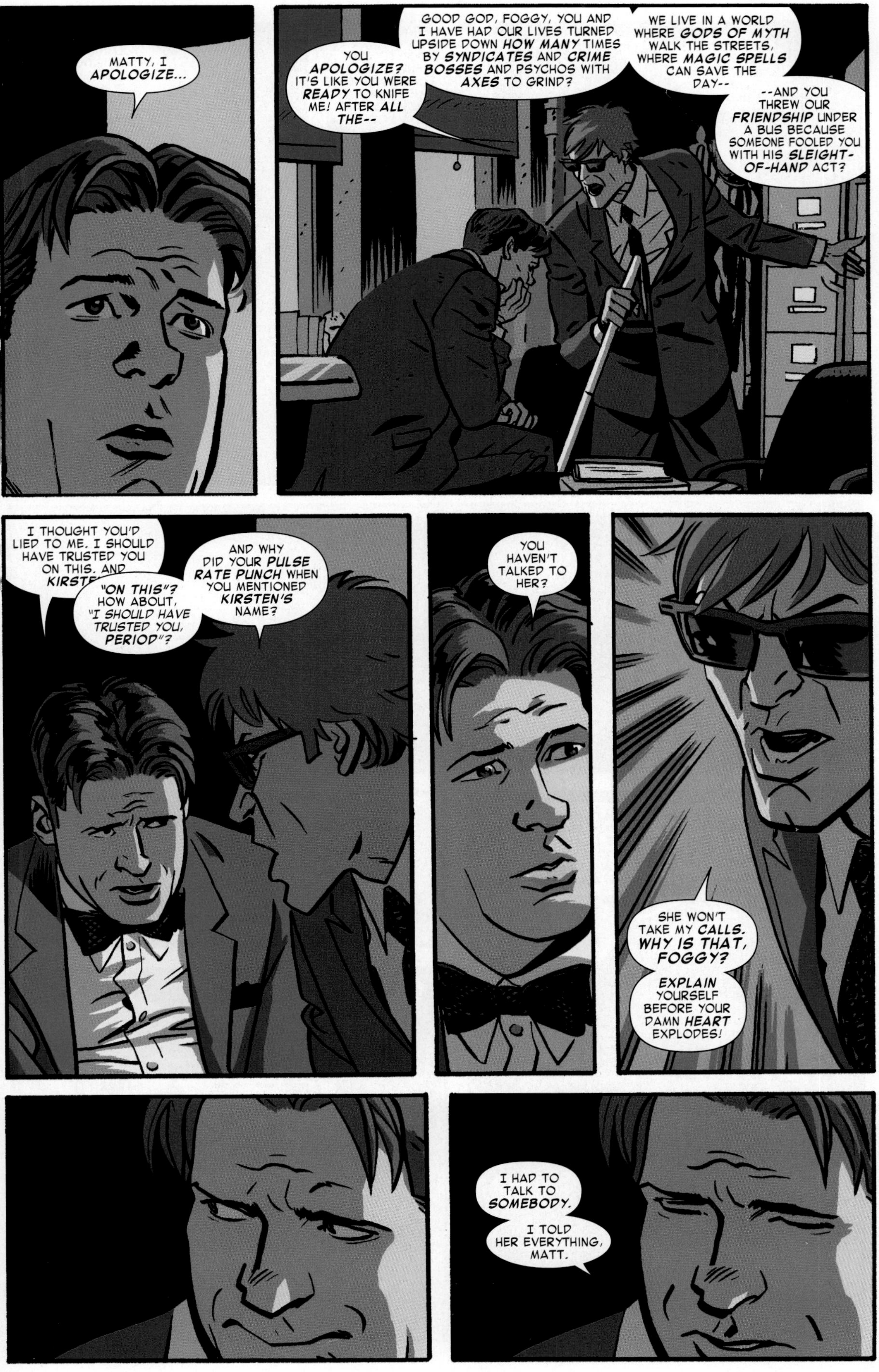
MATTY, I APOLOGIZE...
YOU APOLOGIZE? IT'S LIKE YOU WERE READY TO KNIFE ME! AFTER ALL THE--
GOOD GOD, FOGGY, YOU AND I HAVE HAD OUR LIVES TURNED UPSIDE DOWN HOW MANY TIMES BY SYNDICATES AND CRIME BOSSES AND PSYCHOS WITH AXES TO GRIND?
WE LIVE IN A WORLD WHERE GODS OF MYTH WALK THE STREETS, WHERE MAGIC SPELLS CAN SAVE THE DAY--
--AND YOU THREW OUR FRIENDSHIP UNDER A BUS BECAUSE SOMEONE FOOLED YOU WITH HIS SLEIGHT-OF-HAND ACT?
I THOUGHT YOU'D LIED TO ME. I SHOULD HAVE TRUSTED YOU ON THIS. AND KIRSTE
"ON THIS"? HOW ABOUT, "I SHOULD HAVE TRUSTED YOU, PERIOD"?
AND WHY DID YOUR PULSE RATE PUNCH WHEN YOU MENTIONED KIRSTEN'S NAME?
YOU HAVEN'T TALKED TO HER?
SHE WON'T TAKE MY CALLS. WHY IS THAT, FOGGY?
EXPLAIN YOURSELF BEFORE YOUR DAMN HEART EXPLODES!
I HAD TO TALK TO SOMEBODY.
I TOLD HER EVERYTHING, MATT.

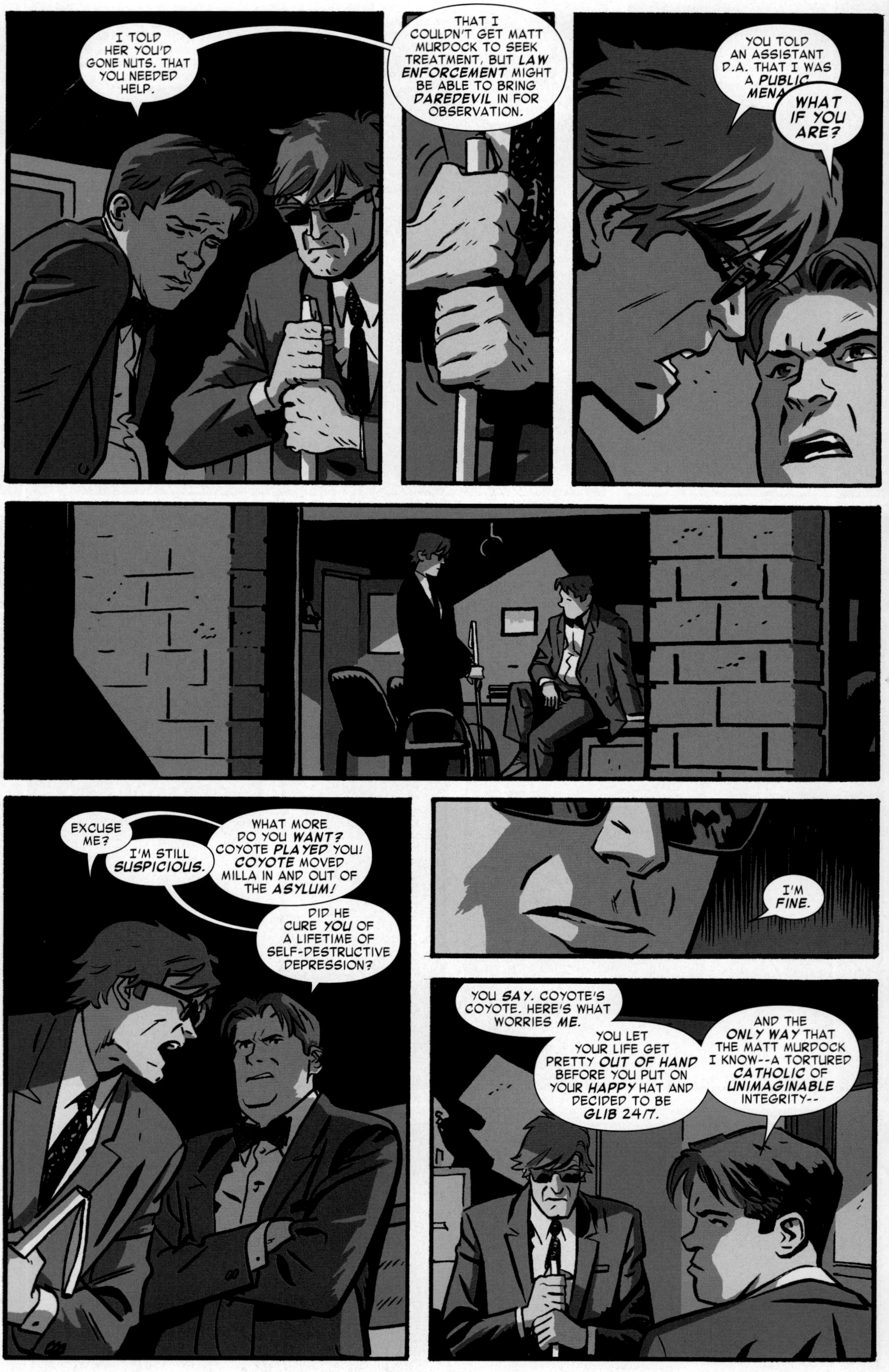

I TOLD HER YOU'D GONE NUTS. THAT YOU NEEDED HELP.
THAT I COULDN'T GET MATT MURDOCK TO SEEK TREATMENT, BUT LAW ENFORCEMENT MIGHT BE ABLE TO BRING DAREDEVIL IN FOR OBSERVATION.
YOU TOLD AN ASSISTANT D.A. THAT I WAS A PUBLIC MENA
WHAT IF YOU ARE?
EXCUSE ME?
I'M STILL SUSPICIOUS.
WHAT MORE DO YOU WANT? COYOTE PLAYED YOU! COYOTE MOVED MILLA IN AND OUT OF THE ASYLUM!
DID HE CURE YOU OF A LIFETIME OF SELF-DESTRUCTIVE DEPRESSION?
I'M FINE.
YOU SAY. COYOTE'S COYOTE. HERE'S WHAT WORRIES ME.
YOU LET YOUR LIFE GET PRETTY OUT OF HAND BEFORE YOU PUT ON YOUR HAPPY HAT AND DECIDED TO BE GLIB 24/7.
AND THE ONLY WAY THAT THE MATT MURDOCK I KNOW--A TORTURED CATHOLIC OF UNIMAGINABLE INTEGRITY--

--COULD SO UTTERLY ABSOLVE HIMSELF OF *RESPONSIBILITY* FOR--FOR *MILLA*--FOR *BULLSEYE'S* MURDER, FOR SOME *REALLY DEVASTATING CHOICES*--

--IS IF HE'S NOT *HIMSELF* SOMEHOW.

...

ANYTHING YOU WANT TO *ADD* TO THAT?

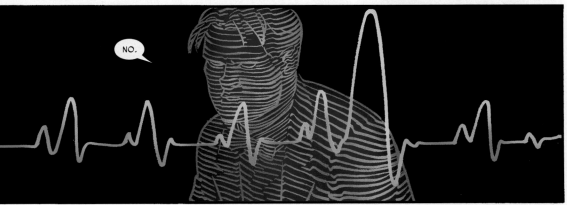

NO.

REGARDLESS, I SHOULDN'T HAVE COLD-SHOULDERED YOU. IF YOU *WANT* HELP, I'M *HERE*. I...I NEED IT FROM YOU *TOO*. LET'S JUST PUT THIS BEHIND US, OKAY?

GO TO HELL, NELSON.

HEY, C'MON. I'VE KNOWN YOU TOO LONG--

I DON'T *CARE*. IF YOU'RE *THAT CONVINCED* THAT I HAVE BEEN IN *NO WAY* COMPELLED TO *ATONE* FOR MY SINS...

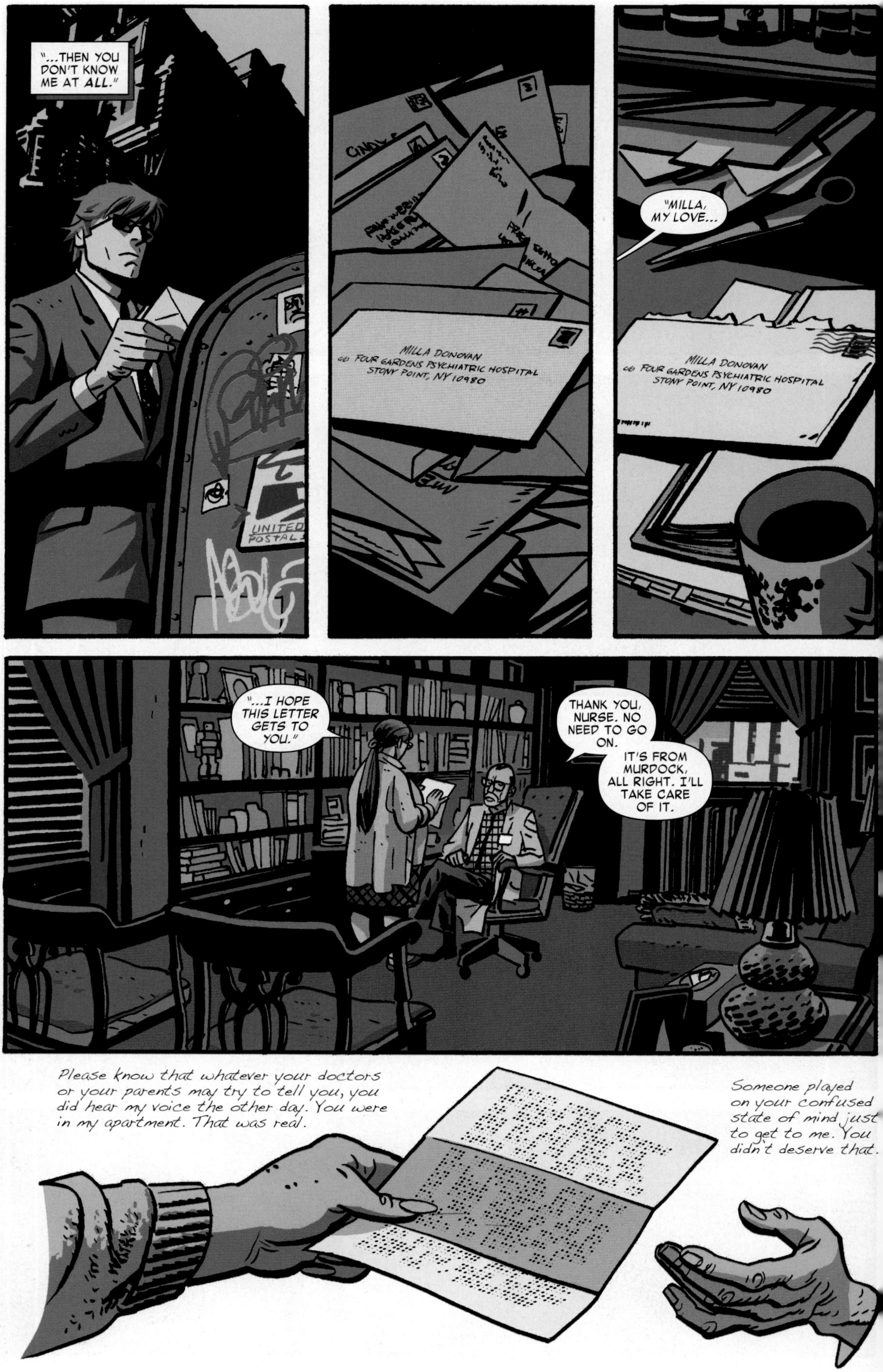

"...THEN YOU DON'T KNOW ME AT ALL."
MILLA DONOVAN c/o FOUR GARDENS PSYCHIATRIC HOSPITAL STONY POINT, NY 10980
"MILLA, MY LOVE...
MILLA DONOVAN c/o FOUR GARDENS PSYCHIATRIC HOSPITAL STONY POINT, NY 10980
"...I HOPE THIS LETTER GETS TO YOU."
THANK YOU, NURSE. NO NEED TO GO ON.
IT'S FROM MURDOCK, ALL RIGHT. I'LL TAKE CARE OF IT.
Please know that whatever your doctors or your parents may try to tell you, you did hear my voice the other day. You were in my apartment. That was real.
Someone played on your confused state of mind just to get to me. You didn't deserve that.

You didn't deserve any of the things that happened to you just because you fell in love with a man who couldn't protect you from his enemies.

If, through some stroke of luck, you are reading this note, don't let your doctors find it. I shouldn't be writing to you at all, I'm told. I should let the wound close.

But you have to know, as I have said before, that I will spend the rest of my days searching for a way to make up for all your pain and suffering.

You have to know that I think of you every day and that I miss you and want you to be well.

MILLA DONOVAN
GARDENS PSYCHIATRIC HOSPITAL
NY POINT, NY 10980

MURDOCK, M

And you have to know that I will never forgive myself for failing you.

Love, Matt
Love, Matt
Love, Matt
Love, Matt
Love, Matt
Love, Matt

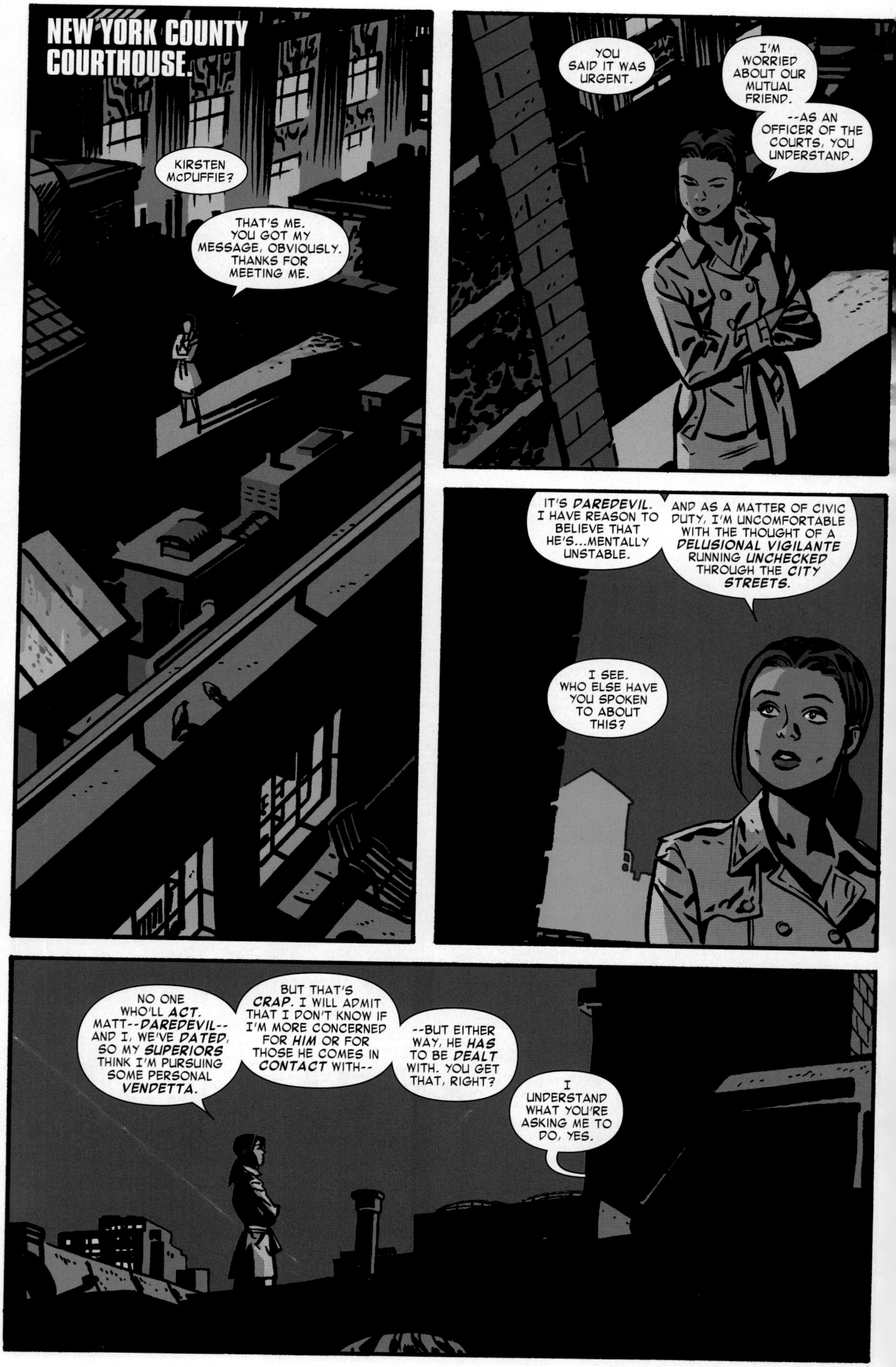
NEW YORK COUNTY COURTHOUSE.
KIRSTEN McDUFFIE?
THAT'S ME. YOU GOT MY MESSAGE, OBVIOUSLY. THANKS FOR MEETING ME.
YOU SAID IT WAS URGENT.
I'M WORRIED ABOUT OUR MUTUAL FRIEND.
--AS AN OFFICER OF THE COURTS, YOU UNDERSTAND.
IT'S DAREDEVIL. I HAVE REASON TO BELIEVE THAT HE'S...MENTALLY UNSTABLE.
AND AS A MATTER OF CIVIC DUTY, I'M UNCOMFORTABLE WITH THE THOUGHT OF A DELUSIONAL VIGILANTE RUNNING UNCHECKED THROUGH THE CITY STREETS.
I SEE. WHO ELSE HAVE YOU SPOKEN TO ABOUT THIS?
NO ONE WHO'LL ACT. MATT--DAREDEVIL--AND I, WE'VE DATED, SO MY SUPERIORS THINK I'M PURSUING SOME PERSONAL VENDETTA.
BUT THAT'S CRAP. I WILL ADMIT THAT I DON'T KNOW IF I'M MORE CONCERNED FOR HIM OR FOR THOSE HE COMES IN CONTACT WITH--
--BUT EITHER WAY, HE HAS TO BE DEALT WITH. YOU GET THAT, RIGHT?
I UNDERSTAND WHAT YOU'RE ASKING ME TO DO, YES.

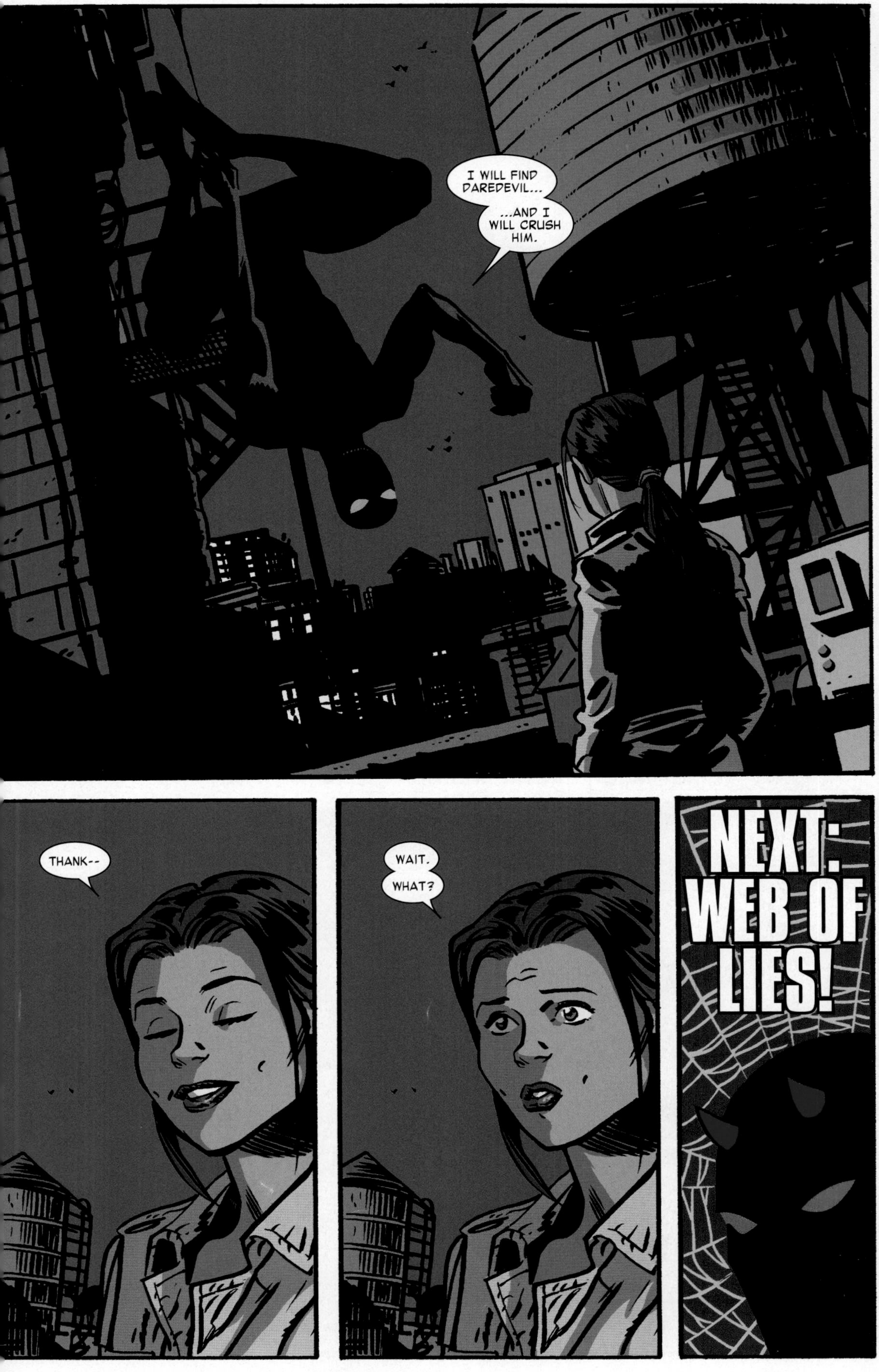
I WILL FIND DAREDEVIL...
...AND I WILL CRUSH HIM.
THANK--
WAIT.
WHAT?
NEXT: WEB OF LIES!

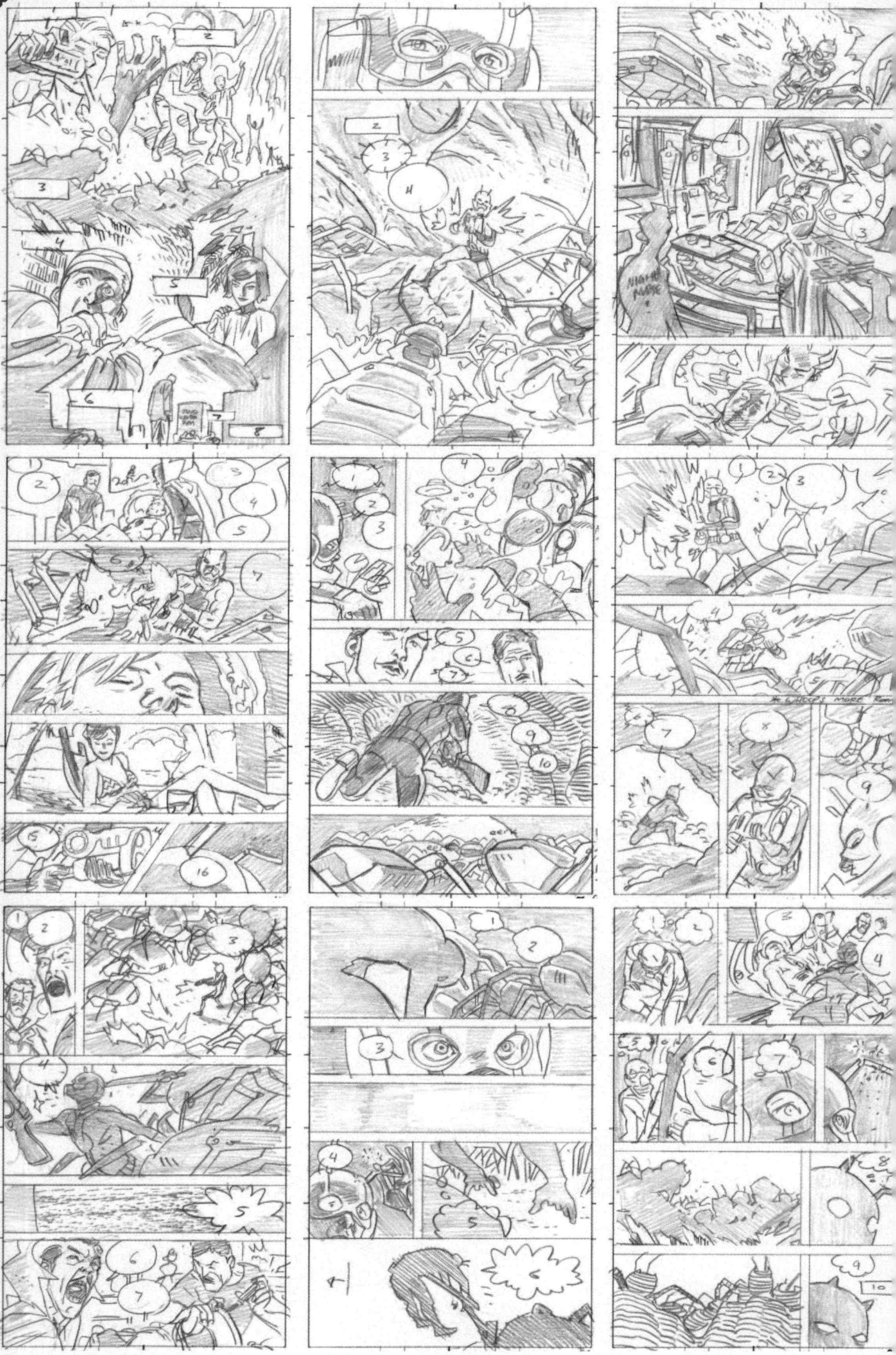

DAREDEVIL #16 ***LAYOUTS BY CHRIS SAMNEE***

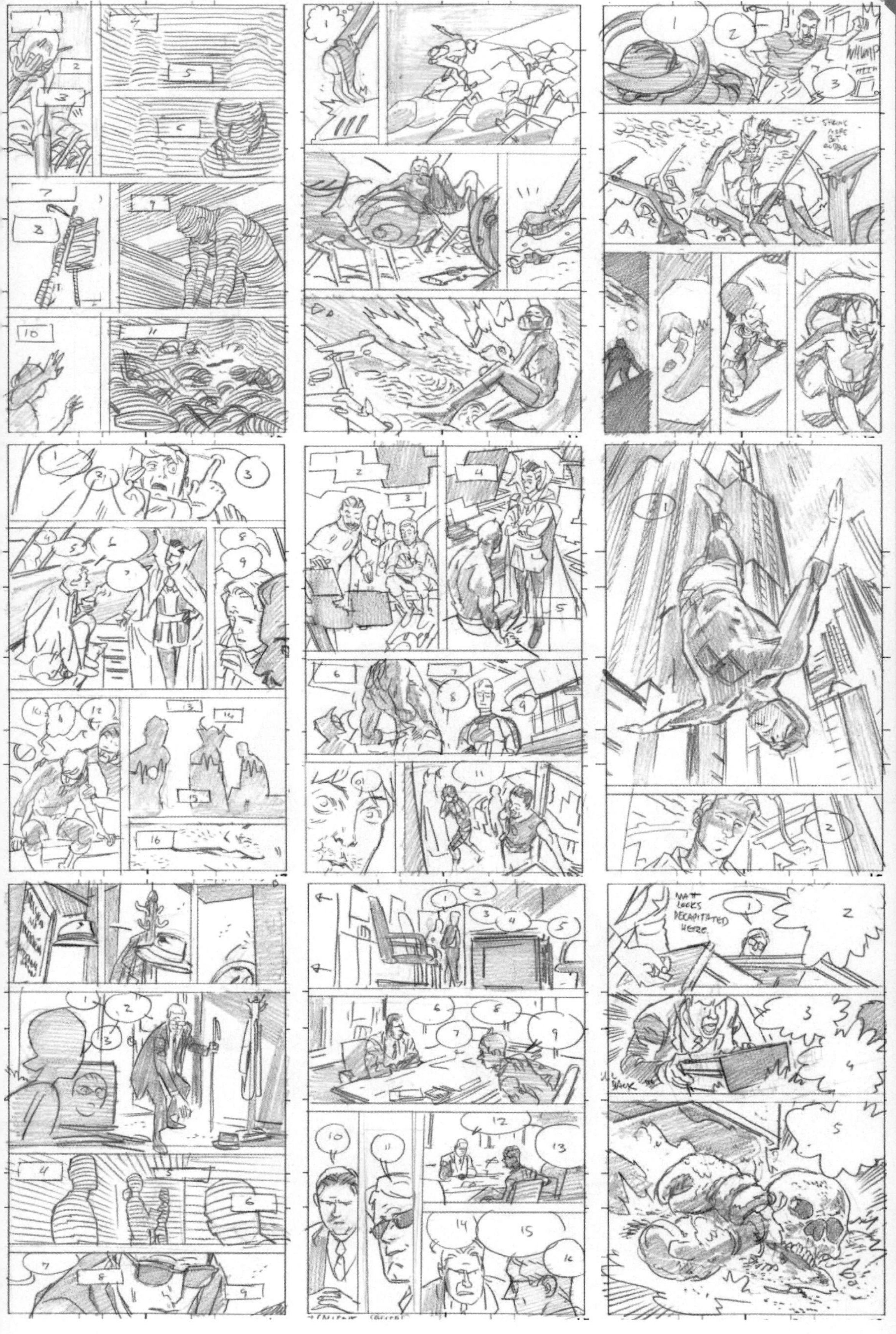
WHUMP
MATT LOOKS DECAPITATED HERE.

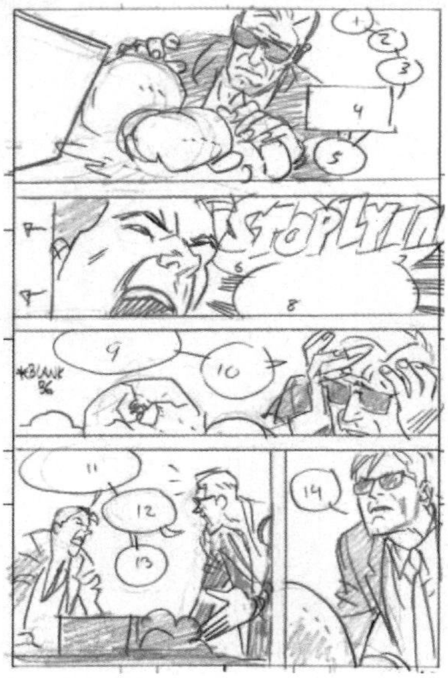

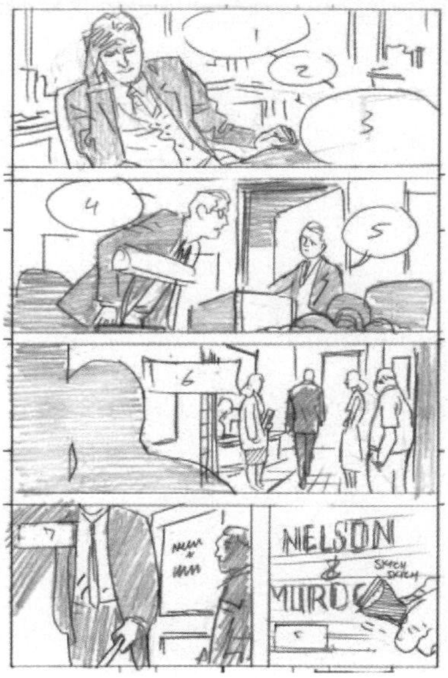

NELSON

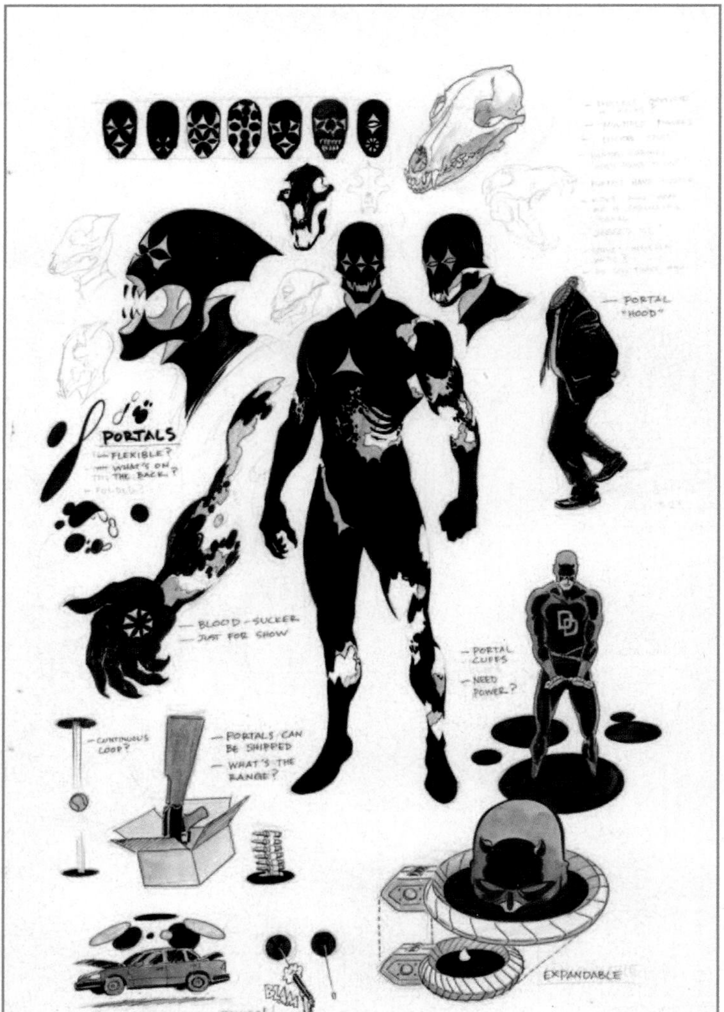

PORTALS
FLEXIBLE?
WHAT'S ON THE BACK?
BLOOD-SUCKER
JUST FOR SHOW
PORTAL "HOOD"
PORTAL CUFFS
NEED POWER?
CONTINUOUS LOOP?
PORTALS CAN BE SHIPPED
WHAT'S THE RANGE?
EXPANDABLE
CAN SUSPEND HEAVY THINGS!

COYOTE CHARACTER AND TECHNOLOGY DESIGNS BY PAOLO RIVERA

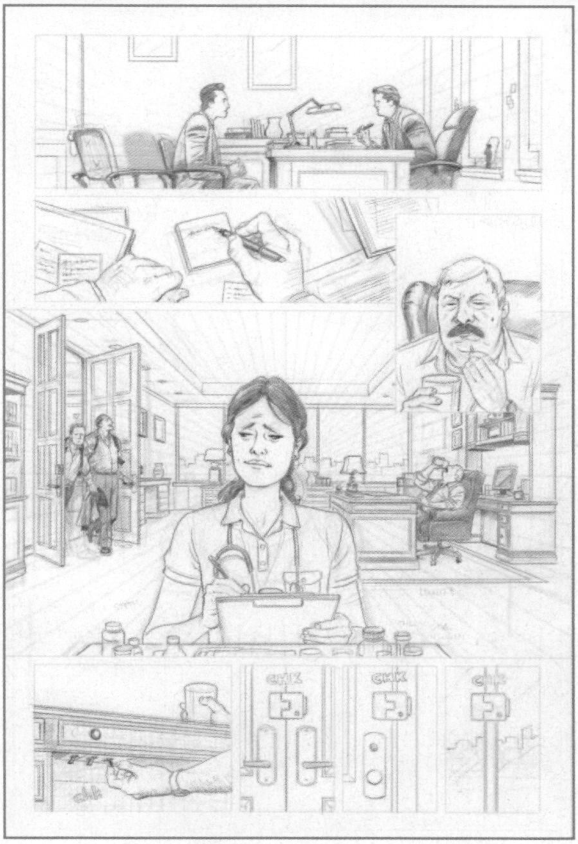

DAREDEVIL #18, PAGE 2 ***UNUSED PENCILS BY PAOLO RIVERA***

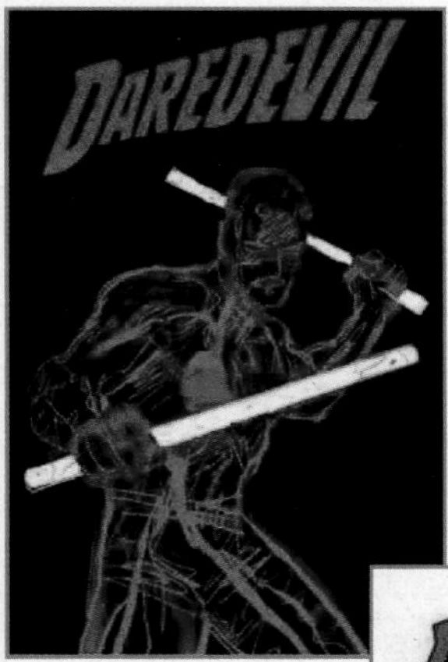
DAREDEVIL

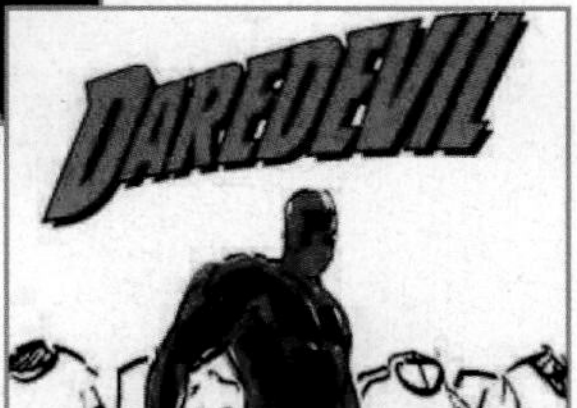
DAREDEVIL

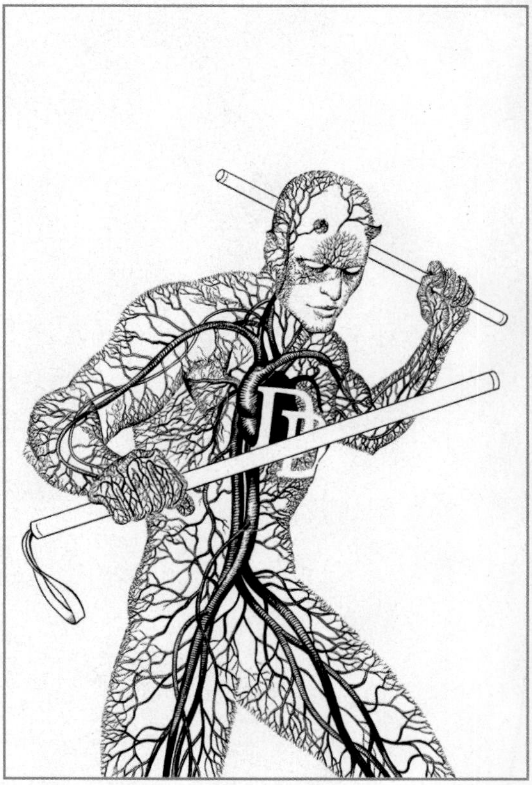

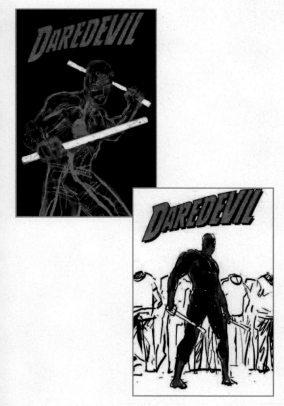

DAREDEVIL #18 ***COVER SKETCHES AND INKS BY PAOLO RIVERA***

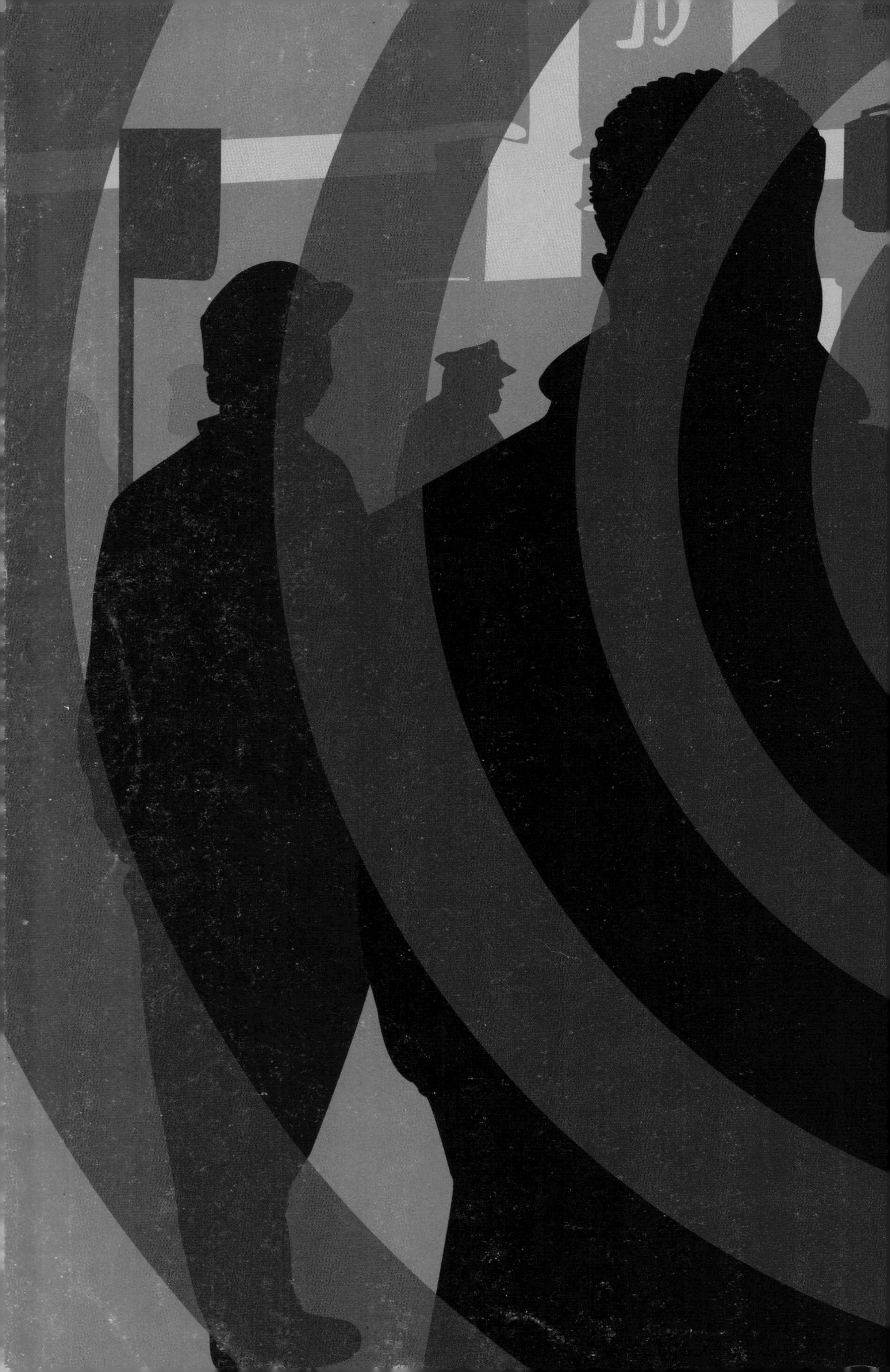